Learning t̶ ̶ ̶ ̶ ̶ ̶
from T̶ ̶ ̶

Learning to Learn from Text

EFFECTIVE READING IN THE CONTENT AREAS

A. Morris

N. Stewart-Dore

ADDISON-WESLEY

Acknowledgements

Our thanks are due to a large number of people and organizations. In particular we should like to mention the Secondary Inservice Branch of the Queensland Department of Education, the Queensland Inservice Education Committee and the Brisbane Inservice Committee.

We are also grateful to the following for permission to use material in this book: George Philip & O'Neil for the chapter entitled 'Commerce' from their book *The Niuginians*, by R.L. Andrews; Lloyd O'Neil for the chapter entitled 'Motivation to Work' from *Social Psychology*, edited by T.C. Teasdale; Jacaranda Wiley for pages 152 and 153 from *Concepts in Science I*, by R.G. Cull and W.A. Drake; and the *Courier Mail* for the article entitled 'One in four get skin cancer', published on 1 December 1981.

Thanks are due to John Park for his Graphic Outline (Stage 1), Suzanne Innes and Lyn Pepper for their Graphic Outline (Stage 2), Ian Down for his ideas on extracting and organizing information, and to those who gave assistance with the classroom examples and exercises in the Appendix.

Doris Hardie deserves thanks for the execution of a considerable typing task.

Our thanks are also due to the many people who have helped us to develop our ideas to this point. To these and all the other friends who have enabled us to get this far, our warmest thanks . . . we hope you approve of our efforts.

Nea and Bert

To our teacher colleagues

First published in 1984 by the
Addison-Wesley Publishing Company
6 Byfield Street, North Ryde, NSW, 2113

(c) 1984 A. Morris and N. Stewart-Dore
ISBN 0 201 13980 4

Printed in Singapore

Contents

Introduction 9

PART I
Reading in the Content Areas 11

Why Focus on Reading in the Content Areas? 13
   TEACHER CONCERNS 13
   WHAT IS READING? 14
   WHY TEACH READING? 18

What is Content Area Reading? 21
   READING TO LEARN 21
   EXPOSITORY VERSUS NARRATIVE MATERIALS 21
   LANGUAGE REGISTERS 22
   CONCLUSION 23

The Need to Focus on Content Area Reading 25
   EFFECTIVE READING IS TIED TO EFFECTIVE TEACHING AND
   LEARNING 25
   EFFECTIVE CONTENT AREA READING CANNOT BE ASSUMED 25
   READING IS A THINKING PROCESS 27
   EFFICIENT READING IS NECESSARY FOR INDEPENDENT LEARNING 27
   WE LEARN BY DOING 29

Communication and Content Area Reading 31
   THE CENTRAL ROLE OF LANGUAGE 31
   THE NATURE OF SUBJECT LANGUAGE AND ITS USE 38
   REGISTER OF SUBJECTS 41
   STRATEGIES FOR EXPERIENCING SUBJECT LANGUAGE 43

PART 2
Reading to Learn: the ERICA Model 45
Stage 1. Preparing for Reading 47

The Structured Overview: Organizing Our Ideas 48
   INTRODUCTION 48
   DEVELOPMENT OF A STRUCTURED OVERVIEW 51
   USE OF THE STRUCTURED OVERVIEW 53
      When Introducing a Topic 53 — For Ongoing Reference 54 — For Revision or
      Assessment 55 — Summary 55 — Activities 56

The Graphic Outline: Surveying the Materials   57

    INTRODUCTION   57
    MATERIALS SUITABLE FOR GRAPHIC OUTLINES   58
    TYPES OF GRAPHIC OUTLINES   58
    CONSTRUCTING A GRAPHIC OUTLINE   64
    USE OF GRAPHIC OUTLINES   82
    VALUE OF GRAPHIC OUTLINES   83
        To the Teacher 83 — To the Student 83
    SUMMARY   84

Learning New Vocabulary   85

    INTRODUCTION   85
    IDENTIFYING CONTENT AREA VOCABULARY   86
    EFFECTS OF NON-SPECIALIZED VOCABULARY   87
    WHICH VOCABULARY SHOULD BE TAUGHT?   87
    THE IMPORTANCE OF CONTEXT CLUES   90
    TEACHING THE USE OF CONTEXT CLUES   92
    CONCLUSION   93
    SUMMARY   94

Stage 2. Thinking Through the Reading   95

Introduction   95
Three-Level Reading Guides   98

    WHAT DO THREE-LEVEL GUIDES LOOK LIKE?   100
    DETERMINING CONTENT OBJECTIVES   102
    CONSTRUCTING A THREE-LEVEL GUIDE   102
        Summary 104
    USING THREE-LEVEL GUIDES   104
    QUALITIES OF 'GOOD' THREE-LEVEL GUIDES   105
    SOME TIPS ON USING THREE-LEVEL GUIDES   106

Cloze Exercises   107

    USING CLOZE TO DEVELOP COMPREHENSION   107
    CLOZE ACTIVITIES VERSUS CLOZE TESTS   108

Stage 3. Extracting and Organizing Information   113

    INTRODUCTION   113
    PROBLEMS CAUSED BY SOME EDUCATIONAL PRACTICES   114
    EXTRACTING INFORMATION   116
    SEEING THE OVERALL PLAN   117
    GETTING INTO THE TEXT — RECOGNIZING TOP-LEVEL STRUC-TURES   118
    SEEING MAIN IDEAS AND SUPPORTING DETAILS   122
    DIAGRAMS AS AIDS TO UNDERSTANDING   134
    OUTLINING   135
    CONCLUSION   139

Stage 4. Translating Information from Reading to Writing 142

INTRODUCTION 142
'Retelling' Experience 142 — How Does This Relate to School Learning? 143
TRANSLATING INFORMATION: WHAT IS IT? 145
WHY TRANSLATE IDEAS THROUGH WRITING? 146
Overcoming Verbatim 'Copying Out' 146 — Making Use of Information 147 — Promoting the Writing Habit 149 — Showing How Reading and Writing Are Interrelated Language/Learning Activities 152
WHAT AUDIENCES ARE THERE FOR STUDENT WRITING? 155
In Class Audience 155 — Audiences in Other Schools 155 — Adult Audiences 155 — Sharing One's Writing with Others 156
DEVELOPING FLEXIBILITY IN COMMUNICATING WHAT HAS BEEN LEARNED 158
HOW IS TRANSLATING INFORMATION ACHIEVED? 159
The Writing Environment: RSVP 159 — Reasons for Writing 160 — Context, Purpose and Audience Determine Form 162
GOING ABOUT WRITING 163
Pre-Writing 163 — Rough Drafts 164 — The Conference Approach 164 — Reading to Review 165 — Redrafting 165 — Editing 166 — Final Copy 166 — Publishing Students' Writing 166 — Response to Writing 166
HOW IS SUCH WRITING ASSESSED? 166
BUT IT MUST TAKE UP A LOT OF TIME? 167

PART 3
Background to the ERICA Model 169

Existing Models 171
SQ3R 172
Development of the ERICA Model 174
SMALL GROUP DISCUSSIONS 176
CONTENT OF THE ERICA STAGES 177
PREPARATION 178
Advance Organizers 179 — Purpose-Setting Questions 179 — Structured Overviews 180 — Text Structures 182 — Surveying 183 — Pre-Teaching Vocabulary 184
THINKING THROUGH 185
Three-Level Reading Guides 186 — Selective Deletion Cloze Activities 186
EXTRACTING AND ORGANIZING INFORMATION 187
Conceptual Overload 188 — Cohesion 188 — Poor Paragraph Structure 188
TRANSLATING INFORMATION 190
The Role of Language in Learning 190 — Reading and Writing: Interrelationships 192 — Integrated Reading and Writing Models 193 — Writing Processes 194

Learning to Learn from Text
PART 4
Appendix 197

Sample Curriculum Units of Work Incorporating ERICA Strategies 199

UNIT 1: Science 201
UNIT 2: History 209
UNIT 3: Geography 213
UNIT 4: Mathematics 219
UNIT 5: Home Economics 230
UNIT 6: English 242

Bibliography 251
Glossary 264
Index 275

Introduction

THIS BOOK AIMS at providing teachers with a clear, step-by-step approach to the teaching of effective reading in Content Areas, which can easily be incorporated into lesson planning and presentation.

PART 1   Looks briefly at what reading is and why teachers will find it profitable to help students develop effective reading strategies in their particular subject areas.

PART 2   Presents the Effective Reading in Content Area (ERICA) teaching model and shows how each strategy within it can be developed and implemented using a variety of subject materials.

PART 3   Examines the theoretical background to the four stages in the ERICA Model and explains the choice of the particular techniques used.

PART 4   Presents sample units of work from several subject areas and year levels, and which incorporate the stages in the ERICA Model.

The purpose of this text is to provide teachers with a model which they can use when planning teaching units that use print resources (textbooks, outlines, handouts, and so on) as part of a teaching strategy. The teaching model consists of four stages.

Preparing
Thinking Through
Extracting and Organizing
Translating

THE ERICA MODEL

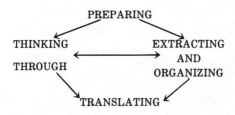

Development of this model took place in the context of inservice workshops with experienced, practising teachers. The aim of these workshops was to identify and trial a series of strategies which would help students develop effective reading skills in content areas. Since the objective of effective reading was always kept to the fore, it became common practice to start by putting the initials ERICA at the top of any planning papers or models. Eventually the initials became synonymous with the project as a whole and the name ERICA was formally adopted.

Although the activities presented are described as reading and learning strategies, they are much more than this because they help students to:

- Think more clearly.
- Learn to extract and organize information.
- Write more effectively.
- Use oral language to clarify and communicate ideas.
- Function more successfully as independent learners.

We recognize that the above claims sound extremely ambitious. Teachers, however, testify that the strategies do work. Some of the ideas put forward are not new, and we acknowledge our debt to their originators as these are introduced.

The main contribution of this text is to offer teachers a working model which can be easily incorporated into any or all subject areas. This putting together and expanding of previously separate ideas about Content Area Reading and language development provides a systematic approach which can be used as the basis for an integrated whole school language/reading policy. We hope that it proves as useful for you as it has done for the many teachers who have helped us develop it.

Bert Morris
Nea Stewart-Dore
1983

PART 1
Reading in Content Areas

Why Focus on Reading in Content Areas?

TEACHER CONCERNS

Many primary, secondary and tertiary teachers are concerned about their students' ability to use reading skills when they are required to apply them outside the context of a 'reading lesson'. Students who 'seem' to be able to read in one situation suddenly cannot do so in a different one. These students may cope quite well in the subject, English, but appear to have difficulty when faced with other subject area materials. Some people read aloud well enough but fail to understand what they read. We say they don't *comprehend*.

Of equal concern to teachers are those students who copy large extracts from articles, notes or books when given a research assignment. Some of these students copy so unthinkingly that they transcribe every word in the passage, even down to page references. For example:

> ... Captain James Smith (see page 221) who accompanied Dr Jones had provided a map (page 342) which showed the exact location of the sunken ship ...

Although the majority of teachers realize that students should be able to express ideas in their own words and consequently discourage such copying, some teachers condone and even encourage the practice. This is unfortunate, because habitual copying discourages the development of both thinking and language skills.

The cry of 'how do I stop my students copying' is closely related to other concerns about the quality of students' final written work. Thus teachers worry about essays which are poorly structured, and which contain confused and badly-expressed ideas.

While concerns about written work may seem divorced from reading, the writing assignments which are set frequently originate in reading. For example, students are required to research information on explorers, foods or transport, and are then expected to prepare an essay or a chart, reviewing this information. The teacher who receives an expressed or poorly-structured piece of writing may well feel that this is a writing problem.

But is it? Could it be that the initial reading was so inefficiently carried out, that the student simply had insufficient information to write an informed and better organized piece?

An experienced secondary school teacher recently wondered whether his Year 12 Economics students were having problems reading articles which he assigned them to study. The teacher was dissatisfied with the quality of the essays which the students wrote after they had studied the set articles. In this case, the teacher exchanged

13

ideas with another staff member whose students were not having the same problems. They talked and discovered that Teacher A did very little to prepare his students to read the articles. He had assumed that they could read well enough to understand them. Teacher B did not make this assumption, and carried out some preparation and purpose-setting exercises with his students *before* assigning the readings. As a result, this group was able to write more informed essays.

When asked, Teacher A's students admitted that they could not understand the articles and felt unable to make adequate summaries, from which to write their essays. Their problem was related to the reading rather than to the writing aspect of the assignment. Lacking specific reading purposes, they felt obliged to analyze the whole article, but were unable to do so. Their writing was poor, because basically they had nothing to write about!

It is in these circumstances that students resort to copying. They know that the information is relevant, but have difficulty *separating the important from the unimportant.* Hence the solution — copy it all!

Admittedly there may be some students who are lazy, who cannot be bothered, and who do not want to do well; perhaps they will copy anyway. However, there are also other students who would like to do well, but who don't know how! These students do not choose to copy. They do so because they have no alternative strategies. It is this second group whom we can help.

WHAT IS READING?

Although we can define reading by describing what it allows us to do, nobody has yet been able to describe exactly what we do when we read. We can say that reading is a process through which we gain access to information which has been represented in a special code. This code allows a writer to transmit a message, which readers then decode according to their prior experiences.

During the last fifteen years, much research has been done on the processes through which we arrive at comprehension. It is now generally acknowledged that reading without understanding is not really reading at all. However, the implications of this research are not clear to many teachers. We need therefore to clarify the difference between *saying words aloud* and *reading for meaning.*

The following passage can be easily 'read aloud' by anyone who has read this text so far. However, very few people, if anyone, can fully understand the author's intended meaning.

> Clopp gogs in turpy and mutto.
> Clip gogs only in mutto.
> Frew gog together in several mutto sturpys and get on very pash.
> Next year however, Clopp will have to make an important decision.
> The place in which frew gogs is to be reorganized and turpy and mutto

styrpys will be goth at different places.
Clopp will then have to decide whether bi wants to gog turpy or mutto. If bi chooses turpy, bi and Clip will no longer be able to gog together. That will make fren higigy because frew have become ogli katars.

Now, what *is* reading? If it means making the correct sound as indicated by the marks on the page, then we can read the passage above because we can say the words aloud. But, can we say that we understand what it means? Obviously not, because words such as frew, gogs and turpy have no meaning in the English language. Thus, although we may be able to make the correct sounds — read aloud accurately — this is no indication, in itself, that we fully understand what we are 'reading'.

The points made in the preceding passage apply equally to real life reading situations. The passage below is an example of a piece of text which could be read aloud by many people, who would have no idea what the author intended.

Totalizing knowledge can't be thought of as attaining ontological totalization as a new totalization of it, therefore dialectical knowledge must itself be a moment of the totalization. That is, totalization has to include its own reflexing retotalization within itself as an essential structure and also as a totalizing process within the process as a whole.

(With apologies to Jean Paul Sartre's *Critique of Dialectical Reasoning*.)

Again we may read the passage aloud even though we may have stumbled a little over 'ontological' or 'retotalization'. However, just because we can 'say' the correct words doesn't mean that we can 'read' with understanding. Think of a foreign language. We can undoubtedly make a good attempt to say these French words aloud, 'Levez la main. S'il vous plait,' but like many people we may have no idea what they mean. If we don't, then we cannot claim to be able to 'read' French.

As teachers however, we often make similar mistakes about our students! We get them to 'read aloud' for us, which they may do quite efficiently, and we then *presume* that they also understand what they have 'read'. Actually they may have no idea what it is about, rather like the vast majority of the population who can say aloud 'ontological totalization' without having the foggiest idea of its meaning.

Efficient reading does obviously include the ability to recognise the symbols and make the correct sounds. In the jargon used in reading, this is called using *grapho-phonic* clues: grapho to do with printed symbols, phonic to do with sounds. However, we must also be able to put meaning to the words. In the first example we came across the words *frew, gogs* and *turpy*. These are nonsense words which do not exist in our language. In the second example we met the word *onto-*

logical, dialectical and *totalization.* These words were difficult for us to understand because
- We were not familiar with them, and so lacked the necessary background knowledge, or *schema* as it is more properly called.
- There were no additional clues in the passages which we could use to help us unlock the meaning.

Clues which relate to our existing knowledge of words are called *semantic clues.* If these are missing then we have to try and work these out from the surrounding words. In other words, if we encounter unknown words as we read we must use *context clues*, or we may go to a glossary, encyclopaedia, or dictionary to get an explanation.

Whereas grapho-phonic clues require only a limited background knowledge about the correct sounds, semantic, or meaning clues, require an enormous background. Besides the grapho-phonic clues (sounds for symbols) and semantic clues (meaning for words) we get other background clues from our knowledge of the language itself.

For example, in our Clopp and Clip story on page 4 you could probably answer the following questions.

What does Clopp gogs in?
What does Clip gogs in?
What do Clopp and Clip gog together?
How do they get on?
What kind of words are the following:
  Clip, Clopp, turpy and mutto
  gogs and goth
  frew, bi and fren
What might the following words mean?
  frew ...., pash ...., bi ....,
  higigy ...., ogli .... and katars
  ....

The first question can be answered simply by completing the sentence.
What does Clopp gogs in?
Answer: Clopp gogs in turpy and mutto.
Similarly, we can answer the second question by finding the key words, 'Clip gogs' and then adding the remaining part of the sentence:
'What does Clip gog in?'
Answer: 'Clip gogs only in mutto.'
Using the same strategy, even though we have no idea what Jean Paul Sartre meant, we can also answer the following questions correctly.
Question 1: What can't totalizing knowledge be thought of?
Answer: Totalizing knowledge ...
Question 2: What must dialectical knowledge be?
Answer: Dialectical knowledge ...

Question 3: What does totalization have to include within itself?
Answer: ...

Although we probably did not *understand* the material we could still answer questions correctly. Why? Again because we simply followed the language or *syntactic clues* contained in the passage.

We could analyze our language skills in more depth, but at this point all we need to realise is that our existing knowledge of language clues helps us to read with understanding. If we are familiar with the language patterns of particular texts, we can use our intuitive knowledge of how language works to answer certain types of questions. As teachers we need to realize that a reader's ability to answer such 'language based' questions like those above *does not mean* that he or she understands the message. We are no nearer to understanding 'ontological totalization' than we were originally, even though we have answered some questions 'correctly'.

We can now begin to see that *we bring far more knowledge 'to' the page than we actually get 'from' it*. Richard Anderson suggests that

Text is gobbledygook unless the reader possesses an interpretive framework to breathe meaning into it.

(Anderson, 1977, p. 423)

It is our background knowledge of language structures, word meanings and sounds, together with our background knowledge of the particular topic described, which helps us make *predictions* about what we are reading. The more we are able to predict what a particular piece of text will be about, the more we are likely to be able to read it with understanding.

Reading is a complex task which involves much more than the ability to match the correct sound with the symbols on the page. Reading should be assessed, not in terms of the appropriateness of the sounds involved, but in terms of the meaning we can get from the printed message.

- We know it demands a great deal of background knowledge which we bring to the print.
- We also know that we use various clues within the text. These clues seem to be related to:
    The meaning of the words, *semantic clues.*
    The structure of the language, *syntactic clues.*
    The letter symbols and their matching sounds (*graphic-phonic clues*).
- We know that it is a very active process which requires the reader to sift through ideas, tying together important ones and discarding unneeded ones.
- We know that we learn to read by reading and that 'good' readers are people who read a lot.

WHY TEACH READING?

Because the notion of universal literacy is taken for granted we tend not to ask ourselves just why we teach reading.

Reading is something which children are expected to master. It's an expectation of what initial schooling is for, as well as being an expectation of citizens in a literate society. Such expectations however, do not fully address the implications of the question. Why teach reading?

Basically, we seek to develop literacy in order that the person may first, be able to function effectively in the society to which he or she aspires, and secondly, that he or she may have access to the body of human experience and knowledge which is preserved in print. The literate person has access to the collected writings and experiences of those people who have contributed to our culture. As a result we can read history or literature, sociology or psychology, economics or law. Alternatively, we can read to find out how to sail a boat, drive a car, build a successful marriage, cook a meal or keep a pet. Literacy makes all these things, and more, available to us.

However these generalizations do little to help the teacher who seeks to help students meet the reading demands made on them in a particular subject. Very rarely do teachers identify the reading demands which are placed on their students.

Because the question '*Why* are we trying to teach the student to read?' is not asked, the subsequent question, 'What *should* we teach our students to read?' is frequently badly answered. Instead of clear purposeful reading programs being developed from the middle-primary school onwards, we find aimless and haphazard reading activities. These frustrate teachers and do little, or nothing, to help children develop those reading skills which are necessary to make effective use of the print resources available to them.

The teaching of reading therefore frequently occurs in a vacuum. We teach reading but we know not why! If we do ask the question 'Why are we teaching reading?', the answers are usually unbalanced in favour of 'developing a love of reading through literature'. Very rarely is a functional outlook adopted, which consciously aims at helping students use text-books, journals, articles and other expository materials in order to gain knowledge, solve a problem or complete a task.

If any doubt exists about the above assertions, ask any group of teachers, primary and secondary, why they teach reading. Alternatively, look through the materials which usually provide the basis of a reading program.

Traditional reading schemes are comprised almost exclusively of story reading, with very little factual reading-to-learn or reading-to-do experiences. Many newer reading schemes, or new editions of older schemes, now make a policy of including a 'pink page' section containing Content Area Reading examples. These are reading passages chosen from subjects such as Science, Social Studies or Mathematics. However, some teachers seem quite unaware of *why* these examples are included. At a school inservice, one of the authors was told that the policy in the school was to miss out the 'pink page' section from the reading scheme used in the school. The staff had decided that, because the scheme demanded too much time if fully implemented, they would miss out the 'pink pages', which aimed at developing comprehension of content area materials. When asked, the teachers admitted that they had never stopped to ask why the content area reading examples were provided!

Primary teachers, who wish to balance their reading program, often have difficulty locating appropriate content area resources. While the reading scheme can be used to provide a story, which most of the class may use at the one time, few schools provide access to multiple copies of content area materials. School libraries have emphasized the collection of a large number of separate titles, designed to provide a range of materials. Where demand for a title is heavy, additional copies are provided, but rarely does this exceed five or six.

The development of an extensive collection is, of course, an admirable aim and remarks made here are in no way intended to deprecate this ideal. However, the narrow application of this rule means that many primary class teachers find difficulty in locating an appropriate set of texts in a content area. Thus primary students rarely sit down as a class or group to look at how an information giving text is organized. This means the class teacher has little chance of preparing his or her children to handle text books efficiently. Thus, when students reach secondary school, they have little prior experience in using the organisational features of text book material as aids to understanding content.

We therefore suggest that primary school reading programs be developed in such a way that the total reading needs of the students are provided for. This is more likely to be accomplished if the teacher asks, 'Why am I teaching reading to these students? What reading demands will be placed on them in the future?' The following diagram illustrates one possible design for a primary school's answer to these questions.

The diagram suggests the kinds of purposes which can underlie a reading program. Many teachers will claim that they already teach those skills and many others as well. However, the point is, that the reasons for teaching these skills are overlooked and teachers end up teaching skills, such as 'finding the main idea or concept in a text', for their own sake, rather than because they contribute to a more general goal. Instead, teachers should be teaching how to identify Main Ideas because this leads to skill in *note-taking* and *summarizing. Reading*

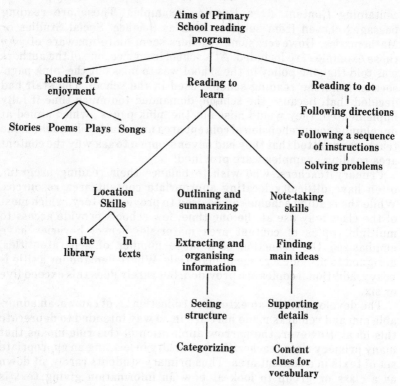

ought not to be taught as a subject but as a process. The process of reading helps us get information, by analyzing print. Reading has to be taught as an *applied* process, which is used in all subjects and so needs to be developed in and through all subjects. Teaching a 'reading' lesson and then teaching a particular subject lesson, without showing how the learned reading skills are related, is an absurd fragmentation of the school curriculum.

To demonstrate that reading skills are simply part of a larger process of getting information from print, we need to teach students how to read in a variety of contexts from Science to Music and from Physical Education to Mathematics. *If we are serious about why we teach reading, then we need to recognize, that the processes of locating, extracting, assessing and organizing information from print, are what we want to develop.* Too often we concentrate upon the content of our subjects and ignore these processes. We should teach reading in order to provide students with a tool which gives them access to the information they need and/or want to get. Anything less than this shows a lack of understanding of the broad purposes of education and represents a failure to provide for the needs of the individual.

What Is Content Area Reading?

READING TO LEARN

As well as looking at 'why' we need to teach reading in content areas, we need to be clear as to 'what' is meant by Content Area Reading.

Content Area Reading is the reading associated with the learning of a particular subject or the performance of a particular subject area task. Thus, if we are studying History, we read historical works and try to learn and understand the factual content. When studying Science we read scientific explanations or instructions. In Cooking we read to follow directions to complete a recipe. While in Accounting we have to cope with a large amount of specialized vocabulary related to commercial concepts. Each area of specialization, Science, Geography, Home Economics, Physical Education, Music, Art and so on, has its own body of literature, which presents the content of that area in a language style of its own. Once we recognize that different bodies of knowledge have their own literature and language style, we can see that the learning implications extend beyond the school scene to the world of work and everyday life. There is the reading associated with Electricians, Lawyers, Motor Mechanics and so on. The list is almost endless.

In most subjects, the reading provided is factual and seeks to inform, explain, or teach. In English however, the situation is frequently more complex. We need to recognize that the English teacher's content reading is frequently different from that in other subject areas. Where subjects such as History usually deal basically in facts, English often deals with life experiences, emotions, feelings and adventures which are usually portrayed in fictional prose. In addition, some teachers of English use media materials such as newspapers which reflect bias and propaganda. In these situations, teachers are also using expository materials so that students face a diversity of types of reading materials within the one subject.

EXPOSITORY VERSUS NARRATIVE MATERIALS

Content area reading materials tend to be *expository* in nature. This means that they try to tell about a subject — to explain and teach. As a result they are mostly factual and present a great deal of information in a very short space. As well as facts, subject materials often present an argument, which the reader is expected to recognize, follow and understand. Many content area materials also include illustrations to support the arguments and facts they present. These illustrations may include *tables, graphs, photographs, maps, line diagrams, cross-sections, charts* and so on. In all cases the reader is expected to

21

be able to cope with the concepts and facts presented in the text, with the style of language and argument adopted by the author and with the range and variety of illustrations provided to support the text.

Baker and Stein in reviewing the research literature on 'The Development of Prose Comprehension Skills' conclude that,

> ... stories have a higher order structure specified by cultural conventions, while expository text structures are more variable and ill-defined. Thus, children can use their story schema to enhance their story comprehension; no such generic knowledge is available for expository prose. Finally, stories are more concrete, with events and characters that the child can identify with, through experience or imagination. Expository material, on the other hand, is typically abstract, dealing with unfamiliar concepts and situations.
> (Baker and Stein, 1981. p. 41)

Subject, or Content Area Materials, differ considerably from the fiction materials which comprise such a large part of many early reading experiences. Fiction materials tend to be *narrative* in nature. Because we encounter so much fiction material from an early age, we intuitively learn what to expect. Thus we can anticipate that the story will have a setting and characters, that there will be a plot, that a number of incidents will be described to develop the plot and illustrate the characters and finally, that there will be a conclusion. These aspects of fiction create what we might call a story grammar, which requires that the narrative be told according to certain rules. (Rumelhart 1976, 1977; Pearson and Camperell 1981.)

When we read narrative materials we have therefore an intuitive set of guidelines for reading such prose. These have developed from hearing and reading thousands and thousands of such stories. Even so we can still find particular authors whose stories present real problems to us, because we find their style unfamiliar and thus difficult to predict (Thorndike, 1977). For example, an author like Tolstoy switches his settings so frequently and introduces so many characters, that the average reader has difficulty in following the plot. The relatively few 'difficult' authors help to make the point that narrative materials in general tend to follow a fairly predictable story grammar.

LANGUAGE REGISTERS

In general, expository materials do not provide us with the same kind of predictable framework that narrative prose does. Although some subjects organise and present their content in certain traditional ways, these traditions are limited to the particular subject and are not generalized across all subjects. For example, Geography books which compare one country with another, frequently employ headings such as Location, Relief, Climate, Vegetation, Population, Transport and Products. Other subjects such as Cooking or Science also have conventional layouts, such as those for recipes and science experiments. These conventions are however, limited to the particular subject and do not carry over to other content areas.

The fact that different subjects present different concepts, arguments, vocabulary and illustrations has lead to the development and refinement of different styles of expression in the various specialist areas. Thus the *language style* and *content* of a text on Accounting is quite different from that found in a Geography text. These styles are technically described as *language registers* and we need to recognize that the language register of one subject is different from, and imposes different demands to, those found in other subjects.

The following examples of language registers illustrate these differences.

From an academic paper on Reading research.

How might a reader's understanding be developed? If we are to avoid the detachment and deferrment of understanding from discourse processing, pedagogy must give due consideration to the nature of discourse processing including variations in schema availability, schema instantiation, top-down/bottom-up processes' communicative contexts, and differential text demands.

(Tierney and Bridge. 1978. p. 123)

From an Economics textbook used in Years 11 and 12.

The LGS ration in LGS over deposits expressed as a percentage, i.e. 44/40 = 110 per cent. But since LGS need only be 25 per cent of deposits, i.e. 25 per cent of $40m = $10m, the bank is able to lend out $44m – $10m = $34m.

(From Gibson, Hermann, Kirkwood and Swieriezuk, *The Australian Economy: An Overview*. Melbourne, Pitman Australia, 1979. p. 187)

From a Mathematics textbook used in Year 8.

A formula is an open sentence which defines a rule connecting variables representing quantities of some kind.

(From: A.G. Priddle and T.H. Davies. *Mathematics: A Systematic Approach*. Wm. Brooks & Co. Brisbane. p. 204)

CONCLUSION

Content area reading is that reading which we need to do in order to learn or to perform some task. This process is usually related to the acquisition of knowledge. The materials provided present and teach facts, argument and concepts. Most content area materials are therefore expository in nature and have a different style and structure from that found in narrative prose. English teachers, who largely *draw upon* fictional materials, use narrative materials for most of their teaching, whereas teachers in other subject areas invariably depend on expository prose to *support* their teaching. The development of specialist studies has led to the growth of subject related language registers, which involve highly specialized language styles, technical vocabulary, and different types of illustration. *These language registers each make quite specific demands on readers, who therefore require great linguistic and cognitive skills and flexibility if they are to effectively cope with one language register after another as they change subjects during the day.*

Although some subjects, such as Science, Physical Education and Home Economics, do have some areas in common, such as physiology and nutrition, they tend to have different bodies of literature which focus on different aspects of the topic and therefore, have quite different styles of expression and presentation. Thus, to the student who is studying these different subjects, they present different reading environments.

The Need To Focus On Content Area Reading

The development of independent learners is an aim to which most teachers would subscribe, yet very little is actually done to promote this ideal. The difficulties of content area reading are not widely recognised and this, in large part, contributes to the lack of assistance provided to students and the consequent misuse of print resources in many classrooms. As well as understanding the difficulties which content area reading poses, teachers should also appreciate the advantages which more efficient use of print resources brings to their classes. In order to help teachers consider these advantages, five reasons are now given which, we believe, clearly demonstrate that teachers do have much to gain from a systematic program designed to improve the reading of content area materials by students.

EFFECTIVE READING IS TIED TO EFFECTIVE TEACHING AND LEARNING

Notwithstanding the growth of television, film and video, print still remains an essential medium for *learning* and *reference*. In fact some people actually claim that literacy is becoming more important as society becomes more complex. (Resnick and Resnick, 1977.)

Print resources have the great advantage in that they are permanent and can be referred to over and over again. Teachers make great use of print resources and at any one time may have textbooks, reference books, teacher handouts, chalk-board notes, overhead transparencies, brochures, newspapers and student notes being used during the study of a topic. Because of this, we need to ensure that reading of these resources is done as efficiently as possible. Both *teacher* and *student* have an important interest in effective reading taking place.

EFFECTIVE CONTENT AREA READING CANNOT BE ASSUMED

Some students read content area materials quite effectively without any extra help from the teacher. However, not all students learn by themselves and a significant number do need help. After all that is what teaching is about! Unfortunately we tend to believe that all students ought to learn effective reading strategies quickly and intuitively. Because we as teachers find reading easy, we have difficulty appreciating that many people need help to learn the reading strategies which we acquired intuitively. It is not that people don't have the capacity to read effectively, but that they have not been taught *how* to read effectively.

Many teachers are sensitive to the fact that students are still developing their reading skills and need to be taught how to apply them appropriately in a range of reading situations. These teachers readily accept that many students need help with content reading. Unfortunately other teachers, either through lack of knowledge, understanding or interest, are very willing to label students who do not read effectively as 'hopeless cases'. Teachers who do this are merely writing-off these students, intimating that it is the students' job to prepare themselves for the reading task.

All teachers need to *recognize and accept* the fact that there will be some students in their classes who need help, if they are to make effective use of the print resources provided. As you read the passage which follows, try to imagine how students *feel* as they try to understand the material which you give them to read every day. This is an important point!

> How might a reader's understanding be developed? If we are to avoid the detachment and deferment of understanding from discourse processing, pedagogy must give due consideration to the nature of discourse processing including variations in schema availability, schema instantiation, top-down/bottom-up processes, communicative contexts and differentiated text demands.
>
> (Tierney and Bridge, 1978. p. 123)

How is it that supposedly literate people cannot understand the passage? The answer is simple. They have not experienced this argument or these concepts before. They are not prepared. *Students face this prospect every day!*

We have to realise that content area reading *varies* not only from *subject to subject* but also from *text to text* and from *year to year.* Students therefore need continuing help! We are not in a situation where we can assume reading efficiency at any age or after any course of remedial reading. The school and the teacher are *by definition* introducing students to material which is unfamiliar and which they are expected to learn from. That is the nature of education.

The teacher's job is to reduce the distance which exists between the student and the printed text. When viewed in this way, it is easier to appreciate that some students need help if they are to make effective use of their print resources. Rather than being described as 'hopeless cases', we can perhaps see them as students who are not 'ready' to interact with and use particular kinds of material and who need help, if they are to develop to the stage where they are ready.

Literacy is a relative concept. For example, a migrant may be highly literate in his or her own language, but illiterate in English. You may be highly literate in your own field, but find reading in another subject beyond you. Ability to read with understanding should therefore not be assumed by the teacher who presents written material in any subject.

READING IS A THINKING PROCESS

If we think about the purposes for which students read content area materials, we will soon realise that a great deal of thinking is involved. We expect students to perform the following tasks:
- Summarize passages or chapters.
- Pick out main ideas and details, building these into an outline.
- Pick out comparison and contrast or cause and effect examples.
- Learn new vocabulary from context clues.
- Distinguish fact from opinion.
- Follow an argument, seeing the logic involved and relating different points to verify the conclusions.
- Decide whether a piece of information is relevant to a topic being researched.

These and other reading tasks are not accomplished without a great deal of thinking. Another point, which we need to recognize, is that in subject areas this thinking is happening within and around the content which the student needs to learn. *Effective reading is therefore effective thinking about the subject*, surely a fundamental content objective, which all teachers strive to attain. Students who do not, or cannot, make effective use of print resources, therefore miss an opportunity to *reflect upon, consider* and *think through* the implications of the concepts presented. It is in the teacher's interests to foster effective reading, since by doing so, students stand a far better chance of understanding and remembering the concepts being taught.

EFFICIENT READING IS NECESSARY FOR INDEPENDENT LEARNING

The Schools Commission Report, *Schooling for 15 and 16 Year Olds* (1980), provides a very useful analysis of current educational practices in Australia. The report notes that the term 'Basic Skills' is often limited to concepts of a very elementary level and asks why the term 'basic skills' could not instead suggest:

> ... the development of skills to a level which allows students to be independent learners, able not only to use appropriate text books, but also to collect and order information and ideas, and structure them into the coherent presentation of an argument ...
> (Schools Commission, 1980. p. 20)

Many teachers would probably claim that these aspirations are beyond the majority of students, but are they? Effective reading is a process which allows us to gain, evaluate and utilize far more information than any one teacher can provide. Every teacher's abilities are limited! In comparison the amount of information available in print is limitless. If we concentrate upon giving knowledge, we are limited to that which we have acquired ourselves and which we have time to impart. *If we encourage students to develop reading and research skills, we provide them with a key to the world.*

The Schools Commission insists that:

> The continuing assumption that the mass of students cannot acquire these skills of research and reasoning must be tackled . . . They require sustained attention, because they have more long-term pay-off for students than additional forgetable information.
>
> (Schools Commission, 1980. p. 20)

As we have already suggested, this process does not occur spontaneously in all students. Obviously the amount of help required will vary from school to school and from class to class. This has probably been where we have been misled. Because we meet some students who can process print information adequately, we tend to assume that this is the norm, the natural occurrence. In fact, the reverse is the case in some schools and may actually be the case overall. In the United States for example, it has been reported that between 90 and 95 per cent of American students are incapable of the reasoned and disciplined thought necessary to analyze and evaluate what they read. The National Assessment of Educational Progress, which reported these satistics, believes that some reasons for students failure to develop thinking and analytical skills are:

- Methods of teaching which rely on teacher-dominated questioning and brief answers from students.
- Multiple choice testing.
- Students' reading habits and the progressive decline in their enjoyment of reading (81 per cent enjoyed reading at age 9, less than 50 per cent at age 13, and only 42.4 per cent at age 17).

The NAEP then goes on to make several recommendations which have particular significance for content area teachers. These are:

- Students should be involved in discussion activities which require them to explain and defend their ideas.
- Extensive writing should be part of all courses and should include organising and relating segments of text to one another.
- Essay questions should be part of all testing.
- Students should be given systematic instruction in writing, including critical thinking and problem solving skills.

(Education USA, 16 November 1981)

We can see from the above, that authoritative educational opinion in Australia and the United States has drawn attention to the need for schools to aim at developing independent information processing skills in their students. If the school and individual teacher set the development of effective reading and research skills as a major objective, then they start from a position of acceptance, where positive action can be taken to develop information processing skills in all students. *Print resources can then be used to develop research and reasoning skills, as well as to transmit a body of knowledge.* For too long we have been content to train students as parrots, able to regurgitate a mass of words. What sense is there in training students to parrot back 'Ontological totalisation is a realisation of a wider totalisation of the whole'? Far better to spend our time in teaching them to research the meaning of this passage and others. After all, the future of our society is dependent upon the skill and inventiveness of its people. Who needs parrots?

WE LEARN BY DOING

Those of us who can dance will recall that we learned to dance by getting up and dancing. Our first efforts may have been preceded by some instruction on the foot movements, relationship to other dancers and so on. Those of us who now dance well, probably have
- Had lots of practise.
- Watched other good dancers and analyzed what they did.
- Had some coaching.
- Learned to subconsciously recognise and react to 'good' dance music.
- Gained a great deal of satisfaction from dancing well.
- Gained a great deal of satisfaction from having our dancing skills recognised and praised.
- Gained a great deal of satisfaction from the social interaction which dancing provides.

People who do not dance will possibly wonder what the above list is all about, while, those who have a dislike of dancing may well disagree entirely on some or all of the points. The point is that those people who do dance learned to dance by dancing. Similarly, those people who play musical instruments, golf, or bridge, who cook, knit, paint, weld, bricklay or whatever, *learned by doing it!* Effective reading of content area materials is in the same category. *We learn to do it by doing it!* Providing help to students in content area reading thus has a quantitative aspect. Students must be given lots of opportunities to practise this type of reading.

Unfortunately this point is not always evident in school practices. Many teachers deny their students the opportunity to use reading material at all. These teachers claim that the books are too difficult or that the students can't read well enough; 'So I tell them what they need to know!' This self defeating practice means that students will not learn to read effectively, if the teacher does all their reading for them.

Learning to Learn from Text

In a major study of secondary school reading practices, Lunzer and Gardner (1979) found that the reading which students were asked to do was invariably in short bursts of only a few *seconds* duration. Rarely, if ever, were they asked to reflect on or become closely involved with the print.

In yet other situations, teachers want their pupils to have notes about particular topics. However, they feel that the students are incapable of making notes for themselves so *the teachers make the notes!* This avoids the issue, because to know how to make notes *students need to be taught.* Putting reading aside and making notes for students is a 'cop-out' by teachers. It denies that,

- Students can learn how to make notes.
- Teachers ought to be teaching students 'how to' do it.

Observation of school systems reveals that most emphasis is placed on the acquisition of subject knowledge and that the role of the processes discussed above is grossly undervalued.

If we want to prepare enquiring and independent learners who are flexible problem solvers, able to adapt to a variety of situations, then we do need to focus on the processes of gaining and applying information. If, on the other hand, we only want people to possess a certain body of knowledge, then we ignore these processes and set about imparting the knowledge. This text presumes that teachers will choose the former objective.

Communication and Content Area Reading

THE CENTRAL ROLE OF LANGUAGE

Learning subject matter in schools is bound up in the language-using environment of classrooms. Curriculum processes have to do, not only with *teacher determined objectives*, but also with *student intentions*, all of which are transmitted through the four language modes: *speaking and listening, reading and writing*. Language environments are created and sustained through *interactions* between teacher, students and subject resources, all of which contribute to the development of a learning climate.

The learning climate may be 'controlled' by teacher dominated or directed language activities, or it may be shaped by the tentative language explorations of students, who are encouraged to freely use their own language to tap experiences and create meaning.

At all stages of its implementation, the ERICA Model (to be described in Part 2) focuses on creating *opportunities* for students to:
- Draw on their own language resources to recall past experience.
- Grapple with new ideas and concepts.
- Perceive relationships between new ideas and concepts.
- Explore meanings.
- Explain and amplify information.
- Reflect on and interpret their reading.
- Express their understanding orally, diagramatically and in writing.

The ERICA Model focuses on student language use in several ways. The most important of these is the use of strategies requiring mixed-ability group discussion. For years teachers have grouped students according to various criteria. Often however, they have failed to recognize and appreciate the enormous benefits to be gained from structured, rather than controlled discussion activities. They have tended to view group-work from a *product* rather than a *process* perspective; as a means to an end when completing tasks, rather than as an interactive, mutually supportive language experience through which they can learn and gain mastery of and control over knowledge.

Teacher perceptions of what constitutes a *discussion* may vary. In one Year 8 English class, the teacher was observed introducing an excerpt from a story about a schoolboy gang fight. The stated purpose of the reading experience (which constituted the teacher reading the excerpt to the class) was 'to discuss the way the gang members felt during the fight'. What followed was a part-class interrogation, through predominantly closed questions about the events described. Few students proffered answers or became engaged in the issues. Most of the class probably recognized that the question-answer technique wasn't leading anywhere, let alone fulfilling even the teacher's intentions! Not much of a 'discussion' was occurring. The students weren't invited to *explore* possibilities — only to provide single answers to the teacher's questions.

While this is an extreme example of non-discussion, it happens all too frequently. Many teachers find it difficult to tolerate discursive talk that is seemingly non-productive and, therefore, possibly time-wasting. When they are in control, they believe they have some chance of 'covering the syllabus', and achieving *their* intentions.

In contrast to this, Barnes (1976) reports instances of small group discussion where the students directed their own search for meaning and understanding. During the process of talking, students were able to draw on and shape the knowledge that they already had about particular topics and to relate it to a new context. They were all encouraged to explore and make sense of something they didn't understand.

Barnes also provides examples of how small groups can go about *organizing their thinking, through language*; how their self-questioning, demands for clarification, repetition and expansion of ideas about or summarizing of a topic, although spontaneous and improvised, need not be shapeless.

Such discussions are usually lengthy and may sound disorganized to an independent listener who stands outside the process. However in our experience, the 'structured' discussion promotes such a high level of student involvement that no-one who observes it closely, could describe it as disorganized or non-productive. Instead teachers frequently feel elated because they have experienced a class in which even normally unresponsive students were involved and contributing. As one Year 10 Home Economics teacher said, 'They are normally a bad class but today I really felt that they were doing what I should always have them doing.'

Richards (1978) points out that unless students recognize the *purposes of group discourse*, they will not see the need to follow-up leads to tease out meanings, and to use new and sometimes bothersome language forms and vocabulary to help them realize new meanings and understandings. Thus, if small group discussion is to be productive, serving to extend students' understanding of subject matter as well as to enhance opportunities to experiment with and use the language in which the subject matter is couched, there needs to be a clear focus for talk and a well-defined purpose for group interactions.

The ERICA Model provides both the focus for talk and defined purposes for group negotiations. Many of the strategies used focus on language-thinking activities such as these:

- Exploring vocabulary and concepts.
- Drawing on knowledge of language structure to uncover meanings.

- Locating specific information.
- Making inferences.
- Identifying relationships between ideas.
- Clarifying understanding.
- Amplifying explanations.
- Justifying points of view.
- Relating the known to the unknown.
- Testing hypotheses.
- Predicting outcomes.
- Investigating possibilities, both linguistic and knowledge-based.

The overriding purposes of language at work in focused group discussions are:

- To think through ideas.
- To extract and organize information.
- To translate information to demonstrate understanding.

In the ERICA Model, language is actively employed as a tool for learning subject matter. It is the students, not the teacher, who do the 'languaging', the thinking, and the negotiation of meaning, to reach understanding. The teacher's role becomes one of setting up the situations and conditions for exploratory talk, by establishing both *focus* and *purpose*, and by fostering a climate for learning.

But why bother with all this talk? Surely subject teaching has to do with transmitting information? Since the teacher has access to the required information, isn't it more economical for the teacher to instruct rather than to leave the information search to students who are 'unknowing'?

It would appear that traditionally this is exactly what teachers do. Flanders (1962) identified the rule of two-thirds:

> In the average classroom someone is talking for two-thirds of the time, two-thirds of the talk is teacher-talk, and two-thirds of the teacher-talk is direct influence.

There is little reason to believe the situation is much different, some twenty years later.

Teacher-talk is characterized by *exposition* and *questioning* — expounding facts and interpretations which are then tested, with students joining in (by invitation only) only to risk a wrong answer to what's in the teacher's mind.

We've all been guilty of this approach: 'No, what I'm thinking of is ...'

Sometimes, of course, we are genuinely surprised when students diverge a little and offer a response which is appropriate, but which had not occurred to us. A teacher who is aware of the potential value of these responses, will seize upon the opportunity to incorporate student contributions. Sadly, many teachers 'cut off' this kind of interaction, preferring to steer 'discussion' along pre-determined routes. Primarily, this may be because they feel insecure with the discussion technique.

Some reasons for teacher insecurity in small group discussion include:
- Limited training.
- A feeling that their teacher-role is being usurped.
- Concern about management/control problems (popularity, 'noise levels').
- Uncertainty about what is being learnt.
- A belief that students need direct instruction.
- Inflexible seating arrangements.
- Concern for the amount of time/organization necessary to conduct group discussions.
- Their personal capacity to differentiate or individualize instruction.
- Domination by vocal students.
- Uncertainty about the value of discussion as a learning tool.
- A belief that 'talking' is not 'working'.
- The fear of being wrong.
- Restricted subject knowledge.
- Limited knowledge of reading/thinking processes.

Lunzer and Gardner (1979) review several group approaches to reading which involve students in various kinds of activities which require them:

> to read in order to solve problems and to reflect, not only on the results of their reading, but also on the thinking and strategies used in arriving at decisions.
>
> (p. 228)

All of the group activities which Lunzer and Gardner describe, as well as those of Stauffer (1970) and Walker (1974), are logical extensions of teachers recognizing the role of the learner in the interactive process of reconstructing the meaning of a text. These authors provide guidelines for establishing the conditions under which learning through reading can occur. All feature specific activities which place language-using demands on students in group situations. All acknowledge the specialized role of the teacher in:
- Selecting appropriate material to be read.
- Formulating desired reading outcomes.
- Guiding discussion by assigning a wide range of purposeful tasks which challenge students to talk to solve problems.
- Fostering a climate conducive to sharing, criticizing and defending ideas.
- Extending the peer group learning.

Classroom teachers are pragmatists who want strategies which they know will *work for them*. However, some fundamental 'issues' need to be faced *before* such group discussion procedures can be put into practice. These include making distinctions between the following issues:

- Teaching and learning *processes*.
- Teacher and student *intentions* to teach and to learn.
- *Roles* in teaching and learning.

If you accept that there are differences and that your *priority* is to help students seek knowledge and understanding, then you should consider the following group discussion implementation procedure:

1. Begin modestly. Experiment with a couple of groups within a class, or alternatively, have students work in pairs. Later, expand to several groups of four to six students.
2. State what you want to be learned. That is, decide on your content objectives. For example, students will probably understand when and why cyclones occur. Let them know what knowledge and understanding they should attain.
3. Establish your *purposes* for group/pair exchange of ideas (discussion). Establish why you want students to interact and what outcomes you expect. *Share your purposes with the students.* Invite them to help you decide why group interaction is a good idea.
4. Determine the task(s) to be worked on. The task(s) should be related directly to your purposes.

For example, in a Year 8 Geography unit on weather and climate, you may want students to understand the effects of cyclonic storms and to know what precautions need to be taken in such an event. You decide to have students undertake a data collection activity, and provide a framework for action in small groups.

CYCLONE ALERT!

Before you start, read these instructions carefully to find out the purpose of the exercise.

It's important for people who live in tropical areas to know what to do when a cyclone is threatening.

(a) In your groups, decide how you will gather information about the steps to follow during a Cyclone Alert. (Your telephone directory will be a useful resource.)
(b) Make a list of organizations that are likely to be most helpful — pool your ideas and record them on a class chart.
(c) Decide *exactly* what information you will ask for. 'Brainstorm' to make sure you don't leave important details out. Make a list of your class ideas.
(d) In small groups select an organization to write to, requesting information to be included on a poster which explains in everyday language:
   (i) what a cyclone alert is;

(ii) what safety precautions should be taken in the event of a cyclone threatening your town.

(e) Write a group letter to your chosen organization setting out your request for information. Discuss your letter with other groups and decide which are the best letters to send.

(f) Appoint a scribe to make a good copy of your class letters.

5. Organize *mixed* ability groups to complete tasks. These groups foster co-operative thinking, talking and exchange of ideas. They allow less-able students to be tutored by their peers, and provide opportunities for students to rehearse what they know. Reiterating and explaining information provides repetition of ideas, and group negotiation is encouraged.

6. Minimize your role as 'transmission' teacher-director-instructor. Assume responsibility for listening-in on conversations, and help students explore possibilities rather than steer them towards closed decisions.

7. Be prepared to accept:
    (a) Discursive talk which is tentative, exploratory and sometimes wandering — it's part of the process of 'thinking through' or thinking aloud. Recognize that you often indulge in similar practices.
    (b) *Negotiation* of ideas as part of the practice of of your subject. Anyone can parrot the thoughts of others, but weighing up evidence and justifying conclusions requires an understanding that any body of knowledge can be modified.
    (c) Suggestions from students as to how problems might be solved.
    (d) A change in your own attitudes toward language, teaching and learning, and a change in your relationship with students.

Barnes (1976) explores the possibilities of group work in classrooms where discussion is sustained by a supportive social climate. He sees the kind of interactive talk emerging from it as one means for students to 'control their own language strategies'. These are some of the kinds of language strategies available to users:

- Thinking aloud.
- Wondering and hypothesizing.
- Trialling and testing ideas.
- Repeating ideas and rephrasing.
- Grouping for the right word.
- Backtracking and modifying.
- Adding and expanding ideas.
- Seizing on ideas from others to make sense of your own.
- Re-interpreting ideas.

Unfortunately, in many classrooms, little opportunity arises to practise these strategies. The to-and-fro, question-response-question, is as regular as it is monotonous. Students in such classrooms are rarely allowed any reasonable opportunities to rehearse or train, in and through language. They enter the 'Grand Slam' tournament of learning, linguistically unfit, unskilled and outmanoeuvred.

Such a tradition of school language use is in striking contrast with what we know about how students learn language and its uses in the first instance. As babies, their every utterance is rewarded, paraded and encouraged. Approximations to adult language and experiments with it are highlights of the progression towards mastery and control of our linguistic system. As a child gains confidence, he or she becomes more adventurous, venturing further afield linguistically and more prepared to take risks with the infinite possibilities of which language is capable. The child uses language for different purposes as needed and as demanded by the different situations. Language becomes the tool for conquering any challenge. It assumes we don't 'teach' young children language power — they learn it for these reasons:

- To make sense of their world.
- To enter into the social communication network.
- To satisfy real needs.

Children learn language by using it in the context of supportive and interactive relationships. Their facility with language grows by constantly attempting to meet new demands — a process that adults encourage, in the early years, at least.

When children enter school, the ground rules for language learning and use often change abruptly. The institutional nature of the school dictates this change to some extent. One teacher simply can't listen simultaneously to the linguistic needs of thirty children. Nevertheless, the coping strategies adopted by many teachers appear extreme and ruthless, to say the least. That is why we suggest alternative classroom organization in the form of small, mixed-ability groups (akin to social/familial grouping), wherein 'talk' can occur in as near to natural language using/language learning situations as possible.

Tough (1973) referred to children's 'disposition to use language' and there's plenty of real-life evidence to support that disposition. Children (and adults, too) use language all the time at home, school and play — for a wide range of purposes. As teachers, our task is to harness that disposition to need to use language and to provide opportunities to practise language use. *The Bullock Report* (1975) recommended that:

> every teacher ... should accept it as part of his responsibility to develop the pupils' reading, writing and speaking ability in and through the subject or activity for which he is responsible.
>
> (p. 237)

Language development as defined by the National Language Development Project (Curriculum Development Centre, Canberra, 1977-81), comprises three interrelated aspects, namely, learning language, learning through language and learning about language. Language use in school subjects subsumes all three of these aspects, as students learn to communicate in and through specialist language, and in the process, learn more of its capacity to express thought, meaning and understanding.

To take responsibility for the language development of students means that teachers need to be aware of:

- The nature of subject language.
- The ways in which subject language is used to express meaning.
- Strategies which ensure that students experience subject language through speaking and writing, as well as through listening and reading.

THE NATURE OF SUBJECT LANGUAGE AND ITS USE

Barnes (1969) refers to Rosen's notion of 'the language of secondary education', as a formal language which holds subject-specific terminology together and which is used for instruction. Typical of such language is the phraseology of instructions, particularly those of assignments or examination-type questions which ask students to do these things.

- Discuss the implications of . . .
- Compare and contrast . . .
- Draw on your experience to illustrate . . .
- Justify your reasons for . . .
- Review the effects of . . .
- Account for . . .
- Explain why . . .

It is often as difficult for students to decipher the intention of such tasks, as it is to organize the ideas necessary to complete them.

As well, there is the non-technical language within which subject concepts are embedded. Gardner (1972) gives an example from Science.

> Gas molecules display *random* motion; we may *predict* their behaviour from *theoretical* considerations, the actual volume of the molecules may be *neglected*.

(The items in italics are not listed in a major Science reference and are regarded as being non-technical words, yet crucial to an understanding of the concepts being conveyed.)

Here are other text examples in which we have identified non-technical items which contribute to a complete and clear understanding of the concepts presented, but which would not be listed in any major subject reference.

YEAR 8: HISTORY
Source: Marvin, M., Marvin, S., and Cappelluti, F.
The Human Adventure, Addison-Wesley, 1976. (p. 128)

Metaphor — RULE by IRON or RULE by the PEOPLE

The invaders with the hard iron weapons who had defeated the Mycenaeans finally settled down in a small village. It *Time* became the city of Sparta. And Sparta never lost the touch *signal* of iron. As it grew, it became a symbol of a hard life. ——→ *Metaphor*

There was some beauty in the Spartan life. Spartan potters had great skill. And there were festivals with *Addition* *Opposing* dances and songs. But mostly life in Sparta was hard. / *Signal* *view* Sparta had enemies on the outside. There were also *signal* enemies within. The Spartans had made slaves of the *Effect* people of a nearby city-state. These slaves would revolt if *signal* they got a chance. So the citizens of Sparta had to be ready to defend themselves. Their children began to train for war when they were seven. They not only learned to use *Addition* weapons. They also learned to put up with pain and *Signals* hardship.

A Spartan boy went barefoot so that[1.] his feet stayed tough. He wore the same short cloak all year so that[2.] he *Elaboration* got used to the changing weather and[3.] could stand the cold *of key* when winter came. He was given just enough to eat. Some- *point by* times he was given too little to eat, so that[4.] he would learn *examples* to go without food. And someone was always nearby, with a whip,[5.] ready to punish him if he made a mistake.

The Spartan's home was not important. He could not marry until he was 20. He could not live with his wife until *Condition* he was 30. Even then he continued to eat with the other men *signal* in a dining hall. When he and his wife had children, he had to give them to the state. All Spartans belonged to the state. Women as well as men trained their bodies. Girls as well as boys were made to grow strong and brave.

The main food of the Spartans was a black broth made of pork, vinegar, and salt. The story was told of an outsider who had been amazed at the Spartan's courage. Then he had a chance to eat with them. After one sip of the black broth, he decided that the Spartans were no braver than anyone else. He felt that anyone who had to eat food like that would just as soon die anyway!

Sparta was like a huge army. It was ruled by a small *Figurative* group of generals. All through Spartan society, when some- *comparison* one higher up gave an order, the order was obeyed without question.

YEAR 8: HISTORY
Source: Marvin, M., Marvin, S., and Cappelluti, F.,
The Human Adventure, Addison-Wesley, 1976. (p. 352)
THE INDUSTRIAL REVOLUTION

Time sequence signal

Weaving and spinning were among the earliest crafts. For

General-ization

many hundreds of years, they were done by people — mostly women — working in their own homes. Then, in England in the 1700s inventors began improving the tools for spinning and weaving. In 1764, a man built a spinning machine and named it after his daughter Jenny. This spinning jenny was quickly improved. Soon no hand was needed

Change signal

Time order signal

Comparison signal

to spin the thread. And instead of being run by foot power, as spinning wheels were, the spinning jenny was run by a water wheel. In 1785, steam took the place of the water wheel. The spinning mill became a modern factory.

More and better thread was being produced. The weaving process had to catch up with the spinning process. The first mechanical loom was built. By 1813, there were about 2,000 mechanical looms in England. By 1833, there were 85,000. The spinning mills and the weaving factories joined to form the beginnings of the modern textile industry. *Textiles* are cloth. The *Industrial Revolution* had also begun.

Time order Signals

In this passage, a number of specific examples are cited and generalizations and allusions derived from them. For example, 'The spinning mill became a *modern factory*', and '*The Industrial Revolution* had also begun'. This additive technique does little to help students make the conceptual leaps necessary to understand concepts like 'modern factories' or the complexities of the so-called 'Industrial Revolution'.

Source: Barr, B.B., and Leyden, M.B., *Life Science*, Addison-Wesley, 1980. (p. 295)
COMPARISON AND CONTRAST IN CELLS

Comparison signal

Each kind of cell has a different job to do. Yet all cells *perform* certain tasks. They *release* energy in *chemical changes* involving sugar. They build new cell parts from other materials that enter the cell. They allow materials to move into or out of the cell. And they try to *react* to changes in their environment that might stop them from doing these tasks.

MOVEMENT IN AND OUT OF CELLS (p. 295)

In all cells a cell membrane *surrounds* the contents of the cell. Anything that enters or leaves the cell must pass through the cell membrane. <u>This includes</u> sugar, oxygen, *Enumeration* water, and carbon dioxide. It <u>also</u> includes the materials cell *signal* need for their other tasks. — *Addition*

Exception,   <u>Not</u> everything is able to pass through the membrane. Of *signal* *signalling* things that can pass through it, they will sometimes pass *comparison* through more easily in one direction. That is, something *Alternative* may enter a cell more easily than leave it. <u>Or</u> something *explanation* may leave a cell more easily than enter it. — *signal*

Italicized items, like those cited by Gardner, help convey the subject information, although they are non-technical items.

These examples, from History and Science resources, also appear to adhere to some prescriptions for lowering the readability level of the text. Note how many ideas are not explicitly linked across sentences. For example, the first text flits from concepts about foot-powered spinning wheels, to water-driven spinning jennies, to the advent of steam and the modern factory. As well, relatively short sentences similar to those given in the passage below, inhibit the flow and linking of contrastive ideas.

Some water organisms have special adaptations that let them live only in fresh water. Others can live only in salt water. A few, such as salmon, are able to live in both. But all water organisms must be able to regulate water in their bodies. Freshwater organisms must stop too much water from entering their systems. Saltwater organisms have the opposite problem. They must keep replacing the water that leaves their systems.

(Barr, B.B., and Leyden, M.B. p. 55)

REGISTER OF SUBJECTS

We are also concerned with the *register of subjects* — varieties of language which students do not use in everyday transactions, but which teachers use in setting contexts for lessons.

Register has to do with the relationship between language (in this case the features of text) and the context of its use, which distinguishs one piece of writing (or oral language) from another. For example language used in the teaching of school subjects differs in its style from the language used in parliamentary debate, precisely because:

- The *setting, purposes* and *topics* vary.
- The *tenor* of language, which marks the relationships between the participants (teacher — student; opposition — government members), differs.
- The *mode* of language marks the *distances* between the participants.

While register can be marked in this way, we cannot identify for certain absolute features of any one register. However, we can predict that some words and structures are more likely to appear in some texts than they are in others. The language used in subject teaching has evolved to meet special needs of economy and precision, which enable teachers and textbook writers to describe, define, explain and record.

Subject language tends to take on a formal, 'public' style, with few idiomatic or colloquial phrases and no clarification of either the origin of information or the target audience for the communication.

As well, terminology used for giving instructions is formal: terms like 'research' not 'find out'; 'observe the relationship between' not 'see how X and Y are connected'; are characteristic of tradition instructional contexts.

Subject register can also be characterized by impersonal language forms — no first or second person pronouns, and a preference for passive voice. For example:

> But Athenian democracy was not perfect democracy. Athenian rule by the people 'meant rule by the citizen'. A citizen was a male over the age of 20 who was born of a free Athenian family. Slaves, who made up one-third of the people in Athens, were not included. Women, who made up half of the citizen class, were left out. So were the many foreigners living in Athens. Fewer than one-tenth of the people of Athens were part of the 'people' of Athenian democracy.
>
> (Marvin, M., Marvin, S., and Cappelluti, F., p. 129)

Certain features of subject language also tend to signal the *functions* of language in classroom situations. Some functions include:

- *Explaining and exemplifying*
  ('Energy is required by the body for the maintenance of essential functions such as . . .')
- *Describing*
  ('The undulating terrain near the coastline . . .')
- *Reporting*
  ('It was found that . . .')
- *Hypothesising*
  ('Perhaps the most economically significant . . .')
- *Defining*
  ('which by a process known as photosynthesis convert inorganic elements into the organic . . .')

These functions may be intertwined in text thereby making the language used even more complex. Richards (1978) suggests however, that from her data collected in various subjects, certain features and functions appear more regularly than others. She suggests:

> For example, in the Biology lessons as many words are used for describing and defining as for all four other functions. Chemistry, on the other

hand, is the most strongly represented of the sciences in the category of explanation ... The experimental nature of Chemistry is reflected in the comparatively high incidence of hypothesis, report/record and recipe.

(p. 93)

The language of Humanities subjects likewise moves from one function to another. In Geography, for example, Richards asserts that it becomes 'increasingly concerned with quantifying rather than describing', while History moves from giving information to interpreting and evaluating evidence. Language reflects this shift.

Subject register and its role in setting up barriers to students' acquisition of knowledge and understanding is immensely complex. Rosen (1967) asks the question:

How can they (students) be helped towards this language in such a way that it develops rather than retards their thinking?

(p. 122)

Lots of talking, thinking and reading activities which promote talk using language to explore subjects, as outlined in the ERICA Model, is one way.

STRATEGIES FOR EXPERIENCING SUBJECT LANGUAGE

Students 'experience' *subject language* constantly, in a passive, receptive manner usually, if Flander's rule of two-thirds is a fact of classrooms.

Students need to become actively involved in the process of making sense of subject content, through talking and solving problems in small groups and by experimenting with language structures and styles in their own writing.

In many classrooms, students listen and respond to 'test' questions and often give up on trying to make sense of subject matter, which they see as being controlled and directed by the teacher. They view their role as one of receivers of information, to be regurgitated in some form on cue — again signalled by the teacher.

Teachers need to adopt those strategies outlined in the ERICA Model, that is to invite students to actively participate in the construction of meaning, help them to explore possibilities and to draw implications from their understanding of subject content.

The Schools' Council publication, *From Information to Understanding: What Children Do with New Ideas*, (Ward Lock, 1976), sums up our thinking with respect to learning through talking, reading and writing as well as listening. In it, the authors maintain that we 'know' only when we have absorbed ideas into our own way of thinking and have explored their possibilities. This involves reorganizing our view of the world, which goes further than just 'getting' information.

Learning to Learn from Text

'Active' learning demands that you do something with the information once you've found it.

Thus, oral and written activities, individually, in pairs and in small mixed-ability groups, which cause students to 'rebuild theories', also help students to:

- Bring their experience of the world to bear on problems.
- Tease out ideas.
- Untangle threads.
- Grapple with information to make sense of it.
- Experience the shaping of knowledge through using language purposefully. These strategies have much to offer in helping students to gain access to knowledge to make it their own.

PART 2
Reading to Learn: the
ERICA Model

In this section we will consider how to implement reading-to-learn strategies in the classroom. The ERICA Model has been developed in co-operation with a large number of teachers and is presented here as a set of strategies, which have been extensively trialled in many class-rooms, at different levels, and in different subject areas. Jargon has been reduced to a minimum in this section, as has reference to the theories which underpin the model. Readers interested in the theoretical bases for the model, will find that Part 3 provides a research based rationale for the various components of the ERICA Model together with recommendations for wider reading.

The ERICA Model consists of four stages.

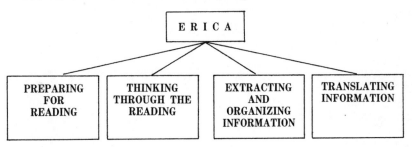

Figure 2.1

The four stages in the model represent the steps which teachers should consider when planning to use reading as an aid to learning. We do not suggest that all four stages *have* to be included in every teaching unit. The materials and the teacher's objectives will determine just which stages are finally included. *However, it is recommended that all four stages be considered when planning a unit of work.* Regular use of the four stages of the ERICA Model will allow the teacher to plan:
- What reading skills will be developed.
- How reading will be used to assist the learning of specific content.

The four stages have been developed in order to help teachers overcome particular problems which many, many teachers face. Figure 2.2 relates specific teacher concerns to each stage of the ERICA Model.

Learning to Learn from Text

TEACHER CONCERN	ERICA STAGE USED
1. Students have difficulty using the text effectively	PREPARING
2. Students can 'read' but do not understand what they read	THINKING THROUGH
3. Students copy rather than change ideas into their own words	EXTRACTING AND ORGANIZING INFORMATION
4. Students cannot summarize or express themselves clearly, and accurately in writing	TRANSLATING

Figure 2.2. Development of the ERICA Model

Stage 1. Preparing for Reading

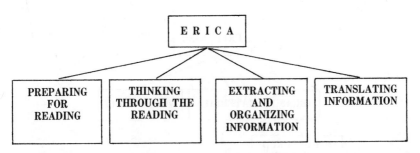

The first stage in developing effective reading in your subject area is to PREPARE BOTH YOURSELF AND YOUR STUDENTS for the reading you want them to carry out. Too often, we assign a piece of reading without first pre-viewing it ourselves, to find out in some detail just what information is presented and what reading skills are required. Perhaps even worse than this, we frequently assign reading without having a definite idea of what we want students to gain from it. Thus, many reading assignments in subject areas lack purpose, are ill-chosen and offer no clear understandable structure to the students. In these circumstances students may well be forgiven for complaining that they don't know what to look for or that they find the text too difficult and can't understand it.

PREPARING STUDENTS FOR A READING ASSIGNMENT: ASPECTS TO CONSIDER

We suggest three aspects of preparation for a reading assignment. The first relates to the ideas (concepts) which are to be learned. The second examines the materials and looks at how the information is presented. The third identifies and categorizes new vocabulary which will be encountered in the text.

The Structured Overview: Organizing Our Ideas

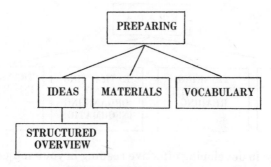

INTRODUCTION

It is known that efficient learners are often efficient readers, who are able to organize ideas. They see *relationships, make associations, see how details and examples can be grouped together in categories, distinguish relevant information and dispense with irrelevant material.*

Efficient learners are able to relate new information to knowledge which is already stored in the mind, so that the new ideas are fitted into existing frameworks. We also know that inefficient learners are often inefficient readers and are less likely to carry out the above activities that efficient learners do consistently.

Thus, when the efficient reader undertakes a reading-to-learn task, it is usually done systematically. This reader looks at the structure of the text, locates the main points and identifies the logical development. Most importantly, the efficient reader only reads as much as he or she needs to in order to find the required information.

In contrast, inefficient readers tend to read entire sections, often in a word-by-word fashion, failing to recognize the meaning units, which are wrapped up in the author's words. These readers lack effective systems for processing information. They are often overwhelmed by the mass of words and are unable to recognize structures or the elements of a logical explanation. Because of this it is important that teachers provide logical frameworks for students, so that they can see how the ideas they are to encounter are developed.

If, at the same time, teachers can tap students' background knowledge, so much the better, for the new information can then be related to known contexts. Reading-to-learn can thus become more objective and systematic, because the readers now have an idea of what is important and can start to discriminate between that which is required and that which is not.

The strategy, which is used to help students begin to organise their ideas, is called a *Structure Overview.* This technique, as described by

Earle (1969), has been extensively researched. (See Part 3.) Similar techniques have been developed under names such as 'concept maps', 'concept webs' and 'concept hierarchies'. All of these techniques basically consist of a set of key words which radiate from an overall concept. Various words are connected together by lines or dots to show clusters which relate to specific aspects of the topic.

Put together, these ideas form an overview of the topic. In this kind of hierarchical structure, more general points are found near the top of the 'tree' and more detailed points towards the bottom. That is, abstract points come higher than concrete details. A Structured Overview will usually, but not necessarily, be arranged as a hierarchy in this way. Of course, you can go over your Structured Overview to amend it as often as you like; new parts can be added and existing ones removed. The following example shows a Structured Overview which could be used to show the organization of concepts related to fruit growing in different climates of the world.

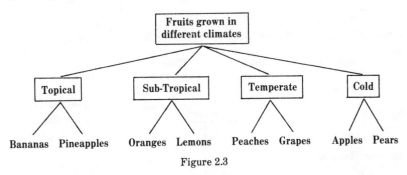

Figure 2.3

Planning a topic in this way provides teachers with a mental framework, which allows them to see which ideas to include and which to leave out. Sometimes, however, we fail to do this planning and accept the plan provided in the text by the author. One of the weaknesses about relying unquestioningly on a print resource to structure our teaching, is that we also rely on the author's conceptual structure. If we fail to think out this underlying structure for ourselves, then we run the risk of teaching in a haphazard fashion; not knowing why we are teaching particular points or how points relate and not having a conceptual framework, around which we can help students organize their learning. In such cases, teaching and learning, become piecemeal.

Moreover, we know that learning is improved by having a logical framework around which it can be organized. This helps us tie new information to existing knowledge so that concepts can be extended, refined and changed in an efficient way, which helps us recall information as we require it. Regular involvement of students in the development of Structured Overviews, shows them how to analyze ideas and helps them see how new material can be categorized.

Examples 2.1 and 2.2 show how information can be presented in the logical framework of Structured Overviews.

Example 2.1. Structured Overview: Family Structures.

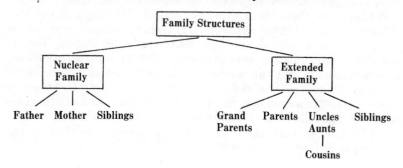

Example 2.2. Structured Overview: Motor Manufacturing.

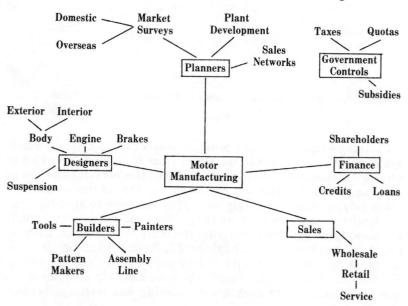

In brief, the aim of the Structured Overview is to provide a conceptual map of a topic in order to help students organize their thoughts as they read-to-learn, and can be defined as an arrangement of key words organized to show that a particular concept comprises a number of related sub-concepts.

DEVELOPMENT OF A STRUCTURED OVERVIEW

When you begin a new topic you may find yourself doodling around on a piece of paper, jotting down a few words to represent the main ideas you want to include. For example, if you are going to teach a unit on Bali, an island in Indonesia, you might start to jot down ideas as follows:

Example 2.3. Bali: rough draft.

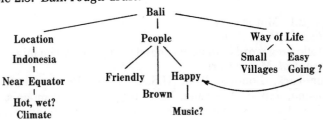

What have you done?

In this case you have noted a main topic, Bali, and then thought of three sub-topics; Location, People and Way of Life. Under these you have noted several points which *might* be developed according to your purposes. This is a Structured Overview. You may, of course, continue to build-up and refine your overview, but the process will remain the same.

Example 2.4. Centres of Population in Australia.

In this example, we start by listing a set of words related to the organization of centres of population in Australia. These can then be arranged in a Structured Overview to show how they can be categorized.

Melbourne, Geelong, Queensland, Toowoomba, Sydney, Victoria, New South Wales, Australia, Brisbane, Wollongong, Wagga Wagga, Newcastle, Ballarat, Bendigo, Townsville, Mount Isa.

One arrangement of these centres could be as follows:

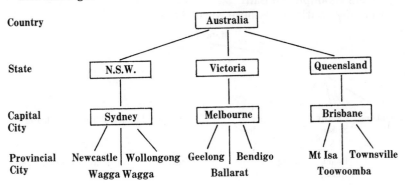

This type of Structured Overview could be used in Social Studies, History, Citizenship Education and other similar courses. For example:

- When talking about different levels of Government in Australia.
- When comparing centres of population.

To confirm your understanding of the development of Structured Overviews, work through this exercise and then compare your result with the prepared Overview.

Exercise 2.1. Motor cars
Individual or Pairs Activity

The following words can be arranged to show how you might look at the concept of 'Motor Cars'.

Motor cars, London Taxi, U.S.A., Italy, France, hatch-back, limousine, Japan, Australia, beach-buggy, special models, types, family-sedan, U.K., Sweden, Europe, German, racing-car, manufacturing centres.

See if you can set these terms out to show how the main concept can be broken down and words grouped together to show particular relationships.

NOTE

It is useful to put each of the terms on a small piece of paper initially. These can be moved around until you have developed your Structured Overview, which can then be copied onto a separate sheet of paper.

Small Group Discussion

- When you have worked out a Structured Overview using all the given words, compare your final arrangement with your neighbours. Try to agree on a best layout for the Structured Overview.
- List the processes you went through in order to arrive at this concensus.
- How did the development of this Structured Overview differ from Example 2.3 Bali?

A possible outline for these words follows.

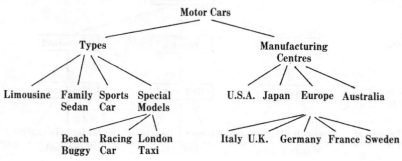

52

USE OF THE STRUCTURED OVERVIEW

When Introducing a Topic

The Structured Overview is used as an *advance organizer to intro-duce readers to a topic,* which they are about to study. The teacher develops the Structured Overview, preferably with the students, to illustrate the concepts which are to be introduced and uses it to show students how these areas can be broken down into a number of cate-gories. The student is thus helped to develop an overall picture of the topic and therefore has a logical framework into which ideas can be slotted.

The teacher can introduce the overview in a number of ways:

Teacher developed

Where the students are unfamiliar with the topic to be considered, the teacher will have to prepare the Structured Overview in advance and will introduce it to the students as a plan of the topic to be studied. This is the case in this text where the authors present you, the reader, with a number of Structured Overviews.

The teacher will frequently have to provide Structured Overviews in this way, since many topics across the curriculum will be largely outside the learners' experiences and need to be conceptualized for them.

Teacher and student developed

The point of Structured Overviews is that they provide a concept-map of a particular topic. The point about independent learning is that learners are able to produce such concept-maps for themselves. The teacher will, therefore, want to develop students thinking to the stage where they can start producing their own Structured Overviews.

Where students are familiar with the concepts and details to be con-sidered, you can use a *brainstorming technique* to get them to pro-duce a list of related words and phrases. These can be listed on the board and the class asked to consider how the list can be reorganized, so as to give an overview of the topic.

For example, the teacher of a Year 10 History class, wanted to intro-duce his class to the World War I campaign which was fought at Gallipoli in Turkey. His class were going to see the movie of the same name and he wanted them to be able to view the film in an objective way.

He asked the class for words they associated with Gallipoli and built up the following list with them. As this event is very familiar to most Year 10 students in Australian schools, they could be expected to have an extensive, although perhaps, unstructured, background to this event. The class's word list, which was put on the board, is shown below.

Learning to Learn from Text

trenches	bravery	poverty	shells
landings	courage	conquest	artillery
bad weather — hot	foolishness	freedom	spies
cold	waste	democracy	traitor
machine guns	unhappiness	casualties	surf
massacre	orphans	hospitals	ambush
terror	indoors	beachhead	

The teacher and the class then developed the following Overview, showing how the words listed could be categorized in order to give an overview of the event.

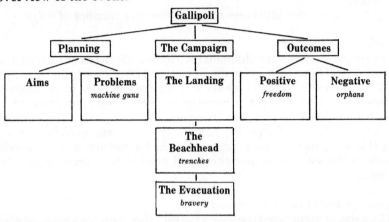

The students then worked alone to fit the details still listed on the board into their Structured Overview. They finally worked in small, mixed-ability groups to compare their work and justify their word placements, and to built up a complete class model on the board.

In this way the teacher introduced the class to the way in which Structured Overviews could be created and led them closer to the point where he could ask them to develop their own overviews.

Student prepared overviews
Student prepared overviews can be prepared in those situations where:
- The topic is sufficiently familiar.
- They know how to execute the strategy.

For Ongoing Reference
The Structured Overview can provide an ongoing reference point for students, against which they can check their progress. The teacher may display the model on a chart or the students can write it in their notebooks. New pieces of information can be added to the overview as study of the topic progresses and a much more detailed 'concept-map'

built up. The Gallipoli example could have been treated in this way had the teacher so desired.

For Revision or Assessment

When revising or assessing a topic, the teacher can ask students to develop a Structured Overview to represent what they have learned. The exercise is an excellent one, because it requires the student to think through the topic to recall the various aspects which have been covered. These then have to be set out and various details then placed in appropriate categories.

Two approaches can be used. The teacher can provide the key concept term and ask the students to analyze this to develop a hierarchy. This is the approach used in the Example 2.3, Bali. In this approach the student works from the 'top' down.

In contrast to this the teacher can work up from the bottom of the model. Instead of providing the key concept at the top, the students are given a number of details and asked to work out a structure. The brainstorming activity in the Gallipoli exercise approximates to this approach.

Summary

- A *Structured Overview* is an arrangement of key words which displays the relationships between component ideas.
- *Structured Overviews* aim at showing the logical relationships between ideas.
- A *Structured Overview* can be used to introduce, conclude or review a topic.
- Interpreting and constructing *Structured Overviews* gives students practice in sorting ideas and seeing relationships in order to categorize them.
- *Structured Overviews* teach students to think logically.
- *Structured Overviews* help teachers clarify their content objectives and so lead to more objective teaching and use of print resources.

Activities

1. Discussion Activity

Read the following statements. Identify those statements which you think can be supported by evidence from the section on *Structured Overviews*. Compare your responses with those of other people. See if you can come to a concensus.

- A *Structured Overview* represents the ideas which the teacher wishes to teach.
- A *Structured Overview* cannot be developed until the teacher has analyzed the print materials which the class are to use.
- *Structured Overviews* are prepared in the form of hierarchies.
- The aim of the *Structured Overview* is to train students to think logically when undertaking research projects.

2. Develop a *Structured Overview* related to a topic which you might have to teach.

3. Develop a lesson plan to show how you would use this overview in a teaching situation.

The Graphic Outline: Surveying the Materials

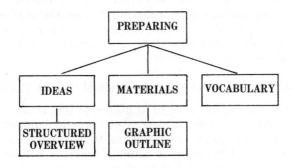

INTRODUCTION

Whereas the *Structured Overview* deals with concepts and shows the interrelationship of ideas within an overall topic, the Graphic Outline deals only with the print materials to be used.

Many teachers are aware of a well known study method called S.Q.3.R. — Survey, Question, Read, Recite, Review. Teachers who have tried to teach their students this method, have found that it is very difficult to get them to learn to survey the text *and* to get them to use the technique consistently.

Surveying means looking through a section of text — usually a chapter — to find out what main points are to be covered, what aids, such as tables and pictures are provided, and finally, how the text is organized. The survey technique has been shown to improve students' ability to use texts profitably. Its value is in preparing for reading because it shows the reader just what is to be encountered.

A reader, who does not survey a text, usually starts at the beginning and plods laboriously through the pages hoping to put the concepts and arguments together during reading.

In contrast, a reader, who surveys effectively, starts intensive reading with an idea of what is to be read and has a structure or framework on which to build. This efficient reader recognizes the logical development, identifies the main points and dispenses with irrelevant material. This reading is active, aggressive, economical and efficient. The content teacher can greatly assist students' reading by helping them view text material in this way. Too many students waste time and effort not knowing what they are looking for, where they are going or when they have arrived at their destination.

To help students learn to survey, teachers can use the Graphic Outline approach which will:

- Ensure that they carry out the survey.
- Provide them with a clear diagram showing what the section surveyed is about and how it is organized.

The use of the Graphic Outline ensures that the student carries out the surveying procedure in an organized manner. Having completed it as an independent activity, before commencing the study of a chapter in class, the student has a mental plan of the chapter to which the ideas found in the text can be related.

MATERIALS SUITABLE FOR GRAPHIC OUTLINES

Graphic Outlines are intended to be used with text books which have headings and sub-headings incorporated in them. Authors use headings and sub-headings as SIGNPOSTS, to direct readers' attention to changes of direction in the organization of concepts. Efficient readers who survey the material before they start to read intensively, recognize these signposts and use them to build up a framework from which to predict the likely content.

TYPES OF GRAPHIC OUTLINES

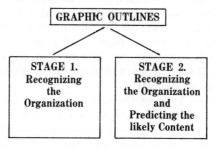

It is valuable to work through two stages when teaching people to use Graphic Outlines.

In Stage 1 the reader *learns to recognize typical structures* which are used in texts. *Narrative materials* have typical structures — story grammars — built into them which readers learn intuitively to recognize. *Expository texts* however do not have such structures, nor are most readers as familiar with them as they are with narrative materials. The Graphic Outline raises the structure of the text to a conscious level, so that the reader becomes familiar with typical organizations more quickly.

Stage 2 is introduced when the reader has acquired a familiarity with typical text structures and is able to complete Graphic Outlines without difficulty. In this stage, the Graphic Outline is modified and the reader is asked to predict what each section is likely to be about. That is, the reader has to first recognize the headings and sub-headings and then reflect on their meanings. Use is made of any graphics provided, illustrations, photographs, tables and so on, but no detailed reading is done at this point. The exercise serves to focus the reader's attention on particular sections within the text, in order to encourage prediction and anticipation of the content. Look over the following examples of Stages 1 and 2 Graphic Outlines and see if you can distinguish the difference.

Example 2.5. Graphic Outline: Stage 1.

SCIENCE: YEAR 8. (As completed by Students)
ROCKS AND MINERALS
Source: Cull and Drake, *Concepts in Science 1*, Chapter 14, Jacaranda Wiley, Brisbane, 3rd ed., 1979.

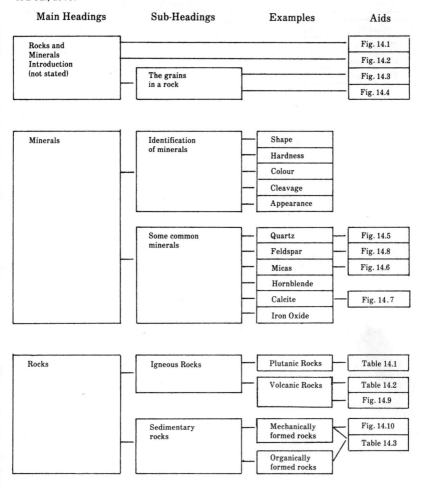

Main Headings	Sub-Headings	Examples	Aids
Rocks and Minerals Introduction (not stated)			Fig. 14.1
			Fig. 14.2
	The grains in a rock		Fig. 14.3
			Fig. 14.4
Minerals	Identification of minerals	Shape	
		Hardness	
		Colour	
		Cleavage	
		Appearance	
	Some common minerals	Quartz	Fig. 14.5
		Feldspar	Fig. 14.8
		Micas	Fig. 14.6
		Hornblende	
		Calcite	Fig. 14.7
		Iron Oxide	
Rocks	Igneous Rocks	Plutanic Rocks	Table 14.1
		Volcanic Rocks	Table 14.2
			Fig. 14.9
	Sedimentary rocks	Mechanically formed rocks	Fig. 14.10
			Table 14.3
		Organically formed rocks	

Learning to Learn from Text

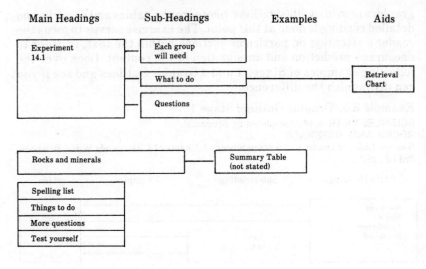

Main Headings	Sub-Headings	Examples	Aids
Experiment 14.1	Each group will need		
	What to do		Retrieval Chart
	Questions		

Rocks and minerals	Summary Table (not stated)

Spelling list

Things to do

More questions

Test yourself

Example 2.6. Graphic Outline: Stage 1.

BIOLOGY: YEAR 10. (As completed by students)
MUSCLES AND MOVEMENT
Source: D. Baldwin, *Human Biology and Health*, Chapter 3, London: Longman, 1978.

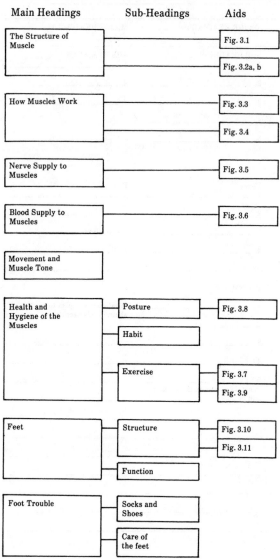

Main Headings	Sub-Headings	Aids

The Structure of Muscle — Fig. 3.1 / Fig. 3.2a, b

How Muscles Work — Fig. 3.3 / Fig. 3.4

Nerve Supply to Muscles — Fig. 3.5

Blood Supply to Muscles — Fig. 3.6

Movement and Muscle Tone

Health and Hygiene of the Muscles — Posture — Fig. 3.8 / Habit / Exercise — Fig. 3.7 / Fig. 3.9

Feet — Structure — Fig. 3.10 / Fig. 3.11 / Function

Foot Trouble — Socks and Shoes / Care of the feet

Example 2.7. Graphic Outline: Stage 2.

HISTORY: YEAR 8. (As presented to students)
Source: Hendy, A. *et al.*, *Foundations*, Chapter 9, Melbourne: Nelson, 1976.

Title: _____

MAJOR HEADING 1	MAJOR HEADING 2	MAJOR HEADING 3
SUB-HEADINGS 1. _____	SUB-HEADINGS 1. _____	SUB-HEADINGS 1. _____
2. _____	2. _____	2. _____
	3. _____	3. _____
	4. _____	
	5. _____	
Map Title _____		
_____	Boxes 1. _____	Box 5 _____
	2. _____	_____
	3. _____	Illustrations
What do you think you will learn in this section?	4. _____	1. _____
	5. _____	2. _____
_____	Illustrations	
_____	1. _____	What do you expect to read about in this Section?
_____	2. _____	_____
_____	3. _____	_____
_____	4. _____	_____
_____	5. _____ What do you think this section will be about?	_____
_____		_____
_____		_____
	_____	_____
	_____	_____
	_____	_____

Example 2.8. Graphic Outline: Stage 2.

SCIENCE, YEAR 8. (As presented to Students)
Source: Stannard, & Williamson, K., EXPLORING SCIENCE 1, Chapter 9, Melbourne:
MacMillan, 1979.

Title: _____

MAJOR HEADING 1	MAJOR HEADING 2	MAJOR HEADING 3
SUB-HEADINGS 1. _____	SUB-HEADINGS 1. _____	SUB-HEADINGS 1. _____
2. _____	2. _____	_____
	3. _____	_____
	4. _____	_____
	5. _____	_____
	6. _____	
I expect this Section to tell me about	In this Section I expect I will find out a lot about	This Section will probably tell me how to

CONSTRUCTING A GRAPHIC OUTLINE

Stage 1

To construct a Graphic Outline for use with your students, you will need to complete the following steps:

1. Look through the chapter or article to see whether it provides such features as headings, sub-headings, diagrams or other supportive illustrations. If it does, then it is suitable for a Graphic Outline approach. *Novels or materials which consist of unbroken prose cannot be treated in this way.*
2. *Identify the main topic headings* in the text. List these headings down the left hand side of a blank page. Space these headings out in proportion to the amount of the text which they occupy.

NOTE

The quality and relevance of headings varies greatly from text to text and students ultimately need to be able to view headings critically. However, at this early stage we simply want to have students recognize the presence and significance of headings within any given layout.

3. Look through each main section of the text and pick out any sub-headings. Add these to your blank page alongside the relevant main headings.
4. Look through the chapter and pick out any aids such as tables, figures and illustrations. List these on your blank page to the right of the sub-heading to which they relate. In poorly organized texts these aids may not be placed appropriately in relation to the written text.
5. When all the main details of the chapter are placed onto your chart, draw a box around each item and draw lines to join up related points. The boxes should be drawn to a scale which indicates the relative importance of that item within the chapter or article. Thus, the main headings will be in big boxes on the left, sub-headings in smaller boxes in the middle alongside the large main-heading box and aids in small boxes on the extreme right of the page. Adjustments to this basic layout should be made to accommodate variations such as sub-sub-headings, examples and so on.

Practice with a few chapters will soon indicate what adjustments are necessary. Practice will also quickly indicate the poor layout and logical sequence of some texts. A typical finished Graphic Outline will look something like this.

Example 2.9. A Typical Graphic Outline.

Subject:
Source:

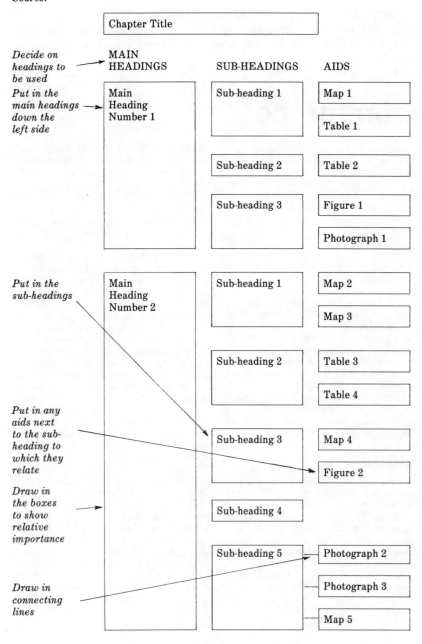

To confirm your understanding of the process of preparing Graphic Outlines, work through the following exercise.

Activity 2.1. Commerce — The Niuginians.
Use this section from a typical school text to attempt your own Graphic Outline. The chapter provided is from a Year 8 Geography textbook.

Commerce

There is a high degree of concentration of commercial crops in a few areas. The plantations are concentrated in the following areas:
1. The Milne Bay district (south-east mainland)
2. The Port Moresby district
3. Popondetta
4. Madang.

There are also plantations scattered in the highlands around Goroka, Mount Hagen, Banz, Minj, and around Wau south of Lae.

A similar concentration is found in the types of commercial crops:
1. About half of the total coconut area is on the mainland, New Ireland, and Bougainville.
2. About 80 per cent of the coffee is grown in the Central Highlands.
3. About 80 per cent of the rubber is grown on the south-east coast of the mainland.

These three commodities plus timber constituted about 94 per cent of the country's exports before the completion of the huge CRA copper mine on Bougainville.

Coffee

The coffee-growing industry in Papua New Guinea has developed very rapidly since it was first grown commercially in the early 1950s. In 1972-73 about 670 000 (60 kg each) with a value of $32 million were exported. About 30 per cent of the coffee is bought by Australia, and another 30 per cent by the United States.

The coffee industry is located in the Central Highlands of the mainland at elevations of 1600-2000 metres. In the high valleys the soils are deep and well drained and there is a markedly seasonal rainfall of 1900 mm per year.

The industry is largely in the hands of the villagers. About 70 per cent of the total production comes from small village plots and the remainder is grown on about 200 plantations.

More than 90 per cent of the coffee grown in Papua New Guinea is Arabica coffee, a high quality variety that is used to blend with other coffee such as Robusta (lowland coffee), of which a small quantity is grown on the lowlands, especially on Bougainville.

Coffee became an important plantation crop only when the highlands were opened to European settlement several years after the war. A coffee plantation requires a minimum of 40 hectares and because this is a crop introduced since the war it has been difficult for would-be planters to obtain enough land for a plantation. It is for this reason, and the fact that the villagers quickly began to grow coffee when it proved to be profitable in the initial period of high prices (after 1950) that villager production outstrips plantation production.

Villager production of coffee is in the form of very small parcels, often widely scattered and remote from roads. Yields are not very high, partly because the villagers often make use of scarce land by planting food crops under the coffee bushes.

On the other hand coffee is a profitable crop in a land-short area; 1 hectare of coffee produces the same income as 7.5 hectares of coconuts or 2.5 hectares of cocoa or rubber

42

(not that these crops can be grown at these altitudes).

Coffee fits in quite well with the traditional farming routine in the highlands. The coffee is picked quite early in the dry season while the subsistence food gardens are not prepared until late in the dry season. Many villages in the coffee districts have communal pulperies where the bean is extracted from the fruit, and most villagers sell their coffee to central factories or to plantation owners for the final processing and grading.

The situation is still changing, however, because in 1964 the Kundiawa Coffee Society in the Chimbu valley was formed with over 10 000 shareholders to process coffee. Since the Society bought a local factory it has been selling more than 2000 tonnes of processed coffee beans each year.

Asaro Coffee Estate

Asaro Coffee is a coffee plantation located 7 kilometres from Goroka along the Highlands Highway towards Mount Hagen.

Area

The plantation is 65 hectares in area, 48 hectares being planted with coffee and the remainder occupied by hilly land, the factory complex, houses, and roads.

Work force

There is a permanent work force of 5 Europeans and about 40 nationals. During the main picking season in June-July-August an additional 150 pickers are brought down

Fig. 31 Collecting cocoa pods on a plantation in the Milne Bay district. The cocoa trees are planted among coconut palms which are grown for two reasons: to provide shade for the cocoa trees, and to provide coconuts. (ANIB photo)

43

The Niuginians

from the Chimbu district to the west. All labour is 'casual'; recruiting is carried out informally. Trucks are sent to the Chimbu district and groups of men — often in lots of 10-12 from any one village — avail themselves of the jobs offered. No contract is entered into and the men move back to their home village whenever they feel inclined.

Until mid-1974 the plantation was legally required to provide everything for the employees: housing, food, matches, tobacco and health facilities, according to a government schedule. Each employee was issued with a blanket, cup, spoon and plate. In practice, most planters provided housing and food and paid the men money instead of providing the rest of the ration (tobacco, paper, etc.).

Regulations have now changed and the planter is able to choose between the old schedule ('full accommodation') or paying wages only ('full wages'). Asaro Coffee follows the latter practice, partly because it is convenient and partly because the employees prefer it.

On one hectare of land near its coffee plantation Asaro Coffee employs 6 men to grow sweet potato. This was started to supply the daily food for the employees but now that no food is required by Asaro Coffee, the sweet potato is sold under contract to the local education authority for food for the school children.

Most of the employees are Chimbus from the Kundiawa district. The locals in the town look after their own coffee. Housing is provided in a compound that accommodates 120 men. The employees are allowed to grow their own food in gardens on estate land near the compound which has fertile soil but is too steep to plant coffee bushes. The main crop grown in the gardens is sweet potato (*kau kau*) with other crops of cassava and corn.

The wives of the permanent work force are employed on the sorting table to remove discoloured and misshapen beans. Most employees work between the official hours of 7.30 a.m. to 4.30 p.m. with an hour for lunch

Fig. 32 Smallholders carrying trays of wet 'parchment' coffee to a European-owned coffee mill near Mount Hagen. Parchment coffee is coffee that still has a thin skin around the bean. (ANIB photo)

but on Asaro Coffee the pickers are paid piecework rates and their earnings vary according to the weight of coffee cherries that they pick.

The Europeans living and working on the estate consist of the managing director, the manager, a book-keeper, a mechanic and a welder. Their families also live on the estate.

Utilities

Drinking water is supplied by rainwater tanks; water for domestic and factory use comes from a small creek leading 8 km down into the plantation from the nearby hills.

Electricity for domestic and factory use until recently was provided by diesel-

44

Fig. 33 Asaro Coffee's factory in its setting of coffee bushes. (RLA photo)

powered generators on the estate but the supply now comes from the Goroka town supply.

Hot air for the coffee driers is provided by burning the parchment hulls that are stripped off the coffee beans before grading and packing; auxiliary heat is provided by burning diesel fuel when necessary.

Production

The coffee bushes are planted 3 metres apart at a density of 1325 per hectare. The average yearly production is 4 tonnes per hectare.

Coffee bushes begin to bear three years after planting. The ripe red cherries are picked mostly in the peak ripening period of June to August and are processed by simple removal of the outside covering by fermentation. In this process the cherries are placed in a concrete vat and covered with water for 72 hours. The skin is removed by a machine containing a number of cutters that strip off the skin and leave the slimy beans for transport to the dryers.

The second stage in processing is the drying and hulling of the beans. The beans are pumped with water from the 'wet factory' (skin-removing vats) to drying machines where warm air is forced through the beans as they are turned mechanically in wide drums. The dry warm beans then pass to a huller where the thin skin ('parchment' or 'hull') is removed by abrasion. The hulls are blown back to the heater where they are used as fuel while the beans pass to the sorting table for quality inspection. The beans are then graded by size and packed. The coffee is sold by contract to a local coffee broker who arranges for transport to Lae and sale to foreign buyers.

During the peak season (June-August) the work force only picks coffee but for the rest of the year there is pruning, desuckering,

The Niuginians

fertilizing (with urea because the plant needs nitrogen and potassium), weeding and general maintenance. The major task is weeding which is carried out with weedicides and hand sprayers.

The importance of small-holders to Asaro Coffee

Like other plantations in the district, Asaro Coffee processes its own coffee and buys other coffee from smallholders in the district to put through its mill.

There are two types of smallholders:

1. The most common type of small-holder is a man with 10 to 100 bushes. This type of farmer picks and sells his coffee to middlemen with trucks who buy along the roads and resell to estates such as Asaro Coffee.

Fig. 34 The exterior of the factory at Asaro Coffee. The women and girls are bringing in the cherries that they picked the previous day from the bushes in their village gardens. (RLA photo)

2. The second type of smallholder has about one hectare of coffee bushes. He may pick and process the cherries to the parchment stage and store the beans to make regular sales to a broker. More commonly, he will take the cherries to an estate mill and pay the estate for processing the cherries to beans, and then sell to an exporter.

Asaro Coffee grows and produces about 450 tonnes of coffee beans per year but purchases of coffee in cherry and parchment form from smallholders and middlemen are about twice this amount. Thus annual production of beans is about 1350 tonnes, one-third grown on Asaro and two-thirds from smallholders.

Fig. 35 Smallholders waiting to sell their coffee cherries to Asaro Coffee. (RLA photo)

Fig. 36 Villager near Goroka picking coffee cherries from the 20 bushes that his village owns. (RLA photo)

46

Commerce

47

The Niuginians

Asaro Coffee buys from about 30 middle-men each day, using a weighbridge to handle the substantial quantities brought in by the trucks between 5 p.m. and 8 p.m.

Resources
Timber

Timber is Papua New Guinea's greatest resource. Forests of various kinds cover about two-thirds of the country and contain very large quantities of timber. The main lumbering areas are the Bulolo valley, the Lae district, New Britain, the Port Moresby district and the Gulf of Papua district.

Since lumbering began in earnest after the war, the most important area has been the Bulolo valley south of Lae where there are valuable stands of klinkii and hoop pines. These tall straight trees, 60 metres high, provide the raw material for a plywood factory which was established in 1954.

Elsewhere there are few pure stands but as the world price of timber continues to rise, it is becoming more worthwhile to log the mixed forests. Most of the timber at present comes from coastal or near coastal locations. Of major help to the establishment of lumbering and plywood manufacture in the Bulolo valley was the construction of a road from Lae to Bulolo and Wau during the war.

Hardwood logs and some sawn hardwood timber are exported, mainly from New

Fig. 37 Chimbus west of the Daulagiri Pass, on the Highlands Highway. This is a typical middle-man's truck, and the middleman is busy buying coffee cherries from people who live too far from a factory to walk there. The road runs in deep narrow valleys with steeply sloping sides. (RLA photo)

48

Britain. There is a possibility that a large export trade will be developed in the near future through Vanimo on the far north-west coast of the mainland, and from other areas on both coasts of New Britain.

About 400 Europeans are engaged in lumbering and sawmilling in 58 establishments. Except in Bulolo the latter are small scale and are generally operated by one or two Europeans with the assistance of about 20 Niuginians.

Mining

The major mineral resource has always been gold and in pre-war years it was the main export, almost entirely from the Morobe district. Dredges, brought in by aircraft and re-assembled on the spot, once worked the Bulolo valley, but since the war production has steadily declined. Now the industry

consists mostly of about 3000 Niuginians working deposits as a source of cash.

Large sums of money have been spent on mineral exploration in Papua and New Guinea, particularly for oil and natural gas, but there is little to show for this activity. Although there were several oil strikes in the 1950s these deposits were minor and no commercial oil discoveries have been made. There are indications of large quantities of natural gas in the Gulf of Papua region. Basic industrial minerals such as coal and iron ore are absent.

By far the most important mineral development has been the establishment of a large scale copper mine and concentration

Fig. 38 Sorting coffee beans by hand in a coffee factory near Mount Hagen. The women are removing beans that are below an acceptable quality. (ANIB photo)

49

plant on Bougainville Island. The mine is exploiting a massive low grade deposit.

Transport

Transportation in Papua New Guinea has two main features: it is scarce and expensive. The standard form of transportation between the main towns is the aeroplane, both for passengers and for all freight except the heaviest and bulkiest goods.

Land transport

There are no railways and even the roads are few and short. The longest and most important road is the recently built Highlands Highway which runs from Lae on the coast, westwards into the Central Highlands to link the three main highland centres of Goroka, Mount Hagen and Mendi with Lae. The road passes through the Markham valley and enters the highlands proper at an altitude of 1600 metres. The distance from Lae to Mendi is 670 kilometres and involves a journey time of nearly three days by bus or truck. In wet weather, travel over the Lae-Goroka sector alone can take several days.

Another major road runs south from Lae to Wau and Bulolo, the chief timber processing centre producing plywood. The most recently built road is the Lae-Madang coast highway, opened in 1977. Elsewhere the roads are very short and serve only the outskirts of the towns.

Shipping

There are a number of great rivers on the mainland — the Sepik, Ramu, Fly, Strickland, Purari — but most are navigable for short distances only and at certain seasons.

Fig. 39 Timber being hauled from the forest in the Bulolo district to the large mill in Bulolo. This type of activity is possible only because of the existence of a road from Bulolo to Lae, and the existence of port facilities at Lae. (Qantas photo)

Fig. 40 This tri-motor Junkers aircraft played a very important part in opening up New Guinea in the 1930s, particularly by transporting gold-mining equipment. Lae was an important service centre for the goldfields. (Australian National Library)

Navigation along the southern rivers is restricted by gorges and waterfalls, sudden changes in water level following torrential rain, and changes in stream channels. Navigation is possible by launch and small boat for several hundred kilometres inland from the mouth of the Sepik and the Fly.

Coastal shipping facilities are little better. On the north coast of the mainland there are long stretches without bays or harbours, and raised coral reefs complicate navigation. Where sheltered inlets are found they cannot be used as ports because the close proximity of mountainous country prevents land access to the inlet. On the south coast there are good harbours east of Kikori but this is a region where strong south-easterlies blow for six months of the year, making conditions hazardous for small craft.

51

The Niuginians

The major ports for foreign trade are Madang (for the highlands), Port Moresby, Rabaul and Lae. More than 100 vessels provide cargo services and limited passenger services between the main ports and the many hundreds of small wharves and landing points.

Air transport

Because of the difficulty of travelling on the land, the aeroplane has been the major means of transport in Papua New Guinea. Even this form of transportation has many problems. Many localities have difficulty finding and clearing even the small amount of land needed for a light plane. Weather conditions over the mountains make flying hazardous as well as severely restricting the number of hours that can be flown on any one day. The mountains present dangers with their great height, constant cloud cover, sudden updrafts and storms.

Transport of export commodities

The main export items are the products of commercial agriculture: copra, coconut oil, desiccated coconut, cocoa, coffee beans, rubber, plywood, logs, and sawn timber.

These are all cheap, bulky commodities and they can be produced only where there is low cost, efficient transport available to move them to exporting points. The cheapest and bulkiest are produced only along the coast where there is access to cheap sea transport.

The main commodity routes are as follows:

1. Copra produced on commercial coconut plantations on New Britain, New Ireland, Bougainville, Milne Bay and Madang districts is moved by coastal ships to the main ports.

Fig. 41 Developing a goldmine on the Merri Creek field in the 1930s. The sluice is being used to wash alluvial gold ore in the wooden box. (Australian National Library)

2. Plywood from Bulolo, and coffee, tea and pyrethrum from the Central Highlands is trucked to Lae for export.
3. Most coffee is trucked to Lae for export.
4. Sawn timber and logs are shipped directly from Cape Hoskins, Vanimo, Madang, Lae, Fulleborne Harbour, Nan Tamby, Bialla and Rabaul.
5. Cocoa grown on the Gazelle Peninsula is shipped in bags to export ports. The main exporting centres are Rabaul, Madang and Lae. From these ports, direct shipment is readily available to the United States, Western Europe, Japan and Australia.

Transport of commodities for domestic use

Taro and yams are still traded in native markets but today Niuginians buy rather than barter, and they use shops or trade stores as well as markets for their requirements.

Economic Development and Trade

Papua New Guinea is an underdeveloped agricultural nation and is likely to remain so for many years despite the recent completion of a copper mine which since 1973 exports copper worth more than all the rest of the exports. All the exports are from primary industries such as farming — especially coffee and coconut — the timber industries, the fishing industries, and mining.

For many years copra was the leading cash crop but in the last few years it has been displaced by coffee. Copra is a crop of the coastal lowlands while coffee is basically a crop of the highlands.

Two important new crops are tea and palm oil. Experimental plantings of tea were made in the early 1950s and the first commercial farms were planted in 1965. Centrally

53

STEPS
1. Survey the chapter to identify the main headings and so identify the different topics covered.
2. Pick out any sub-headings.
   You should now be able to recognize the way in which the author has organized the information provided.
3. Finally, look at the illustrations provided.
   Are these numbered? To which sub-sections do they refer?
4. From this 'picture' of the chapter, decide on the headings you will use in your Graphic Outline.
5. Write the headings you have decided on across the top of the page. Remember this is a Stage 1 Graphic Outline to show the readers what the chapter is about and how it is organized.
6. The heading 'Main Headings' should be written at the top-left of your page. In this column you can now insert the main headings you have identified, but before you start to put them down, you should note two things.
   (a) The chapter opens with an introductory section which is not headed. Build this into your Graphic Outline by putting 'Introduction' (*no heading given*) as the first item in your Main Headings column.
   (b) Note that there are five Main Headings plus 'Introduction' to go into your left-hand column. Plan your spacings so that there is sufficient space between the Main Headings to allow you to put the sub-headings in the next column.
7. You now list the Main Headings in the left-hand column.
8. Next, insert the sub-headings in column 2. As you do this, allow sufficient space between them so that you will be able to add in the correct number of boxes for the illustrations, which are to be listed in column 3.
9. In column 3, insert the illustrations — Fig. 31, Fig. 32 and so on — adjacent to the sub-heading which each illustrates.
10. You now have a rough plan of the chapter. Re-do the Graphic Outline to allow more appropriate spacings and so present a clearer copy.

NOTE

Make sure that this completed copy has instructions for your readers.

Remember to draw boxes around each of the items on your page so that the size of the box clearly indicates the importance of an item in relation to others.

Draw lines to connect the boxes of items which are related.

11. Finally, make out the blank sheet for your students to fill in.

Now, compare your working with the following finished model.

Example 2.10. Graphic Outline.

Subject:
Source:

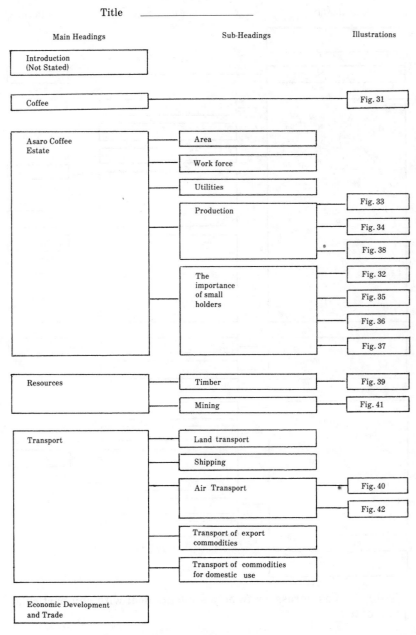

Title _____

| Main Headings | Sub-Headings | Illustrations |

Introduction (Not Stated)

Coffee — Fig. 31

Asaro Coffee Estate
- Area
- Work force
- Utilities
- Production — Fig. 33 / Fig. 34 / Fig. 38
- The importance of small holders — Fig. 32 / Fig. 35 / Fig. 36 / Fig. 37

Resources
- Timber — Fig. 39
- Mining — Fig. 41

Transport
- Land transport
- Shipping
- Air Transport — Fig. 40 / Fig. 42
- Transport of export commodities
- Transport of commodities for domestic use

Economic Development and Trade

Example 2.11. Final Graphic Outline: Stage 1, which will be handed out in class.

Source: R. L. Andrews' *The Niuginians*, Chapter 9, 'Commerce'.

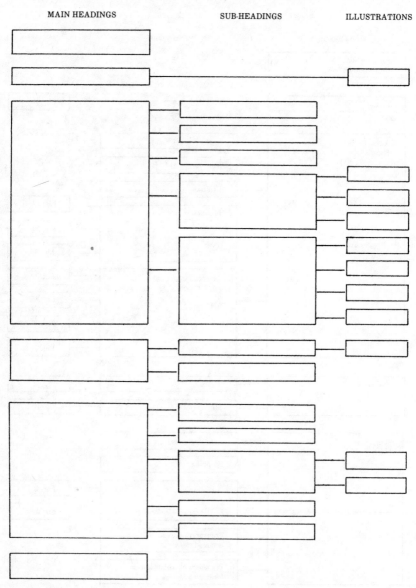

Add clues as necessary to help students deal with any particular piece of text.

Example 2.12. A Stage 2 Graphic Outline for the same chapter we have just used.

MAIN HEADING 1.	MAIN HEADING 2.	MAIN HEADING 3.	MAIN HEADING 4.	MAIN HEADING 5.	MAIN HEADING 6.
		Sub-Headings	*Sub-Headings*	*Sub-Headings*	
		1.	1.	1.	
		2.	2.	2.	
		3.	*Illustration*	3.	*Illustration*
		4.	1.	4.	1.
This Section will tell me	In this Section I will find out about	5.	This could be an important Section. It will tell me about	5.	In this last Section I think I will find out about
		Illustrations		*Illustration*	
		1.		1.	
		2.			
		3.			
		4.		The second largest Section will be important because	
		5.			
		6.			
		7.			
		This is the main Section. It will tell me			

NOTE Although this is cramped it gives an overview of the chapter. Columns could be done separately if more writing space is required.

USE OF GRAPHIC OUTLINES

At the beginning of a new unit of work, the teacher should survey the print resources to be used to see whether any of them are suitable for a Graphic Outline. Remember, this activity can only be carried out with material which uses Headings and Sub-Headings to mark-off different sections within the text. Efficient readers recognize these headings as SIGNPOSTS, which can guide them through an unfamiliar text. You will recognize the need for signposting, if you can recall trying to find your own way around a strange city; good signposting will have helped you, poor signposting will have hindered you.

If the print resource employs signposts, then the teacher should prepare a blank Graphic Outline as already described. Some texts have highly complex organizational systems, whilst others are very simply organized. In either of these cases, it will be necessary to include sufficient clues on your Graphic Outline to help students to work out the organizational system used. The teacher must consider both the material to be used and the class's facility with Graphic Outlines, when deciding what clues to provide.

When the activity is first introduced, the teacher will need to guide the class through it and should make the point, that the purpose of the task is to learn how to survey materials before starting to read-to-learn.

Whilst filling in a Graphic Outline, readers get the feel of the text and in that process, learn a lot about its content.

Having started the class off by showing them how to fill in the first few boxes, the teacher can then allow the students to work together in twos and threes to complete the outline. As the class does this, the teacher should move among the groups to give help and note difficulties. Should any aspects cause general problems, work should be stopped and the point cleared up, so that the class can complete the activity.

Once the class is familiar with the Graphic Outline concept, students can work independently to complete the activity. Class time can then be used to discuss the text organization which *students* have identified. However, if some students find it difficult to complete the Graphic Outlines, it will be necessary to help them complete the activity as a group, *before* the general class discussion takes place.

The point to be remembered is that this is a TEACHING strategy. You are teaching your students how to PROCESS text, by showing them how it is organized. If you do not take sufficient time to ensure that all your students know how to do this task, then they will not be able to apply this processing skill. Regular and careful attention to Graphic Outline activities helps students learn how to SURVEY. This processing skill will improve their ability to use expository materials more efficiently.

VALUE OF GRAPHIC OUTLINES

To the Teacher

Graphic Outlines are as valuable to the teacher, as they are to the student. Preparation of a Graphic Outline forces the teacher to look closely at the structure of the piece of text to be used. When teachers first prepare a Graphic Outline, often they find that there is a lot more — or perhaps a lot less — to a text than they had previously realized.

For example, in the chapter which we used to make our Graphic Outline, did you notice anything about the illustrations which were included? Perhaps when you first surveyed the chapter you noted that twelve photographs were provided. You may have even thought that these were intended as features to enhance the chapter.

Look back at the Graphic Outline, which we prepared, to see how these illustrations related to the topics discussed. You can see that the photographs relate to only six of the fifteen possible points to which they could have been tied. Perhaps it was not necessary to illustrate that ten points which did not have photographs accompanying them. On the other hand, perhaps all the points should have been illustrated, in which case this text might be now regarded as having a deficiency.

The point here is to make you aware of the chapter's organization. A Graphic Outline quickly reveals the structure of the text being studied, any illogical structures, gaps in the information or aids provided, and superfluous padding, which bears no relationship to your intended teaching objectives.

If you go back to the chapter on Commerce again, you could ask yourself why Figure 31 was included. Have you worked out why a photograph, which illustrates the collection of cocoa pods and the mingling of cocoa trees and coconut palms, was included in a section on coffee growing without an adequate explanation? If you did not even notice this apparently out-of-place photograph, you should recognize that in your own assessment of this piece of the text you have overlooked this point. You will improve your critical faculty by making up a number of Graphic Outlines and asking yourself these questions, 'What use will this text be to me in class?' and 'What will I need to add or delete before I can use it as a teaching aid?'

To the Student

Graphic Outlines are used to teach students how to SURVEY a text efficiently. Surveying:

- Shows students the author's organization and presentation of ideas.
- Shows them which topics they are to meet and how these are organized.
- Starts them off with a mental framework into which they can SLOT new information.

- Gets them to set purposes for reading and then focuses their reading on these purposes.
- Introduces them to systematic organizational features, which can be followed when they start to make notes as they study independently.
- Shows them that some materials are well organized and others are poorly organized. This helps them become more critical as readers and helps to breakdown the blind acceptance and trust of the printed word which many people have.
- Teaches students how to use headings as SIGNPOSTS which will help them find their way around the unfamiliar 'city' — the chapters found in textbooks.

SUMMARY

- Surveying is a well-known study skill, which helps a reader develop a mental image of the content and organization of a piece of text *before* trying to read-to-learn.
- *Graphic Outlines* offer a means for teaching students how to survey text efficiently before they start to read-to-learn.
- Two kinds of *Graphic Outline* activities have been suggested
    Stage I outlines introduce readers to the organizational structure of texts.
    Stage II outlines also introduce readers to the organization of a text but they further require the reader to predict what the material will be about.
- *Graphic Outlines* are designed for use with print resources which provide headings and sub-headings to break up the text into meaningful units.
- *Graphic Outlines* help teachers assess print resources more objectively.
- Students should be taught how to complete *Graphic Outlines* in class before they are given them as independent activities.
- Students, who find it difficult to complete *Graphic Outlines* alone, should be given assistance in small-group discussions.
- *Graphic Outlines*, which students have completed, should be followed by small-group discussions to ensure that errors are quickly recognized and corrected.
- *Graphic Outlines* can be used to teach students how to take notes, so giving them a plan of the author's organization.

Learning New Vocabulary: Using Context Clues

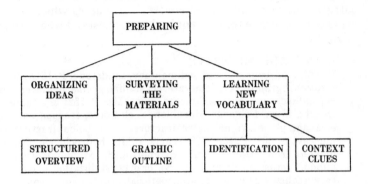

INTRODUCTION

The final area of preparation is that of *vocabulary*. Reading texts which incorporate a lot of unknown words, can be difficult and frustrating and can cause many readers to give up before they really get started.

The use of specialized vocabulary in the various subject areas is one of the distinguishing characteristics of Content Area Reading. Not only are new terms, such as *epiglottis, refraction, sedimentary, erosion* and *asset* introduced, but known words can also acquire new meanings, for instance *post, adopt, court, scallop* and *yarn*.

Specialized subject vocabularies are necessary, because each specific subject text carries very precise meanings and thus allows students of that subject to communicate with each other in clear unambiguous terms. By the nature of its many vocabularies, Content Area Reading presents a high level of reading difficulty.

The acquisition and understanding of specialized vocabularies also includes symbols, such as those used in Mathematics and Music, and which are basic keys to understanding each subject. Since it is the role of the subject teacher to introduce this new specialized vocabulary, it must be the subject teacher who teaches students how to recognize and use it.

The literature on the teaching of reading has long recognized the need for special emphasis to be placed on the ways in which new words are introduced. However, some content area writers overlook the need to provide readers with assistance in learning new vocabulary and tend to overload them with far too many new terms at the one time, even failing to provide adequate explanations on occasions.

IDENTIFYING CONTENT AREA VOCABULARY

Having determined the print resource to be used, the teacher should now systematically list all the specialized terms or words introduced. The following list, from a Year 8 Science textbook, clearly demonstrates the large amount of *content vocabulary* which the reader of this quite average text is required to understand when studying this material.

ROCKS AND MINERALS
P. 150: landscape, cores,* sedimentary, sandstone. P. 151: grains, illustration,* granite, conglomerate, crystalline grains, flat faces,* molten, crystallizes, igneous, sediments, minerals. P. 152: crystalline form, Quartz, Mica, Feldspar, Hornblende, cleavage, transparent, opaque, cleavage planes, right angles, fractures,* conchoidal fracture, biotite, muscovite, 60°. P. 153: 75°, reacts, dilute hydrochloric acid, carbon dioxide, Iron Oxide, limanite, magnetite. P. 154: metamorphic, determined,* potassium dichromate, water of crystallization, decomposition, recrystallizes, asbestos, molten material, erupt, magma, solidify, solidifies, intrusive, extrusive, Plutonic rocks, Pluto, gabbro, dolerite. P. 155: Rhyolite, flow bands,* porous, Pumice, Basalt, lava, Volcanic rocks, Mechanically. P 156: Deposited,* deposition, Organically formed, Conglomerate, Sandstone, Shale, banding,* marine organisms, secrete, Calcium carbonate, finely textured, overlying, percolating.
*Words previously encountered which now have a different (CONTEXTUAL) meaning.
Source: Cull, R.G. and Drake, W.A., *Concepts in Science 1*, 3rd ed. (1979), Chapter 14 Jacaranda Press, Brisbane.

Activity 2.2.

1. Read through the following extract and list those words you think may cause difficulty for a reader unfamiliar with the content.

   The continental margins are deeply incised by submarine canyons which serve as routes for sediment transportation away from the continental shelves. The sediments are deposited in ocean trenches or on the abyssal ocean floor, where they build up continental rives.
   Wyllie, P.. *The Dynamic Earth*, 1971.

2. Which of the words on your list are explained in the passage and which are not?

3. Which of the words on your list do you think are essential to an understanding of the passage? Have all these words been explained satisfactorily?

By completing this activity, you have just done what every teacher, who assigns reading, should do before asking students to read a passage. Because the understanding of words is so fundamental to efficient reading, it is essential that teachers pre-view materials to see just what words are introduced and how they are explained.

The specialized vocabulary of Content Area Reading is so related to an understanding of the concepts, that the misunderstanding of even a single word can lead to a complete misinterpretation of the points being made. The provision of too many unknown words in a text moves the material completely beyond the reach of the average student.

EFFECTS OF NON-SPECIALIZED VOCABULARY

While a teacher can reasonably be expected to teach specialized words as part of an understanding of a subject, he or she cannot be expected to deal with a large number of general vocabulary items. When selecting print resources, the teacher should assess not only the subject specific words which are to be taught, but also the non-specific words which will have to be assumed. *If the material contains too many of the latter in relation to the ability of the class, it should be set aside and a more suitable print resource provided.*

WHICH VOCABULARY SHOULD BE TAUGHT?

Identifying difficult vocabulary is simple enough, but the teacher is still left with the problem of which words to emphasize in class lessons. There are more than eighty words and terms in the preceding list from *Concepts in Science 1*, but obviously they cannot all be given special attention in limited class time. The teacher must decide which words have already been taught, which therefore will only need revising, and those that will not be really important and could be minimally explained in passing. Once words of these types are eliminated, the list will be substantially reduced and will start to become manageable. The remaining words can then be categorized into **must**, **should** and **could** words.

The list of **must** words includes those which the teacher considers must be recognized and understood at sight if the student is to have a basic understanding of the subject or topic. These are the *essential* words which the teacher must concentrate upon in the classroom.

The list of **should** words includes those which, although not essential, are nevertheless highly significant and a student should really know them to do well in that subject. Must and Should words are frequently difficult to separate and the teacher's final decision will depend primarily upon content objectives, time available and the ability of the class.

The list of **could** words include those which a good student would know, but which are not necessary for a basic understanding of the topic. These are words which the teacher will use in passing, offering a brief explanation if it is seen to be necessary.

Breaking the initial list of new words down in this fashion reduces the load on the teacher by placing a priority on the words which need special attention. As we have seen, many subjects introduce a very large number of words and there is no possibility of the teacher teaching all of them. Establishing priorities for vocabulary enables the teacher to focus upon those words which are vital to an understanding of the subject, thus maximizing use of the time available.

Figure 2.3 Vocabulary Identification Chart

Text: Concepts in Science 1.   Chapter: 14   Pages: 150-156

Word	Page	Definition or Context Clues Provided	IMPORTANCE			Student Vocabulary Exercise	Teacher Glossary
			Must	Should	Could		
landscape	150			✔			
cores	150			✔			
sedimentary	150	✔	✔			✔	
sandstone	150	✔	✔				
grains	151	✔	✔			✔	
illustration	151			✔			
granite	151	✔	✔				✔
conglomerate	151	✔	✔			✔	
crystalline grains	151	✔	✔			✔	
flat faces	151				✔		
molten	151		✔				✔
crystallizes	151		✔				✔
igneous	151	✔	✔			✔	
sediments	151	✔	✔			✔	
minerals	151		✔				✔
crystalline form	152				✔		
quartz	152	✔		✔			
mica	152	✔		✔			
feldspar	152	✔		✔			
hornblende	152	✔		✔			
cleavage	152	✔	✔			✔	
transparent	152		✔				✔
opaque	152		✔				✔

Teachers, who regularly try to identify difficult vocabulary, have found the Vocabulary Identification Chart to be extremely helpful. Use of the chart allows the teacher to plan what is to be done about each identified word. The exercise of placing these words into **must, should** and **could** categories forces the teacher to assess the demands of the vocabulary load. This exercise will demonstrate to teachers the size and difficulty of the vocabulary load which their everyday subject texts impose.

To complete the final two columns (Student Exercise and Teacher Glossary), the teacher must look closely at the definitions or context clues which accompany or support each important word or term. Where words or terms are contextualized or defined adequately in the text, they can be assigned in a pre-reading activity for the students to work out their meanings. If the definitions and/or context clues are sufficiently clear, this type of exercise can be set as an independent activity. If they appear too hard for such independent work, but are within the students' abilities, the meanings can be worked out in group discussions in class with teacher help. If they are too difficult even for this, they should be included in a teacher-made glossary which is provided for the students and used when each word or term is encountered.

Figure 2.3 shows how some of the words in a Science chapter might be identified and assessed using a Vocabulary Identification Chart. The words listed in column 7, will be assigned for independent work and students will be expected to identify the definitions or context clues provided in the text. Use of this technique means that:

• The teacher is conscious of the vocabulary load.
• The teacher assigns a priority to content vocabulary.
• Students' vocabulary acquisition becomes objective, and systematic.
• Students are taught to recognize and use definitions and context clues.

Activity 2.2

Although the information shown on the Vocabulary Identification Chart appears straightforward, a number of significant issues are presented. Read through the following sets of statements which require you to reflect on these issues at three levels. Place a tick beside those which you can agree with, according to the different instructions given for each level. Discuss your choices with a colleague and see if you can agree on which statements might be acceptable. Compare your responses with those of your colleagues.

Level 1: Tick those statements which accurately represent the information given in Figure 2.3. Be prepared to justify your answers.
 −1. Only two words are adequately defined in the text.
 −2. The teacher plans to provide a glossary to explain the meaning of each Must word.
 −3. A comprehensive index is provided.

Level 2: Tick those statements which can be inferred from the chart. Discuss your answers with a colleague. Be prepared to justify your choices.
 −1. The teacher is not prepared to accept word definitions given by the author.
 −2. The author and the teacher do not agree on the relative importance of the words listed.
 −3. The text cannot be used effectively without a great deal of teacher input.
 −4. The author did not consider that the reader might wish to look up the meanings of words.

Level 3: Tick those statements which you think could be supported by evidence given in the Vocabulary Identification Chart. Justify your choices to a colleague and try to agree on the statements which can be accepted.

—1. A poorly organized index does not encourage efficient study habits.

—2. The contents of a teacher-prepared glossary are determined more by the author than by the teacher.

—3. This text will only be as good as the teacher makes it.

THE IMPORTANCE OF CONTEXT CLUES

It is important to realize that being able to recognize context clues which explain new vocabulary, is a most important reading skill. Efficient readers recognize context clues automatically and, because you are probably an efficient reader, you may not realize that some people are not able to do so.

Although most basic reading schemes provide some exercises in the use of context clues, students are rarely shown how to apply this skill to content area material. Efficient readers transfer skills from learning-to-read to reading-to-learn situations and can make the connections for themselves. However, less-efficient readers often fail to transfer those skills and need guidance to take advantage of the context clues provided in a text.

There are two important reasons for subject teachers providing students with regular practice in *locating* and *interpreting* context clues.

1. So that students are able to use context clues and thus become independent learners.

2. So that teachers can utilize their teaching time more effectively.

The practice of telling students the meanings of words which are well explained in context, deprives them of valuable language learning experiences, through which they locate context clues and explore and interpret meanings for themselves.

The following examples taken from the Addison-Wesley Science Program shows how varied context clues can be. Although this program highlights new technical words by using *italics* and draws the teacher's attention to them in the Teacher's Manual, the kinds of context clues provided vary tremendously. While this lack of consistency may initially make it difficult for readers to determine meanings, in the long-run the ability to identify a variety of clues becomes an advantage.

In using such a text the teacher's task is to draw students' attention to the context clues as they occur. The students' task is then to use these clues to confirm meanings for themselves.

Activity 2.3
1. Look through the following examples and identify any new words which are introduced.
2. Identify the context clue(s) for each word.
3. Compare the context clues provided and see if you can recognize any similarities between the types of explanations given.

Vocabulary Context Clues:
Source: *Addison-Wesley Science Series, Level 6*, Addison-Wesley, 1980.

Changes in species. Individuals change as they grow older. *Species*, or kinds of living things, change, too. But often species change very slowly. And so people do not live long enough to observe the change taking place. Scientists have made inferences about changes in species based on their study of fossils.

(p. 8)

... few species living today lived millions of years ago. Most species living then became *extinct*. They died out. Other species, often something like them, took their places.

(p. 8)

Dandelions, and other plants, too, are successful when they can *adapt* to changes in their environment. If conditions around them favour tall plants, then the dandelions grow tall. But if conditions around them favour short plants, they remain short. Being able to adapt is important.

(p. 10)

SOMETHING TO THINK ABOUT
Plants that live only one year, and then die, are called *annuals*. Annuals produce seeds that continue the species. But *perennials* live through more than two growing seasons. They do not have to produce seeds each year for the species to survive.

(p. 13)

Endangered species. Today many species of animals have become few in number. Their numbers have become so smal that the species are in danger of becoming extinct. And so they are called *endangered species*. Some plants, too, are endangered species. Endangered species may be able to survive if people protect them.

(p. 14)

OUR CLOSED SYSTEM — Lesson 4
A scuba diver takes along one or two tanks of air. The air may last as long as an hour or two. But then, the diver must come to the surface to breathe. Scuba divers cannot reuse, or *recycle*, their own oxygen supply.

(p. 20)

Neither the space traveller nor the scuba diver is completely independent. Neither the spaceship nor the scuba diving outfit is a completely *self-contained* system.

(p. 21)

TEACHING THE USE OF CONTEXT CLUES

Teaching students to use context clues is a sadly neglected practice. Not only is the practice neglected in many classrooms, but the need to do so is often not even recognized by those who prepare texts. The role of context clues in clarifying meaning also implies that the reader will need to refer to the contextual definition on other occasions. *Thus all important words should not only be defined in context but should also be listed in an index.*

As an interesting exercise, look through a selection of content area textbooks and evaluate the *quality* of each index. Some books do not even provide one! However, some — even those for quite young children — provide both an index and a glossary. Where these two features exist, the teacher should ensure that they are well used. Moreover, the teacher should recognize that one purpose of the index is to refer the reader to the *context clues*, which explain the meaning of terms as they are introduced.

Having previewed a section of text which is to be used in a reading-to-learn situation, the teacher should know which important new words are to be learned and should have identified those which are sufficiently well-explained at the students' level of understanding. Students can be asked to look up the meanings *given in the text* for themselves. This should be done in class in small groups until students learn what is expected of them. After this, the activity can be assigned for independent work followed by review in class.

When setting activities of this type, teachers should give students clear directions for finding words in the text. Page, paragraph and line references should be given so that students can identify context clues quickly and then interpret them. There is no point in having students wade through page after page of text trying to find a word before they begin considering context clues. The following activity is based on the Addison-Wesley materials used in Activity 2.3.

Sample Independent Activity

You will need to learn the meanings of the following terms to understand the topic you are about to study. Each of the terms is well explained in the text.

1. Locate each term and write out the context clues which explain its meaning.
2. Then, in your own words, write out an explanation of each term

The first one has been done for you as an example.

    species: (page 8, paragraph 1, line 2).

1. Species, *or kinds of living things*.
2. All living things belong to different species, for example, dogs and cats.

    extinct: (page 8, paragraph 2, line 4).

Reading to Learn: the ERICA Model

adapt: (page 10, paragraph 3, line 2).
annuals: (page 13, paragraph 1, line 2).
perennials: (page 13, paragraph 1, line 3).
endangered species: (page 19, paragraph 1, line 5).
recycle: (page 20, paragraph 1, line 4).
self-contained: (page 21, paragraph 4, line 4).

NOTE

When students are familiar with this word referencing system, the reference can be reduced to the numbers only, as in 8:1:2.

An alternative way of organizing the above activity is in chart form as set out in Figure 2.4.

Figure 2.4

TERM	PAGE	CONTEXT CLUES GIVEN	YOUR EXPLANATION
Species	8:1:2	or, kinds of living things	All living things belong to different species, for example, dogs and cats
extinct	8:2:4		
annuals	13:1:2		
perennials	13:1:3		
endangered species			
recycle			
self-contained			

As with all other activities in the ERICA Model, it is essential that this activity be carried out in, or followed up by, small, mixed-ability group discussions. This is essential because not only does it allow meanings to be clarified, but it also allows students to:

- Point out the various context clues to each other.
- Discuss the accuracy of personal explanations.
- Use the new technical terminology in meaningful contexts.

CONCLUSION

Many techniques have been developed for teaching new vocabulary in subject areas. In so far as all teachers 'use' new vocabulary in the course of teaching their subjects, it can be said that teachers 'teach' the vocabulary of their subject. However, what is often overlooked is the significance of context clues to the reader. As already pointed out, the use of context clues is of crucial importance and must be taught. Sometimes there are words which cannot be explained adequately through context clues. These words require special treatment. Whichever method is adopted, the teacher should realize that unknown words serve as stumbling blocks to immature readers, who are trying to come to grips with the conceptual presentations in content area readings. Effective reading will be enhanced when adequate vocabulary preparation is carried out.

SUMMARY

- *Content Vocabulary* is that collection of specialized terms which represents concepts within a subject.
- *Content Vocabulary* allows quick and accurate communication of subject concepts.
- A simple word can have quite different specialized meanings in different subjects.
- To read effectively in a subject it is essential to understand its specialized vocabulary.
- The meanings of specialized terms are often explained in the context.
- Efficient readers recognize and interpret context clues as they occur.
- Knowledge of words and use of context clues can be improved through systematic teaching.
- Meanings of new terms are best taught in context and not in isolation.
- The subject teacher is the only teacher who knows which words are essential to an understanding of that subject.
- The subject teacher must teach the *vocabulary* of the subject because nobody else will.
- The teacher cannot hope to teach all the terms to be encountered in a subject and must rank words to be taught.
- The teacher needs to preview print materials to be assigned for reading, to determine their specialized vocabulary load.
- Glossaries should be provided by the teacher to explain words which are not explained adequately in context.
- Glossaries should be written in everyday language.
- Specialized words necessary for an understanding of the subject should be used frequently by the students.
- Small-group discussions provide opportunities for students to use *Content Vocabulary*.

Stage 2. Thinking Through the Reading

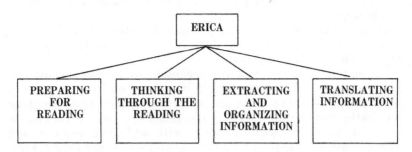

Teacher concern:
'My students can read but they don't understand what they read'.
Problem area:
Comprehension

Introduction

In a long-term study of secondary school classrooms, Lunzer and Gardner (1979) observed that very few instances were found where students were encouraged to 'reflect' upon the text material they used and that reading in class usually consisted of short, sharp bursts of reading, lasting only a few seconds.

These British observations are supported by Durkin (1978) in the United States who, in a review of primary school practices, found that comprehension was very rarely taught. Instead most comprehension 'lessons' were, in fact, comprehension 'tests'. Students were repeatedly asked to answer questions to demonstrate their understanding of passages read. Very rarely did the lesson set out to teach them how to gather information and draw conclusions from it. Most of the teachers observed approached understanding text (comprehension) as an end product. Very few tackled reading in terms of its comprehending process — reflecting on and using print to realize meaning.

The ERICA Model provides a number of activities which help students reflect on or *think-through* their reading. This *thinking-through process* has proved to be most effective in developing comprehension and, as a spin-off, *is usually highly motivating*. Instead of setting students the task of reading a passage and assuming that this will be done efficiently, *thinking-through* provides in-class activities which help the teacher guide and monitor the students' comprehension of texts.

Some subject teachers initially claim that they do not have sufficient time for such activities. However, before passing judgement, why not think about what is involved.

The material to be studied will be content area material chosen by you, the teacher. This material will introduce concepts you wish to develop. The skills of picking out relevant information and weighing and synthesizing it will be practised in relation to your current teaching aims. Providing your students with additional practice and guidance will work to their long-term advantage in your subject area. In the process, you will be helping them to become more efficient learners, because you have taught them how to find and evaluate information in your subject area. Can you afford *not* to teach process?

Attempting to learn 'facts' without a solid understanding of them is of very doubtful value, yet teachers continually press to 'get-through-the-syllabus' without giving any attention to how well students understand the body of factual information being presented. It is usually these same teachers who continue to bemoan the extent to which students forget all they were 'taught' in earlier years.

In the following section, you will be introduced to some in-class activities which require students to go over a piece of the text from which the teacher wants them to learn. They will go over this passage not once but several times; they will think about what it *means*, not just what it *says*; and they will debate with other students their reasons for reaching certain conclusions.

The suggested activities are intended to be used in small mixed-ability groups. Our experience shows that streaming students into low or high ability groups within the class for discussion, is not as productive as using mixed-ability groups. In these mixed groups, not only do the allegedly 'less-able' students get a chance to hear *how* the other students arrive at their answers, but they also get a chance to give their own reasons and to have these accepted or corrected on the spot. Such 'peer tutoring' situations allow all students to clarify their thoughts, see clues in the text which they missed on the first read through and hear other opinions and interpretations. Students who express themselves very poorly in writing have a chance to say what they mean, while students who do not usually join in class-sized discussions feel less pressured and can join in these small group debates.

Thinking through reading suggests that:

- Various activities can be devised which involve students in much deeper reflection upon the print and its meanings.

- Directed discussions can help students think through a given passage, thus clarifying their reasoning and improving their critical reading skills.
- Students can learn from each other through an interactive, dynamic and stimulating experience.
- Students of mixed abilities can profitably work together in small groups.

Here are some teachers' comments which echo these points:

'After teaching Science and History for twelve years I felt for the first time that I was actually teaching my students to think.'

'I have worked as a Resource Teacher for four years during which time I have continually advised teachers to find easier textbooks because readability was too high. I now find that if I use different techniques, students can make effective use of texts which they are not supposed to be able to read because the books are too difficult for them.'

'To my amazement slow children who never normally contribute anything, suddenly become involved, expressing ideas and reasoning of which I thought them incapable.'

'My class discussions have now become purposeful with more students involved, more time spent on the task and with much more insight into the implications of the text being derived.'

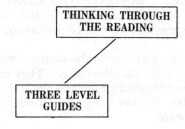

Three-Level Reading Guides

Three Level Reading Guides were developed by Herber (1970) as a means of improving comprehension. Herber reasoned that to comprehend, readers first have to *locate* information and see what the author actually says. They then have to *interpret* what the author might mean, and finally, they have to be able to *use* this information. This provides a three-step, or three level, model of comprehension:

1. *Literal Comprehension: reading on the lines* to see what is actually said.
2. *Interpretive Comprehension: reading between the lines* to make inferences about what the author might mean.
3. *Applied Comprehension: reading beyond the lines* to make associations with other knowledge, to solve problems and to modify existing perceptions.

These three levels of comprehension form the stages of Herber's Three Level Guides. The first level focuses on the Literal Level and shows students the *actual information* provided in the text they are using. Accurate identification of relevant information is always important, but it is absolutely crucial in subjects such as Mathematics, Science, Commerical Studies and Music. The Literal Level work is used to show students the precise information needed to arrive at certain conclusions.

Level two, the Interpretive Level, provides students with an opportunity to *reflect on* pieces of literal information. They may combine several literally stated ideas to reach a conclusion or see that, because one fact is stated, a number of other facts may also be inferred. For example, a passage may state:

'Australia's principal export is now coal.'

Inferences which might be drawn are that:
- Australia has other exports besides coal.
- Coal has not always been Australia's main export.
- Coal as an export, is gaining in importance overseas.
- Australia's coal industry is very competitive compared with that of other countries in terms of both price and quality.

Level two work requires students to *think through* the implications of what is stated literally. The teacher thus consciously prompts students to think, rather than to mindlessly parrot and regurgitate facts.

The third level of the guide encourages students to *think beyond* the text. Instead of leaving the given text information to stand by itself, the applied level of the guide moves students to the stage where the information can be related to other situations and broader contexts. For instance, the statement about Australia's coal exports was used to suggest inferences which can be made about it. A levei three statement would take students beyond such inferences to look at generalized notions such as these.

'Countries need to export in order to earn money from abroad.'

This statement opens up for discussion the area of foreign earnings and balance of payments. On the other hand, the statement 'Australia, the lucky country', leads students to examine the implications of Australia's vast energy reserves and natural resources.

Three-Level Guides are useful in improving comprehension for several reasons. First, they show students which information the teacher wants to focus on. *Items of information provided in a piece of text are not equally important and the text needs to be read selectively*. Because many students find it difficult to make this selection for themselves, large numbers of them copy chunks of irrelevant prose or perhaps worse, do not write anything at all. The guides allow the teacher to select literal statements in the text, draw inferences based on these statements and then expand these ideas to embrace wider generalizations and ideas. Students thus think through the implications of a piece of text, illustration, diagram or musical score and see how critical and thoughtful reading helps them develop a deeper understanding of concepts. This process contrasts with mere regurgitation of facts.

A further benefit of Three-Level Guides derives from their use with small mixed-ability groups. Instead of less-able readers being left to struggle through the text by themselves, they benefit from immediate peer-teaching. The text being considered is processed again and again, with students reading it aloud to each other and picking out the sections which justify particular conclusions. The less-able readers therefore have the relevant passages read to them repeatedly; they hear how more-able readers reason and see how they skim the passage to selectively choose supportive statements. Background experiences are shared and interpretations are weighed, valued and judged. Mixed-ability group discussion therefore provides a far more immediate, intensive and personalized form of instruction than the teacher can ever hope to offer.

A third major benefit of Three-Level Guides lies in the areas of language and reasoning. By depending on small-group discussions as contexts for justifying choices, the guides require students to become involved in a considerable amount of verbal exchange. Ideas are formulated, shared and refined more effectively in a group situation than in traditional teacher led discussions. More participants get more opportunities to interact and receive more immediate feedback. Having to justify one's choices and then listen to other students justify their choices, promotes much more thinking than the comprehension questions which traditionally follow a reading exercise. Students can clarify their ideas verbally before being asked to commit them to paper and have them assessed.

Three-Level Guides therefore provide teachers with a very powerful means of guiding reading and the subsequent writing. Instead of a hopeful instruction to 'read', teachers using the guides have a chance to hear students 'think aloud' as they talk through each level. Stumbling blocks are quickly identified and students' reasoning strategies exposed. In addition, the guides are highly motivating, because students learn that they have an opportunity to share and clarify ideas which they can later incorporate into their own written work.

WHAT DO THREE-LEVEL GUIDES LOOK LIKE?

First
Three-Level Guides consist of a series of statements *not* questions. The statements are directed at these three levels of comprehension — Literal, Interpretive and Applied.

Second
The statements used in the guide are separated into the three levels and therefore appear as three separate blocks. Students learn that some information is explicitly stated and some only inferred and that both of these kinds of understandings can be developed and used in ways that extend beyond the printed page they actually have in front of them.

Third
The statements may be developed around a section in a book, in which case a student receives only one sheet with the statements on it. Alternatively, the teacher may prepare a summary of a text which becomes the passage to be studied using the guide. In this case, the student receives copies of the shorter text summary and the guide. Guides can also be used to help students think through diagrams, pictures, musical scores, mathematics problems, poems or any genre at all.

The following example is a guide based on a teacher-written summary of information from several references.

Read the summary and then complete the Three-Level Guide.

Reading to Learn: the ERICA Model

THE MACDONNELL RANGES

The MacDonnell Ranges in the Northern Territory of Australia are surrounded by a vast area of near desert lands. There are rugged mountain ranges running east-west with wide gently-sloped valleys between. North and south of the mountains are broad, undulating lands covered with spinifex and mulga.

The land here is constantly dry and hot. Rainfall is not reliable and there are frequent droughts when the blazing sun shines down day after day for years. When the rain does come, grasses and flowers spring to life and a new land is born.

People who live in this area raise cattle. Because of the harsh conditions, the number of cattle per square kilometre is very low and averages between one and five beasts. Imagine one cow needing anywhere between 60 and 320 hectares to feed itself. Obviously with such a low stocking-rate, properties have to be very large and are measured in tens and even hundreds of thousands of hectares.

In drought years, station owners suffer heavy losses. Water holes dry up and cattle die of starvation and thirst. Between 1960 and 1966, the number of cattle was halved in some areas. The station owners restock their properties in good years and try to rebuild their herds. Unfortunately, this takes time because the land also has to recover.

Level 1. Tick the statements which focus on what the author says in this summary. When you have made your decisions, discuss your choices and your reasons with your group.
- (a) The MacDonnell Ranges are rugged mountains.
- (b) The MacDonnell Ranges are in a very hot-dry area.
- (c) Droughts can last for a few days.
- (d) People who live here raise sheep.
- (e) The harsh conditions keep the number of cattle down.
- (f) Properties are very large.
- (g) Cattle drink from water-holes.
- (h) The land also has to recover.
- (i) Station owners rebuild their herds in good years.

Level 2. Tick the statements which you think mean what the author meant in the summary. Discuss your choices with your group, and be prepared to justify them.
- (a) The MacDonnell Ranges are very isolated, lonely places.
- (b) Grasses and flowers seed themselves naturally.
- (c) Grass and flower seeds are long lived.
- (d) Cattle in the MacDonnell Range country are very hardy.
- (e) People who live on properties in this area have no close neighbours.
- (f) Raising cattle in the MacDonnell Ranges is not a very reliable business.
- (g) The years 1960-1966 were drought years.
- (h) A new land was born in the MacDonnell Ranges in 1967.

Level 3. Tick the statements which you think the author would support. Be ready to give your reasons when you discuss your choices.
- (a) People have to learn to take the rough with the smooth.

— (b) Cattle from the MacDonnell Ranges probably need fattening-up somewhere else before being sent to market.

— (c) Children who live on large cattle properties probably get very little schooling.

Having completed the guide by ticking the statements with which you agree, work in groups of no more than six to *compare responses* and to develop a group concensus.

The MacDonnell Ranges example was designed to encourage consideration of the hardships of life in outback Australia. Most Australians now live in cities and have no concept of how families on outback cattle stations exist.

DETERMINING CONTENT OBJECTIVES

Before starting to develop a Three-Level Guide first determine the content objectives. This is an essential step because it gives the Three-Level Guide direction and purpose. Most teachers find this step to be a new experience. They realize that previously they have often let the print dictate their purposes for using it. These teachers find the Three-Level Guide approach much more satisfying because they can now use the print resource to suit *their* purposes. So, first decide where you want to go!

In the Three-Level Guide you have just completed, attention was first drawn to the physical landscape, the climate, the distances involved and the uncertainty of the cattle industry. The reader then had to consider what type of cattle could survive in this environment and whether people living on these properties could lack city advantages such as schools and neighbours.

The ultimate class discussion which results from using this particular guide normally leads to a much more informed, more considered and better balanced view than that obtained when a traditional question-answer technique is used for the same material.

This occurs because the teacher had in mind a distinct objective before he or she started to prepare it. The points raised in it therefore lead in a particular direction. Guides which are prepared without a clear objective in mind are usually loose and directionless. Their Level 1 and Level 2 statements pick out points haphazardly and do not build up to logical conclusions. Do you recognize the point previously made in the introduction to this section?

Comprehending needs to be taught not assumed.

CONSTRUCTING A THREE-LEVEL GUIDE

Having determined the content objectives it's now possible to develop a Three-Level Guide. In your mind, the guide should be rather like an arrowhead.

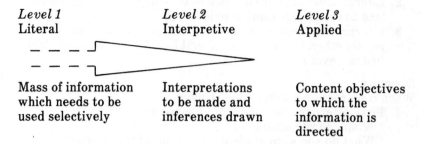

Level 1	*Level 2*	*Level 3*
Literal	Interpretive	Applied

Mass of information which needs to be used selectively	Interpretations to be made and inferences drawn	Content objectives to which the information is directed

The arrowhead points towards the content objectives — the knowledge base which we want to reach. *The Literal Level provides a mass of information which has to be sifted through and used selectively.* Rarely will all this information be needed and students will need to be taught that they have to be selective and discard irrelevant ideas.

The Interpretive Level is the stage where ideas are refined. This is the reflective stage where we look behind the words on the page and start to 'put two and two together to make five'. The arrowhead narrows here and shows us that a lot of ideas and examples lead only to a single point or concept. All the words, all the fine phrases, all the masses of information must be refined and sharpened until they culminate in one unifying notion.

What does this mean in terms of constructing a Three-Level Guide? How do we proceed? You have read the explanation, can you now list the stages of construction?

Q: Which Level do you construct first?   ....

Q: Which comes next?   ....

Try to work this construction order out for yourself. Once you 'see' the logic of it, you will always use it and will be able to develop tight and purposeful guides.

You should have listed the order of construction as follows:

> First: Applied Level, Level 3.
> Second: Literal Level, Level 1.
> Third: Interpretive Level, Level 2.

Thus, to see what a Three-Level Guide is directed towards, always read the Applied Level statements first. That way you know its objectives.

The order of construction is therefore determined by:

1. The need to decide on the content objectives, which you are aim-

ing for. These determine your Applied Level statements and mean you start by writing these first.
2. Literal Level facts are decided next. Which 'bits' of information lead towards your content objectives?
3. Interpretive Level is constructed last. At this point you start to put together, to 'chunk' the Literal Level facts you have identified in Level 1.

Summary

When constructing a Three Level Guide:
1. First determine your content objectives.
    What are you aiming for?
    What do you want students to get out of the reading?
    Do not feel constrained by the text, but rather, think of the wider implications and of going beyond the text and making generalizations.
2. Write your *Applied Level statements* first.
    Aim these at your content objectives, the main ideas, concepts, and generalizations that will take the student beyond the text.
3. Now write your *Literal Level statements*.
    Which information, given in the text, leads to the concept on which you have based your Applied Level statements?
4. Finally, write your *Interpretive Level statements*.
    Design these to help students make inferences about what the author actually says. This is called 'reading between the lines'. If you find this difficult, ask yourself,
    'what does the print say?'
    Then ask,   'what does that mean?'
    or   'what doesn't it say?'
    For example, a text might say:
    'John shivered and said, "I wish it were summer".'
    Some inferences which might be drawn from this are:
    (a) John was cold.
    (b) John likes hot weather.
    (c) It was winter.
    (d) John was not wearing heavy clothes to keep him warm.

USING THREE-LEVEL GUIDES

1. *Choose* an important component of a topic.
    Construction and use of a Three-Level Guide is too demanding a task to waste time on for no purpose. Develop guides for passages of text where an important point is being made or where students are having difficulty. One Mathematics teacher used a guide when she found her students were having difficulty understanding *Integers*. The smile on her face after the lesson showed how pleased she was with the outcome.

2. *Allow* sufficient time to complete the guide in one session.
   The length of the passage and the number of statements provided will need to be adjusted to fit the time available. As an example, the MacDonnell Ranges guide can be completed in one forty-five minute period. Hard and fast rules cannot be laid down, because different classes respond differently to the same guide.

3. *Ensure* that each student first works alone to complete the guide. Stress the need for students to be able to give reasons for their choices. Many students read casually and superficially and will need encouraging to reason things out for themselves.

DO NOT MISS OUT THIS STAGE!

4. *Ensure* that students work in mixed-ability groups of no more than five students to discuss their answers and their reasons for those answers. Always have them reach a concensus.

DO NOT MISS OUT THIS STAGE!

5. *Do* circulate around the class to identify areas of disagreement or misunderstanding. Refer to these situations when reviewing the guide as a class activity, after students have had sufficient discussion time.

6. *Do not* review statements which have been generally agreed upon unless there is a particular point you wish to stress.

7. *Do not* interfere with the discussions!
   The idea is to get the students talking rather than for you to have an extra chance to tell them what you think.

8. *Do* use the guides to show how to analyze a text to focus on relevant information, how to combine various pieces of information and how to make inferences.

QUALITIES OF 'GOOD' THREE-LEVEL GUIDES

These include statements which:
- Promote discussion, are open to a variety of interpretations and which take the reader into and beyond the print.
- Lead from what the print says, to what it can mean and to what its application can be.
- Focus on relevant information and show the reader that she or he can read selectively and so reject information irrelevant to the task at hand.
- Lead to the teacher's content objectives rather than to merely follow the text sequence.

As well, 'Good' three-level guides are well set out so that students do not have to flip through many pages, but can engage in the thought processes logically and without interruption.

SOME TIPS ON USING THREE-LEVEL GUIDES

- *Do not* prepare a guide to cover too many pages in a text book. Turning pages back and forth can be very frustrating and tends to make the exercise tedious.
- *Do* use mixed-ability groups. This is one exercise where your less-efficient readers can receive help when and where they need it. They will soon join in and make a useful contribution to the group.
- *Limit groups* to four to six students. Large numbers inhibit participation.
- When you start using Guides, *take one level at a time. Do not* expect students to work through all three levels at one sitting. It will take students some time to get used to the differences between the levels of tasks involved. Many readers, including teachers, are sloppy in their assessment of what is and what is not said by an author. Do stress the difference between:

(a) What the author actually says.
(b) What the reader has to infer.
(c) What the reader thinks and what the author is getting at.

Cloze Exercises

```
                    ┌──────────────────┐
        ┌──────────│ THINKING THROUGH │──────────┐
        │          │   THE READING    │          │
┌───────────────┐  └──────────────────┘  ┌──────────────┐
│  THREE-LEVEL  │                         │    CLOZE     │
│    GUIDES     │                         │  EXERCISES   │
└───────────────┘                         └──────────────┘
```

The second 'Thinking Through' activity is the *Selective Deletion* cloze exercise. *Cloze* is a procedure in which words are deleted from a passage. Blank spaces of standard length, usually twelve to fifteen letter spaces, are left to show where words have been deleted. Readers are then asked to fill in each blank space with the word or words which they think make the best sense.

Here is a typical cloze exercise:

Fill in each blank in the following passage with the *one* word which you think makes the best sense. *When you have finished*, work in your group to decide which words are the best for each space.

EROSION AND DEPOSITION

Rivers are responsible for many of the landscape features we see today. For many thousands of years, rivers have been (1)_____ away the mountains to (2)_____ valleys. This is called erosion and we say that rivers (3)_____ land which they pass over. The river carries (4)_____ the rock pebbles and soil particles which it has (5)_____, sometimes for many kilometres and sometimes even out to sea. When the river reaches (6)_____ land it slows down and begins to (7)_____ the many rock, sand and soil particles which it has (8)_____ along from where they were eroded. (9)_____ pieces are deposited as gravels and the fine (10)_____ particles as silt. The deposited materials gradually build up and (11)_____ the river to overflow and find new channels. Over the years, rivers (12)_____ about a great deal (13)_____ valleys (14)_____ the hills and building up flat fertile plains on the (15)_____ ground. The (16)_____ of erosion and deposition can be seen in many places and are still going on (17)_____. See if there is any evidence of (18)_____ erosion or deposition near where you live after there has been some heavy rain.

NOTE

The numbers are inserted to help ease of location when discussing alternatives.

USING CLOZE TO DEVELOP COMPREHENSION

Cloze is particularly useful in identifying those readers who read word-by-word. Because these readers do not read in meaningful 'chunks', they find it very difficult to understand the gist of a text. They fail to recognize the clues to meaning which are available in the passage. Often, these are the students of whom their teachers say:

'They can read (aloud) but they don't understand what they read.'

When faced with a difficulty in their reading, as, for example, in a cloze exercise, some readers make up their mind about a deleted word on the basis of the information they have collected up to that point. They do not read on to pick up extra context clues. Their errors often fit the previous word but not the following one.

In our example above, word-by-word readers might complete the first two spaces in the following way:

For many thousands of years rivers have been (1)   flowing   away from the mountains to (2)   sea   valleys.

The first word selected may make sense when related to the sentence beginning, but it becomes unacceptable when one reads on to find the words, 'away' and 'valley'.

Errors of this type give us a clue about how some readers react when they meet a word they do not recognize. Their decision about the meaning of the word is made on the basis of incomplete information.

Goodman (1967) and Smith (1971) would perhaps argue that such readers are the product of reading teaching which emphasizes individual words, rather than methods which emphasize reading in meaningful chunks by making use of the variety of clues provided in the context.

However, if we deliberately use cloze to force readers to 'read-around' for extra clues *and then* put them into small-group discussions to justify their choices and hear other students' alternatives, we encourage more thoughtful reading. We also demonstrate over-and-over again the techniques which more efficient readers in the group use to find extra clues. The less-able reader is thus provided with individual guidance and help, as and when it is needed, and is also given efficient models from which to learn.

NOTE

Using cloze in this way, requires the teacher to delete words for which clues remain in the text. THIS IS ESSENTIAL! The purpose of these exercises is to show readers how more thoughtful and more wide-ranging reading will reveal clues which help them understand a particular point.

We are trying to promote more reflective rather than superficial reading. The selection of words to be deleted therefore cannot be taken lightly and each must be carefully considered before being left out.

CLOZE ACTIVITIES VERSUS CLOZE TESTS

Many teachers will be familiar with the use of cloze as a test of reading ability or even of readability. Even more teachers will feel that they are experienced users of cloze because they frequently design tests in which they leave out words in order to test whether students can insert the 'correct' piece of information. Passage A falls into this category.

It is important for teachers, who are experienced in these forms of cloze, to realize that the cloze activities recommended in the ERICA Model serve a different purpose, namely, improving reading performance by developing a reader's ability to locate and combine clues contained in prose passages. Passage B falls into this category.

If cloze is to be used to develop comprehension, then the cloze activities themselves must be prepared with this in mind.

The following passages demonstrate the difference between cloze tests and cloze activities as recommended in the ERICA Model.

PASSAGE A: PYRAMID OF CHEOPS
A few facts on the Pyramid of Cheops.
1. It is made out of _____ blocks.
2. These blocks are made of _____.
3. Each block weighs about _____ tonnes.
4. The pyramid stands about _____ metres high.

PASSAGE B: PYRAMID OF CHEOPS
A few facts on the pyramid of _____.
1. It is made out of 2,300,000 _____.
2. These blocks are _____ of limestone.
3. Each block _____ about 2.5 tonnes.
4. The _____ stands about 420 metres _____.

In Passage A no clues are available in the text to help the reader work out which words have been left out. Deletions of this type only test the reader's previous knowledge. In Passage B however, we see how the same passage can be used in an entirely different way. In this example, the words deleted or suitable alternatives can all be worked out by using the remaining clues.

Activities similar to Passage B, combined with small-group discussions, can help to teach the use of context clues. They demonstrate how *reading-around* will reveal extra clues, from which the reader obtains a fuller and deeper understanding of a written passage.

On the other hand, Passage A types may be useful as revision activities. They do little to develop the use of context clues, but do require the recall of previously encountered information. *While this type of cloze activity may be used as a test, it cannot be regarded as helping to improve comprehension.*

In the examples of cloze activities, 2.4 to 2.9, decide for yourself whether each is a comprehension or a test type activity.

Activity 2.4

Fill in each blank space in the passage below with the one word which has been left out. Note, there is only one correct word for each space.

A mother, father and son located in the lowest socio-economic bracket are discussing what the child will do at the end of this year, his (1)_____ year at school.

The father receives an (2)_____ (3)_____ while the mother is a (4)_____ (5)_____ The boy is the eldest of (6)_____ children who range in age from 15 years to (7)_____ years. What will the boy and his parents decide to do?

Activity 2.5

Fill in each blank in the following passage with the one word you think makes most sense. Work by yourself and think about why you chose each word. When you have finished, compare your ideas with those of your partner and decide which words fit best.

A mother, father and son located in the (1)_____ socio-economic bracket are discussing what the child will do at the (2)_____ of this year, his (3)_____ year at school. The (4)_____ receives an invalid pension while the mother is a part-time cleaner. The boy is the (5)_____ of eight children who range in age from 15 years to 2 years. What will the boy and his parents decide to do?

Activity 2.6

Fill in each blank in the following passage with the one word you think makes most sense. Work by yourself and think about why you chose each word. When you have finished, compare your ideas with those of your partner and decide which words fit best.

The Force That Stops Motion

Investigation 1 showed three things:

1. To (1)_____ a rubber band, you use a force.
2. A stretched rubber band can (2)_____ movement.
   In (3)_____ words, it can exert a (4)_____.
3. The bigger the stretch, the (5)_____ the force.

The force of a stretched rubber band can move a block of wood. (6)_____, the block does (7)_____ move far across the table. It soon (8)_____ down and stops. Why does it (9)_____?

If you want to stop anything, you have to exert a force (10)_____ to the way it is moving. With the (11)_____ block, it seems that the (12)_____ force acting is the force exerted by the (13)_____ rubber band. (14)_____ there must be (15)_____ force. The block is touching the table top. The (16)_____ that (17)_____ the block moving must be caused by the (18)_____ surfaces (19)_____ together. This (20)_____ is called friction.

110

Reading to Learn: the ERICA Model

Activity 2.7

Fill in each blank in the following activity with the one word you think makes most sense. Work by yourself and think about why you chose each word. When you have finished, compare your ideas with those of your partner and decide which words fit best.

Expansion and Contraction

Your local garage mechanic will probably be able to tell you how he fits a new ring gear to a flywheel. This is often done by (1)_____ the ring until it (2)_____ enough to slip easily over the flywheel. As the ring cools and (3)_____ it will fit (4)_____ in place. The iron rims of wagon wheels were once fitted in this way. The steel tyres of a railway truck are (5)_____ attached by this method.

Applying part of our principle in (6)_____ way, a motor builder often fits the inside sleeve of a cylinder by cooling the sleeve in liquid air. He then slides it (7)_____ the (8)_____. Here (9)_____ produces a very tight fit.

Many examples of metals expanding and (10)_____ can be located by the (11)_____ the metal makes as it is (12)_____ or cooled. An iron roof or an iron garage creaks loudly as it (13)_____ up after a (14)_____ or as it (15)_____ after a hot day. An electric iron also makes a noise as it heats up and creaking noises then remind us that the metal is (16)_____ as it cools. New fence wires (17)_____ never be drawn tight on a (18)_____ day, if they were they would probably (19)_____ as the wire (20)_____ as the sun went down and the temperature dropped.

These are only some of the effects of expansion and contraction caused by substances being heated or cooled. You can probably think of many more.

NOTE

This was used after students had completed in-class experiments on heat and so were familiar with the concepts described.

Activity 2.8

Fill in each blank in the following exercise with the one word you think makes most sense. Work by yourself and think about why you chose each word. When you have finished, compare your ideas with those of your partner and decide which words fit best.

How a Thermometer Works

You have seen that a thermometer is designed to measure temperatures over a range of values. In order to do this it has to have a scale which has definite (fixed) points. The (1)_____ also has to have something inside it which moves along the (2)_____ to show us any (3)_____ in temperature.

The thermometers we have used have had the (4)_____

Learning to Learn from Text

point of ice as the (5)_____ fixed point and the boiling point of
(6)_____ as the upper (7)_____ point of their
(8)_____. In these thermometers, mercury has been used to
(9)_____ changes in temperature.

When the temperature (10)_____ the mercury expands and
moves (11)_____ the scale to show us this rise in temperature.
When the temperature falls, the mercury (12)_____ and moves
(13)_____ the scale and shows a lower temperature.

A mercury thermometer is made of a glass tube which has thick
walls. At the bottom of the thermometer is a small bulb which holds
the (14)_____. The bulb is made of very thin glass so that any
changes in (15)_____ quickly affect the (16)_____ and
(17)_____ it to move up or down the scale. Inside the thermometer the mercury moves up and down a very, very
(18)_____ tube, which is only as thick as a hair. This
(19)_____ has had all the air sucked out of it so that the
mercury can (20)_____ move up and down.

NOTE

This was used after students had handled and used mercury-in-
glass thermometers.

Activity 2.9

Fill in the blanks in the following passage with the *one* word which has
been deleted from the original text.

There are two kinds of statistics (1)_____ and (2)_____.
(3)_____ statistics are used to tell us what (4)_____ in
the measurement, while (5)_____ statistics are used to determine whether a given result is a (6)_____ one or is due to
(7)_____.

There are three measures of central tendency — the
(8)_____, (9)_____, and (10)_____. The
(11)_____ is the most frequently appearing score in the distribution; the (12)_____ is the score that divides the distribution
exactly in half; and the (13)_____ is the arithmetic average. Of
these three measures, the (14)_____ is the most reliable and of
greatest use.

Stage 3. Extracting and Organizing Information

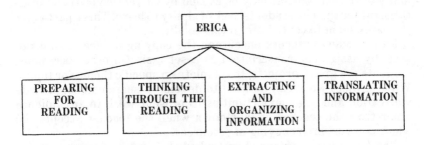

INTRODUCTION

How many times have you heard these comments in your staff room?

'My students copy out large chunks of text.'
'My students can't distinguish the important points from the irrelevant details.'
'Instead of writing a clear concise summary, my students try to tell me everything they can find on the topic.'

These are concerns of this third stage of the ERICA Model.

We have already looked at the stages of Preparing and Thinking Through, and have asked these questions.

- How can we prepare readers so that they can make better use of their texts?
- How can we help readers understand what they read?

Now we need to consider how we can help readers select and use information given in a text. *Remember*, by 'text', we mean *all* the print resources used, not just textbooks.

It is all very well to be able to understand what a passage is about, but understanding is of little value if use cannot be made of this knowledge. Even though readers will be better able to get meaning from the text if the stages of Preparing and Thinking Through have been followed, we still need to consider how we can help them become more efficient at Extracting and Organizing the information they need.

Many students are overwhelmed by the mass of information they encounter and seem unable to distinguish 'the wood from the trees'. Often these students do find the relevant section of a text, but then resort to verbatim copying of large slabs of text, rather than selecting the necessary pertinent points. Effective note-taking is frequently beyond students who cannot differentiate between main points and supporting details or examples.

PROBLEMS CAUSED BY SOME EDUCATIONAL PRACTICES

Many of these problems may be caused by current educational practices, rather than by students' lack of ability to learn. Three particular practices seem to contribute to this condition.

Firstly many teachers encourage the copying of large chunks of text, by assigning transcription as a set task. On other occasions, students are given 'projects' to complete on specific themes or topics. While project work can be used to develop research skills, provide motivation and offer opportunities to present work to an audience other than the teacher, it falls down when the teacher accepts the wholesale verbatim copying of resources.

The absurdity of this is shown when the copied passage contains reference to some other source or section of the original text. The practice is unfortunately prevalent in tertiary institutions, as well as in schools. One student handed in an assignment which she purported to be her own work, but which contained the following extract.

> The use of learning centres, learning packets and units *such as those described in this chapter*, can be viewed as a positive sign.

The chapter referred to was one in the book from which the student had copied. A fatal mistake for the plagiarist!

Teachers, who do not discourage copying of this nature by insisting on a summary in the student's own words, are doing the student a grave disservice. Not only is plagiarism fostered, but thinking and the ability to select and translate ideas into one's own words are inhibited and are hence not treated as worthwhile skills to develop.

A second practice, which encourages copying and poor note-taking ability, is the seemingly growing practice of teachers preparing all notes for students. Much criticism has been levelled at textbooks which are too difficult for students to use and some are undoubtedly too difficult. Consequently their choice represents either poor text selection or a lack of available alternatives. However, many which have been labelled as 'too difficult' might have been placed in the 'useful' category, if only the students had been given more guidance in how to use them efficiently.

A lack of suitable textbooks has caused many teachers to write their own notes. These are handed, or worse dictated, to students who are then expected to rote learn them. The problem with this practice is *not* that teacher-made notes are deficient, but that it doesn't teach students how to make notes for themselves from a text. The practice represents a stress on the *content* being transmitted, rather than on the *process* by which this information is acquired.

If you believe, as we do, that it is important to help students become independent learners, who can process print information for themselves, then you will recognize the need to teach this processing in class. To this end, showing students how to make notes and involving them in the active process of producing notes, will be far more beneficial than continually providing teacher-made notes for students to regurgitate.

The third practice which contributes to students' inability to process print is, in fact, one of omission. In general, educators fail to recognize the need to teach students how to extract and organize ideas for themselves, consequently they do not teach them how to do it. The fault is one of omission. Teachers and schools who recognize this need, actively teach the processing skills required to extract and organize information. Their students *do* learn how to work independently, which demonstrates the long-term value of such programs. Unfortunately, such teachers and schools are scarce and most students do not receive the guidance they need.

The following examples demonstrate how our ability to process information is improved when we know what to look for.

Example 2.13
Allow yourself five seconds to look at the pattern below. What word exists in the pattern?

If you have difficulty picking out the word which is shown, try to avoid looking at the four black figures. If you still have difficulty, look at the three spaces *between* the black figures.

The solution is obvious when you know what to look for.

Example 2.14
Which 2 three-digit numbers come next in this sequence?
71, 421, 283, 542, 495, 663, ___, ___.
If the problem is difficult it's *not* because your Mathematical ability is inadequate, but because you don't know what to look for.
If you find the problem difficult, look at the row of figures as a whole and ignore the spaces between them.
Do you need some more help?
Imagine you are counting up in one of the multiplication tables you once learned. Do you still have a problem?
Try counting up in sevens. The next two numbers will be made up of the next number in the 7's table, 70, 77, and 84 and will look like this: 707, 784.
Again, the solution is obvious when you know what to look for.

Example 2.15

Which three-digit numbers follow next in this sequence?
91, 827, 364, 554, 637, ___, ___.
There was no difficulty that time: 281, 909.

These three examples illustrate the following point. *Processing information is difficult if you have no guidelines to follow, if you do not know what to look for and if you do not practice the task.*

However, once you know what to look for, the task becomes much simpler and you can approach similar problems with some confidence. Activities, which show students how to analyze texts and provide them with practice in this task, can be built into regular subject learning activities. The short-term benefit is that students learn from the print resource provided. The long-term benefit is that students learn processes which can be applied to other situations, hence they become more independent learners.

EXTRACTING INFORMATION

If we could imagine an idealized essay structure it might look something like this:

INTRODUCTORY PARAGRAPH
Lists three main points to be discussed

PARAGRAPH 2
TOPIC SENTENCE – POINT   1
Supporting Sentences   1
                          2
                          3
                          4

PARAGRAPH 3
TOPIC SENTENCE – POINT   2
Supporting Sentences   1
                          2

PARAGRAPH 4
TOPIC SENTENCE – POINT   3
Supporting Sentences   1
                          2

CONCLUDING PARAGRAPH
Restates three main points and may formally draw a conclusion.

In the above example, each of the five paragraphs has a specific purpose. A topic sentence is presented at the beginning of each paragraph and supporting sentences flow from it. The structure shows cohesion and logic as it develops from the introduction through the three explanatory paragraphs to the conclusion.

If all of the print resources provided in schools followed an idealized structure like this, then the teacher's job would be greatly simplified. Students could be taught to label the opening sentence as a topic sentence and then look for the details provided in the sentences which followed. Note-taking would be greatly simplified, because the structure would be consistent and ideas could be extracted and organized simultaneously.

However, the great majority of print resources — books, articles, newspapers, magazines and journals — do not follow an idealized structure. Rather than being consistent in their organizational structure they are consistent only in their inconsistency. Authors' styles, subject matter and the publishers' needs, all result in a tremendously varied organization of materials. This lack of consistency makes extracting and organizing information difficult, which perhaps explains why methods for doing so are infrequently taught.

However, print resources comprise ideas which authors have written and it is the readers' task to identify them. Some principles of idea organization include:

- Main ideas are supported by less important examples.
- Ideas are contrasted one with another.
- Causes are explained in terms of their effects.
- Directions are given.
- Items are listed.
- Solutions are given to problems.

The teacher's role is to teach readers to focus on the most important features of the text as the basis for closer analysis. Just as you were able to pick out 'Tie' or work out the two number sequences when you knew what to look for, so readers are better able to identify the ideas set before them when they know the structural organization of the text in which the information is embedded.

SEEING THE OVERALL PLAN

When we read-to-learn we usually have to tackle a fairly lengthy section of prose. It might be a chapter in a book, an article from a journal or newspaper, or perhaps a complete story. Most print information is presented in long sections, because it refers to a substantial topic being studied. For example, a History class may have to consider a chapter on nineteenth century Imperialism, while an Art class may have to deal with a chapter reviewing twentieth century art movements.

When we begin to help students extract information, it is important to start with a general overview of the relevant chapter, section or article. This concept has already been introduced in discussing the use of Structured Overviews as a preparatory activity. The Structured Overview illustrates how a topic can be represented in diagrammatic form to show its sub-topics. It can also be developed to reveal the component parts of a sub-topic.

Whereas the Structured Overview relates to the topic being studied, the Graphic Outline introduces the reader to how an author has presented this topic in the text being considered.

Students who approach a topic or a text through either the Structured Overview or Graphic Outline, or both, have already started the process of Extracting and Organizing information. These strategies provide readers with a *cognitive* map of the information they are to process. Although these are global viewpoints, they provide readers with a *framework* into and around which the information to be read can be fitted.

Think back to the three examples earlier in this chapter when you may have struggled to recognize 'Tie' or to work out the number sequences until you had 'frameworks' or 'keys' for knowing what to look for. The Structured Overview and the Graphic Outline can both act as keys in this sense. They show readers which topics and subtopics are to be encountered, how they relate to each other and how the text is organized.

GETTING INTO THE TEXT — RECOGNIZING TOP-LEVEL STRUCTURES

We need to realize that ideas are expressed by the author in an overall global sense and also in a point-by-point, detailed sense. The overall, or macro framework, underlies the larger unit, the book, article or chapter. As an author plans a text, he or she starts with a basic structure or framework inside which the material is to be presented. The reader who recognizes this underlying structure is able to relate smaller sections of the text to the total picture.

It has been widely suggested that several top-level structures are very commonly used and that students can be taught to recognize these. For a discussion of some of the research which supports this argument, see pages 182-183.

The most commonly suggested ones are:
- Comparison-Contrast
- Cause-Effect
- Attribution
- Problem-Solution

These top-level structures are found both at the macro-level, that is, underlying the whole section, article or chapter, and also at the micro-level, that is, within smaller units such as paragraphs and sentences. We suggest that teachers concentrate initially on helping students recognize top-level structures at the macro-level rather than the smaller micro-units. The reason for this is that the larger overall framework underlies the whole text. The larger framework gives purpose and direction and helps readers understand the relevance of the smaller sections.

However, even at the paragraph level the author may use a variety of structures, sometimes within the one paragraph, to emphasize a particular point. Students who are introduced too quickly to differing organizational pattern-structures at the micro-level can be easily confused.

These examples will help to demonstrate these top-level structure points.

Example 2.16
Source: Andrews, R.L. *A Geography of Natural Landscapes*. 2nd edn. Geo. Philip & O'Neil, Melbourne, 1973. Chapter 1.
Topic: Equatorial Rainforest Landscape in Malaysia.
    In this chapter, the author seeks to draw a *contrast* between
- Equatorial rainforests which have not been commercially developed.
- Equatorial rainforests which have been commercially developed.

Thus the top-level structure used for the chapter is one of COMPARISON – CONTRAST and can be diagrammed in this way.

```
            ┌─────────────────────────┐
            │ LAND USE IN MALAYSIA     │
            └─────────────────────────┘
                 ╱              ╲
    ┌────────────────┐   ┌────────────────┐
    │ TRADITIONAL,   │   │ MODERN,        │
    │ UNDEVELOPED    │   │ COMMERCIALLY   │
    │ RAINFOREST.    │   │ DEVELOPED      │
    │                │   │ RAINFOREST.    │
    └────────────────┘   └────────────────┘
```

However, the author does not provide an organizational diagram similar to the one above and embeds his overall plan in the body of the text as follows:

Under-developed Rain-Forest	Very few people live in the rainforest. In Malaysia where the forest now mainly covers only the highlands and rough country, about 100,000 *orang asli* (aborigines) live in the forest. These people are primitive hunters and gatherers and mostly belong to the Sen tribe.
Commercially Developed	In the rest of Malaysia, the main uses of the land are for rubber-growing, tin-mining and the growing of rice, oil palm, pineapples and coconuts.
Undeveloped Rain-Forest	There are still a few people in East Malaysia who are shifting farmers who have not altered their environment very much. The most important group of people who live this way are the Ibans of Sarawak.

(p. 4)

and . . .

Contrast   The studies that follow are representative of two
Signal   important landscapes and ways of life in the equa-
               torial rainforest environment.

(p. 5)

The author then illustrates these two uses of equatorial rainforest by way of case studies. To illustrate the traditional rainforest farm, the author describes the life of the Iban people of Sarawak. Then, to illustrate a modern commercially affected rainforest environment, he describes the rubber-growing areas on the west coast of Malaysia.

The shift from one side of the contrast pattern to the other is not highlighted and is explained in the text in these terms.

Contrast   In contrast to the underdeveloped, undisturbed
Signal   appearance of the equatorial rainforest landscape in
Undeveloped   most of Sarawak, (see Ibans), the rubber-growing dis-
Commercially   trict of Malaysia has undergone many changes since
Developed   the introduction of the rubber tree.

(pp. 5-6)

Readers need to recognize the significance of the words 'in contrast to' and to appreciate that this marks a fundamental transition point within the text. This could easily be missed because the author in his Preface says:

I hope that by the time a student works his way through this book — and I stress 'student', not teacher . . .

Those teachers who provide no guidance to students thereby rely on them finding such underlying structures for themselves. In these circumstances it would be little wonder if students floundered, not knowing what to look for, and focused on superficial details rather than the underlying logic. Thus, the value of the author's underlying structure can be lost, if neither the teacher nor the student recognizes its presence and function within the text.

In the Geography text already discussed, it would be easy to concentrate on the lists of different features described, without putting them into either comparison-contrast or cause-effect structures. The result would be unfortunate, because not only would the author's point be missed, but also the comparison-contrast structure would not be used. Especially since it is this structure which has been shown to be a more powerful learning aid than the listing structure. (Meyer, 1975.)

Example 2.17
Source: Cull, R.G., and Drake, W.A. *Concepts in Science 1*. 3rd Ed.
   Jacaranda Press, Brisbane, 1979. Chapter 14.
Topic: Rocks and Minerals.

In this example, the authors explain some differences between igneous and sedimentary rocks. These differences — comparison-contrast structure — are explained in the text in terms of how the two rock types are formed, how long they take to form and where they are formed. Some examples of each are then given.

When teaching this topic, the teacher could ask the students to look for the kinds of things the author tells us about the different rock types. These could then be listed under headings.

Types	Formed By	How Formed	Where Formed	Time to Form	Features	Examples

Using this procedure, the class should work with the teacher to analyze what the author has described. Remember that at this point, we are only categorizing major points made in the text. Details can be added later. *The purpose is to prompt students to think about the way the text information can be grouped and arranged.*

Having built up categories through listing the headings, the teacher can now assign the task of finding the details which the author has provided. The following diagram has been successfully used to help students analyse this section of the text.

ROCKS   EXTRACTING INFORMATION

         Formed by   Types   How and   Time to   Features   Examples
                              Where   Form
                              Formed?

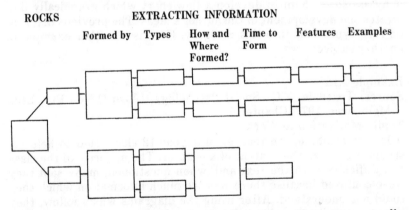

This diagram shows very clearly that the authors are actually describing not two, but *four* types of rock, because each of the two main categories is itself divided into two sub-types.

By using this diagram, students will see what the text is saying. Without the diagram, the reader has to create mental pictures of what the text is describing and as you can see from the diagram, this would be a very complex process. With the diagram, however, the reader has a chance to take each piece of information and slot it into the appropriate box, gradually building up the whole picture as the text is processed. In addition to separating the various pieces of information, the diagram also presents it in parallel strands, so that the different rock types can be compared or contrasted at any point. Teaching students to make visual analyses in this way provides them, not only with a means of restructuring prose passages, but also with a valuable aid to learning, since the visual display forms a succinct summary of the information presented.

SEEING MAIN IDEAS AND SUPPORTING DETAILS

As already stated, many students find it very difficult to distinguish between the main points and the details which support them. Students may have this difficulty, because they lack an overall perspective of the topic being presented and so have no framework into which information can be fitted. The examples already given suggest how the teacher might help students develop appropriate cognitive maps, to help them establish such a framework.

In the last example on rock types, we moved from the macro or overall view, to the micro or detailed view. Having been presented with the overview diagram, students can then sift through the textual explanation to find relevant details.

Where students find it difficult to pick out the main points in the flow of a prose passage, the teacher can help them come to grips with it by assisting them to develop a flow-chart which graphically illustrates the development of the author's ideas. The previous diagram on rock types falls into this category. Here is a further example in another subject area.

Example 2.18
Source: Teasdale, T.C., Social Psychology, Lloyd O'Neil Pty. Ltd., Melbourne, 1977. Chapter 6.
Topic: Motivation to Work.

In this example, the teacher of a Year 12 class tried to help his students analyze the content of a chapter. The majority of the class had difficulty with the text and, when questioned, many said they were confused because there was too much information which they could not understand. After using the diagrams which follow, they then said the diagrams helped them see what it was all about. By using the diagrams they were able to break-up the text into meaningful chunks with which they could cope.

The chapter considers theories about motivation to work. The teacher prepared a diagram for each theory and the students worked through the text to fill in relevant details. The two following diagrams show the different structures underlying the theories. Since the Herzberg Theory is explained in terms of a research project, the diagram first asks students to establish some points about this work.

Examples of Herzberg's Satisfiers and Dissatisfiers are then given.

In contrast, McGregor's 'x' and 'y' Theory is divided into two types of management philosophy and different points about each one are then listed.

The class's response to using these diagrams was very positive. Of twenty-three students in the group, twenty-one said the diagrams were a great help because they showed them what to look for in the text. The two who disagreed were both excellent students who felt they did not need such structured assistance. Less-able students however, completed far more work than normal. As a consequence of their more positive involvement, they did not cause their usual disruptions.

6. Motivation to Work

People behave differently at work: some work hard while others do as little as possible; some derive great pleasure and satisfaction from work while others express their distaste for it. People differ in abilities, and this determines how well they will be able to perform in their work and which job they are best suited for. People also differ in interests and *motivation*, and this determines which kinds of work they prefer to do and how industrious they will be in their job.

This section will concern itself with workers and the motivation to work. In Unit 1, the theory of motivation was discussed, and in particular, the theory of A. Maslow. Here, we shall apply the theory, investigate other theories and concern ourselves with those inner forces which energise and move the individual into certain channels of behaviour which are directed towards accomplishing goals.

6.1 The historical perspective

One of the earliest ideas about what motivates man was the concept of *hedonism*. The Greek philosopher Epicurus who lived in the third century B.C. proposed the theory that pleasure was man's ultimate goal, and as such was a determinant of behaviour. The British philosopher Jeremy Bentham (1748–1832) advanced the concept of hedonism as the explanation of all behaviour. It could be argued that Bentham is the inspiration for the Australian way of life, in which the pursuit of pleasure — surfing, barbecues, races, football, beer drinking — figures so strongly.

The main difficulty with Bentham, however, is that he did not explain *why* people seek pleasure. The first person to shed light in this area was E. L. Thorndike (1911). He argued that of all the responses a person made to a situation, those which resulted in satisfying or pleasurable consequences were strengthened. Those which led to uncomfortable or unpleasant outcomes were weakened. The strengthened responses become more probable, the weakened responses less probable. This theory, based on past consequences, became known as the *law of effect*. What is important to Thorndike's theory is the point that work and effort occur not in order to achieve some future satisfaction but only because satisfaction *has* already been experienced. It does not answer, however, the question, 'why are the consequences of a response pleasurable or unpleasurable?'.

We have seen, by use of Maslows hierarchy of needs, that an explanation of this question is tied to the idea of physiological needs. The individuals is seen as having basic needs such as hunger and thirst, and pleasure resulted from the reduction of these drives. At this stage, the *law of effect*, or reinforcements, would become important. For example, a baby's behaviour immediately prior to a feed would be strengthened, because of the positive reinforcement.

For the remainder of this section, we will look at the theories that attempt to specify the drives that motivate the individual at work.

6.2 Herzberg's motivation-hygiene theory

Frederick Herzberg's theories have had a profound effect on the thinking of many people, especially business managers. Herzberg (1959) claimed that man has two sets of needs:

(a) his need as an animal to avoid pain
(b) his need as a human to grow psychologically.

From the responses of 200 engineers and accountants who represented a cross-section of Pittsburgh industry, Herzberg was able to identify sources of satisfaction and dissatisfaction. His research design was simple and was built around two questions:

(a) Can you describe, in detail, when you felt exceptionally good about your job?
(b) Can you describe, in detail, when you felt exceptionally bad about your job?

Analyses of the responses showed that:

(i)   The subjects most often mentioned job experiences or factors related to a *good feeling* about the job in terms of job *content* (content factors).
(ii) Factors or experiences mentioned in connection with a *bad feeling* about the job were most often related to the *surrounding* or *peripheral aspects* of the job (context factors).

Herzberg classified the content factors as *satisfiers* (*i.e.* intrinsic factors found in work itself), while the context factors were called *dissatisfiers* (*i.e.* extrinsic factors found in the environment of work). (See *Figure 7.11.*)

Herzberg was thus able to identify nine needs which, if not fulfilled, lead to job dissatisfaction but which, whether fulfilled or not, have little effect on positive job attitude. (Herzberg called these dissatisfiers *hygiene factors* because they are *preventative* actions taken to remove sources of dissatisfaction from the environment, just as sanitation removes potential threats to health from the physical environment.)

Herzberg also identified achievement, recognition, responsibility, advancement and the work itself as strong determiners of job satisfaction. He called them *motivators*, and he believed that they led to job satisfaction because of a need for growth, or in Maslow's terms, 'self-actualisation'. He claimed that the work itself, responsibility and advancement were the most important job satisfiers, and the essential factors in motivating the individual to superior effort and performance. (Students are recommended at this stage to return to Unit 1 to Maslow's hierarchy of needs. It can be seen that if organisations wish to motivate the behaviour of their employees so that efficiency and greater production result, they must ensure that all lower order needs are being met or partially met. They can then concentrate on satisfying the higher order needs.)

Herzberg's theory is of particular use in pointing out to management that factors such as working conditions, salary and supervision, which are commonly believed to be motivators, are, in fact, of no value in inducing a worker to achieve a greater output. These factors, if satisfied, remove negative attitudes and dissatisfaction. According to Herzberg, if management wishes to motivate its workers it must provide opportunities for achievement and peer recognition.

6.3 McGregor's Theory X and Theory Y

Douglas McGregor's proposal links Maslow's needs to reality. He recognises that workers, whether they are motivated or otherwise, invariably function within a management organisation.

McGregor (1970) proposes two types of management philosophy, and he describes them as *Theory X* and *Theory Y*. He believes that if management adopted his Theory X (the traditional view of direction and control), it would meet the physiological needs of the workers but ignore all the other needs. Theory X assumes that the average worker prefers to be directed, to avoid responsibility, has little ambition, and wants security above all.

Reading to Learn: the ERICA Model

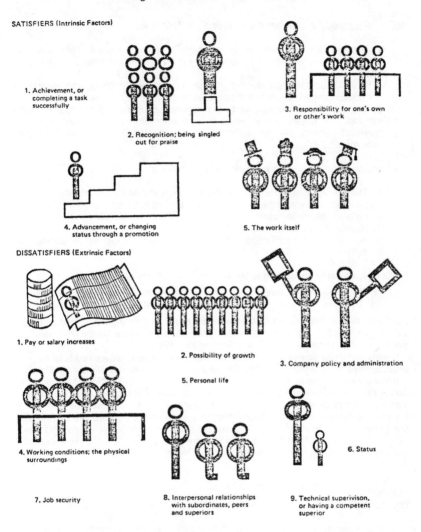

SATISFIERS (Intrinsic Factors)

1. Achievement, or completing a task successfully

2. Recognition; being singled out for praise

3. Responsibility for one's own or other's work

4. Advancement, or changing status through a promotion

5. The work itself

DISSATISFIERS (Extrinsic Factors)

1. Pay or salary increases

2. Possibility of growth

3. Company policy and administration

5. Personal life

4. Working conditions; the physical surroundings

6. Status

7. Job security

8. Interpersonal relationships with subordinates, peers and superiors

9. Technical superivison, or having a competent superior

Fig. 7.11   *The satisfaction and dissatisfaction factors* Adapted from F. Herzberg *et al.* (1959)

Learning to Learn from Text

Theory X

McGregor outlines the three basic principles of his Theory X:

1. Management is responsible for organising the elements of productive enterprise — money, materials, equipment, people — in the interest of economic ends.

2. With respect to people, this is a process of directing their efforts, motivating them, controlling their actions, modifying their behaviour to fit the needs of the organisation.

3. Without this active interaction by management, people would be passive — even resistant — to organisational needs. They must therefore be persuaded, rewarded, punished, controlled — their activities must be directed. This is the management's task. (pp. 307.8)

In addition to this theory, there are several assumptions:

4. The average man is by nature indolent — he works as little as possible.

5. He lacks ambition, dislikes responsibility, prefers to be led.

6. He is inherently self-centred, indifferent to organisational needs.

7. He is by nature resistant to change.

8. He is gullible, not very bright, the ready dupe of the charlatan and the demagogue. (p. 308)

The management can respond to this type of worker in one of two ways:

(a) By being strong, using threats and coercion to get the workers to perform.

(b) By being 'soft' and permissive; by maintaining harmony.

As a motivator, the strong management can result in restricting output and increasing antagonism, thus actually undermining the management's influence. On the other hand, soft management produces harmony but ineffective employees.

Clearly, both approaches are irrelevant because they ignore Maslow's needs for personal worth and needs for self-actualisation. The very roots of motivation are ignored in Theory X.

If management were to adopt Theory Y, which emphasises the individual and organisation, workers would be motivated to achieve their goals by directing their efforts towards the success of the organisation. Management would also attempt to motivate the individual so that he became involved with, and committed to, the goals of the organisation. This would be brought about by encouraging the individual to expand his knowledge, to increase his level of skill, and by giving him and opportunity to increase his ingenuity. The most significant rewards that the worker can realise are Maslow's highest needs: self-actualisation and self-esteem.

Theory Y

The main points of McGregor's Theory Y are:

1. Management is responsible for organising the elements of productive enterprise — money, materials, equipment, people — in the interest of economic ends.

2. People are *not* by nature passive or resistant to organisational needs. They have become so as a result of experience in organisations.

3. The motivation, the potential for development, the capacity for assuming responsibility, the readiness to direct behaviour towards organisational goals are all present in people. Management does not put them there. It is a responsibility of management to make it possible for people to recognise and develop these human characteristics for themselves.

4. The essential task of management is to arrange organisational conditions and methods of operation so that people can achieve their own goals *best* by directing *their own* efforts towards organisational objectives. (p. 315)

In effect, McGregor's Theory X and Theory Y are descriptive of two styles of leadership: the authoritarian is Theory X, while the democratic, approachable manager is described in Theory Y. McGregor would argue that poor motivation arises because management most often follows Theory X. In other words, if workers behave with apathy, it is the fault of management, not the employees. Do you agree with McGregor?

6.4 McClelland and achievement motivation

According to D. McClelland (1961), most people can be divided into two broad groups: a minority which is ambitious and works hard to achieve, and a vast majority that really doesn't care very much. McClelland has estimated that about 10 per cent of American people are strongly motivated towards achievement. To Australians this may seem rather a low figure, since Americans are taught to think of themselves as being a nation of achievers.

According to McClelland, the most convincing sign of a strong achievement motive is the tendency of a person, when he is free to relax and let his mind be 'idle', to think about ways to accomplish something difficult and significant.

The achievement motive is revealed in certain occupations in particular. It is likely to be found in sales and marketing positions, managerial positions of all kinds, in academic institutions, and among independent businessmen.

There are three major characteristics of the self-motivated achiever:

    (a) strategies are set and followed
    (b) moderate goals are set
    (c) immediate feedback is demanded.

(a) The self-motivated achiever tends to set at a surprisingly early age strategies which he follows throughout life. He sets his own goals; he will not drift aimlessly; he rarely seeks advice or help (except from *experts* who can provide needed skills or information). If he wins or is successful, he wants the credit; but if he loses, he accepts the blame. Either way, he wants the victory or defeat to be his.

(b) The self-motivated achiever prefers goals that are neither too easy to achieve, nor so difficult that in achieving them he would be credited with luck rather than ability. He seeks a hard, *practical* challenge. Above all, he will strain his abilities to win.

(c) The self-motivated achiever seeks immediate feedback (almost). That is, he wants measurements of how well he is progressing towards his goal. He wants this information at all times.

McClelland believes that achievement motivation is latent and untapped in most organisations. He maintains that 'achievement characteristics' should be built into more jobs: formal responsibility, individual participation in the selecting of productivity targets, moderate goals, and fast, clear feedback on the results.

On the other hand, McClelland believes that many 'achievers' are hindered in their performance by inappropriate supervisory practices. Work goals should not be imposed on the achiever, but, rather, he should be given a voice in the setting of them. He does not need specific directions and controls, only general guidance. And at all times, the achiever needs constant feedback of a detailed and frank nature as to how well he is performing in his work.

(At this stage the student is recommended to read McClelland's article in the *Readings*.)

HERZBERG'S MOTIVATION HYGIENE THEORY.

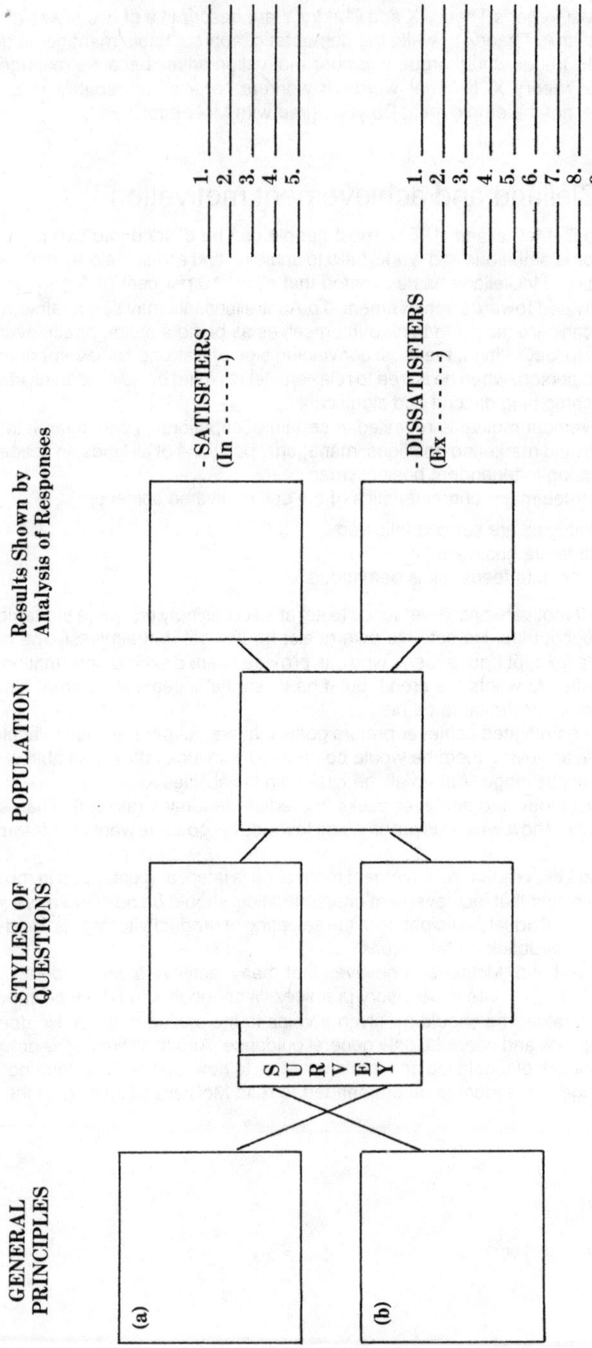

GENERAL PRINCIPLES	STYLES OF QUESTIONS	POPULATION	Results Shown by Analysis of Responses

(a)

(b)

S U R V E Y

— SATISFIERS
(In - - - - - -)

1. _____
2. _____
3. _____
4. _____
5. _____

— DISSATISFIERS
(Ex - - - - - -)

1. _____
2. _____
3. _____
4. _____
5. _____
6. _____
7. _____
8. _____
9. _____

Prepared by I. Down

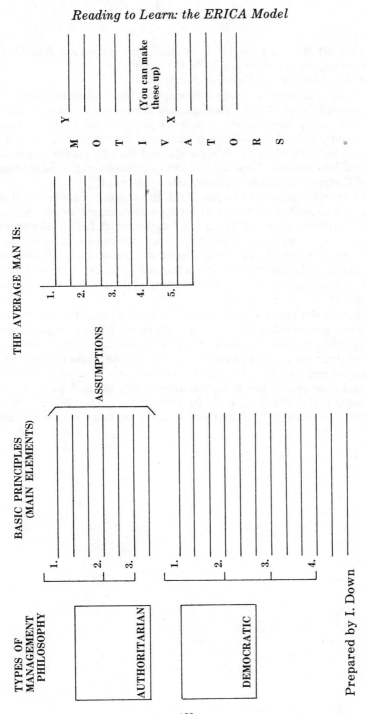

MCGREGOR'S THEORY — X and THEORY — Y.

THE AVERAGE MAN IS:

1.

2.

3.

4.

5.

MOTIVATORS

Y

X

(You can make these up)

ASSUMPTIONS

BASIC PRINCIPLES
(MAIN ELEMENTS)

1.

2.

3.

1.

2.

3.

4.

TYPES OF
MANAGEMENT
PHILOSOPHY

AUTHORITARIAN

DEMOCRATIC

Prepared by I. Down

Example 2.19
Source: Cull, R.G., and Drake, W.A., *Concepts in Science 1*. 3rd Ed., Jacaranda Press, Brisbane, 1979. (Chapter 14)
Topic: Identification of Common Minerals.

Many text passages provide information about different classes or categories of things. Thus, a passage may describe two, three or more categories and provide five, six or more pieces of information about each category. To deal with such masses of information is very difficult, so readers struggle to separate and classify all the separate pieces of information. The Cull and Drake passage on the 'Identification of Common Minerals' demonstrates this point.

Six minerals, Quartz, Feldspar, Mica, Hornblende, Calcite and Iron Oxide are described in terms of a range of characteristics such as shape, hardness, colour, cleavage and appearance. Left in the prose passage, the reader has to constantly back-track and hold a lot of information in memory if any comparisons are to be made. However, translation of the same information into a *Retrieval Chart* as shown below, allows instantaneous identification of details and comparison of qualities.

Although the chart is very simple in appearance, it is surprising how few teachers think of converting information into a graphic form presentation. It would appear that few people naturally recognize that information given in prose passages can be broken down into categories and details. Once these two variables — type of mineral and characteristic — are recognized, they can be used to form the horizontal and vertical axes of a Retrieval Chart. The trick is rather like the examples of 'Tie' and the number sequences used earlier.

Figure 14.3: A piece of granite. Note the crystalline nature of the grains. They have sharp edges and flat surfaces.

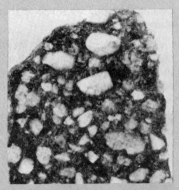

Figure 14.4: A piece of conglomerate. Note the partly rounded nature of the large grains. The rounding was caused by the grains' tumbling along the bed of a mountain stream. They finally came to rest on the bed of a lake, where they were cemented together to form a rock.

Identification of minerals

What are some of the things about minerals that help us to identify them in rocks?

Shape. Some minerals can be identified by their crystalline form. For example, mica always occurs as flaky crystals.

Hardness. Quartz is a hard mineral, whereas mica is soft.

Colour. Feldspar is light-coloured; hornblende is almost black.

Cleavage. This is the way a piece of a mineral tends to break when struck with a hard object. For example, calcite splits easily and always keeps the same shape. We say it has excellent cleavage. Quartz, on the other hand, breaks irregularly. We say it has no cleavage.

Appearance. Quartz is transparent like glass, but feldspar is opaque.

Some common minerals

Quartz is a transparent mineral that is very hard: it scratches steel. It forms six-sided crystals but has no cleavage planes like calcite. (Cleavage planes are the flat surfaces formed when the mineral breaks.) If struck, quartz fractures with a curved surface (this is called conchoidal fracture).

Feldspar is harder than calcite but softer than quartz. It has two cleavage planes almost at right angles. Grains of feldspar often show parallel lines on their surfaces. Feldspar is light-coloured, occurring in rocks as white, pink or yellow crystals.

Micas are very soft minerals. They may be scratched by a fingernail. They flake easily; thin sheets may be peeled off a mica. There are two common kinds of mica — biotite, which is black, and muscovite, which is white.

Hornblende is dark in colour and almost as hard as feldspar. It has two cleavage planes at about 60° to each other. It is usually duller in appearance than black mica.

Calcite is a white mineral, harder than mica but softer than feldspar. It has three cleavage planes at 75° to each other. It reacts with dilute hydrochloric acid to produce bubbles of gas (carbon dioxide).

Iron oxide. Haematite, limonite and magnetite are all oxides of iron. Haematite is reddish-grey, limonite is yellow and magnetite is black.

Figure 14.5: A crystal of quartz. Quartz crystals have six sides and do not break cleanly.

Figure 14.6: Flakes of mica crystals. Mica is a soft mineral that flakes very easily.

Figure 14.7: A piece of calcite that has been shattered by a blow from a hammer. Calcite breaks into flat-sided pieces with faces that are at about 75° to each other.

Figure 14.8: A piece of rock containing a crystal of feldspar. Notice the flat faces of the crystal, which are almost at right angles to one another.

IDENTIFICATION OF COMMON MINERALS

	QUARTZ	FELDSPAR	MICA	HORNBLENDS	CALCITE	IRON OXIDE
Shape						
Hardness						
Colour						
Cleavage						
Appearance						

Figure 2.5.

Once teachers and students are introduced to the concept they can 'see' it very easily.

Try the following example from Merritt (1975).

Example 2.20

CLASSES AND PROPERTIES:

Milk and butter are an important source for Vitamin A. Other sources include fish-liver oils and certain vegetables — carrots, tomatoes and dark green leafy vegetables are particularly valuable sources. Vitamin D is also found in fish-liver oil, butter, cheese, milk and eggs. Vitamin C is found in fresh fruit and vegetables. Wholemeal bread, yeast, liver and dairy foods contain Vitamin B.

Which two variables can be used as the axes of a Retrieval Chart? Place these variables along the horizontal and vertical axes and complete a Retrieval Chart to display the information given in the paragraph. Compare your chart with that of a colleague. You will find it advantageous to place one of these variables on the vertical axis, because it offers the chance to include more characteristics. Which one is it? Here is one suggestion for this Retrieval Chart.

FOODS	VITAMIN A	VITAMIN B	VITAMIN C	VITAMIN D	
Milk					
Butter					
Fish-liver oil					
Carrots					
Tomatoes		°			
Dark green leafy vegetables					
Cheese					
Milk					
Eggs					
Fresh vegetables					
Fresh fruit					
Bread, Yeast					

Figure 2.6.

DIAGRAMS AS AIDS TO UNDERSTANDING

The diagramming techniques which have been introduced can be ends in themselves or they can serve as means to other ends. For example, take the Mathematics teacher who asks students to produce a graph, or the Geography teacher who wants students to draw a climate chart. In both instances, the diagram produced is an end in itself. The reader's task is to turn prose text into a visual display. Where the teacher sets the task, students simply have to carry out the transformation. However, where readers have to determine the form of the illustration for themselves, the task becomes much more difficult. Merritt's example of the vitamin value of certain foods is a case in point. Few teachers seem to spontaneously conceptualize the simple Retrieval Chart format into which this material can be converted. The reason appears to be that they are not used to converting prose information into visual displays.

Much more use could and should be made of transforming prose information into visual forms. Rather than telling students what graphic display format to use, the teacher should require them to think up their own. Students can work on this task in small-groups as recommended for earlier ERICA strategies.

The value of creating graphic formats is twofold.

1. It stimulates understanding because it requires so much re-reading and checking of facts.
2. It provides the teacher with a very effective way of checking students' understanding.

The diagrams produced clearly indicate whether the readers have grasped the points made in the text. Quality of drawing is not important. *It is understanding which is being monitored, not draftmanship.* A variety of graphics could be produced by students. For example:

- Retrieval Charts
- Pie Charts
- Bar Graphs
- Flow Charts
- Time Lines
- Maps
- Structured Overviews

In all these cases, each illustration is produced for its own sake. The task has been to transform print information into a diagram. However, several other benefits also result.

1. Students develop the skill of examining prose passages with a view to changing the information into diagrams. The technique works well and students quickly learn to scan a passage and say, 'This could be turned into a diagram!'.
2. Understanding is promoted because, to create suitable diagrams, readers must identify the important points and eliminate the irrelevant ones. Production of diagrams encourages readers to see logical hierarchies and relationships among ideas in a text. For example:
   - One idea is more important than another and must be placed above it.
   - One process must precede another and so must be placed before it.
3. Small-group discussions help students learn from each other. Students, who do not understand and who would be afraid to ask for help in a large-group context, have the benefit of immediate peer tutoring in language which makes sense to them. The teacher is then free to move around groups giving assistance as required.

OUTLINING

One of the main reasons for helping students make effective use of their print resources is to assist them to function as independent learners. This overriding aim is the reason we have suggested throughout this book, that teachers concentrate less on the content they are teaching and more on the *process* of how information is gained. Nowhere is this process more apparent than in the ability to extract and organize information from the printed page. Some of the techniques introduced — the Structured Overview, the Graphic Outline and the use of vocabulary context clues — will remain with the students and help them become more efficient readers. Although these are valuable techniques in their own right, they really come together when readers get down to the nitty-gritty task of pulling the mass of printed information apart.

As we have seen, some diagrams can be produced as end products which summarize the text passage and need no further elaboration. In most cases, however, the teacher will require students to do something more than draw a diagram. The ultimate task may be to answer a question, write an essay or prepare a prose summary. In this cases, a conventional *outline* similar to teacher-made notes, may be a more appropriate form of information display.

Outlining requires students to select main ideas and then categorize details into sub-sets of these ideas. Because this is not an easy task, this section on Extracting and Organizing information is an extremely important one.

How often do we set out to teach students the *process* of making notes and producing what we will now call *Skeleton Outlines*? Not very often! It is placed in the 'assumed' basket. We assume that students can make notes. After all, we frequently give them notes so they should know how to make them for themselves. Unfortunately, knowing 'how-to' and actually carrying out such a task are two entirely different things. You may have read to this point and feel you 'know-how-to' prepare and carry out all the activities suggested to date. However, if you have not yet tried the techniques for yourself you still have a long way to go. This is a trap into which many teachers fall. Ideas may sound very simple in theory, but when they try them out for themselves they realize that they have not understood the process at all. *Assuming that students can make notes comes into this category.*

Outlining, therefore needs to be practised by students in the classroom, if teachers expect them to follow-up their readings by completing tasks such as essay writing. Students can't write essays if they have nothing to write about. The Year 12 teacher two helped his class work out the chapter on the 'Social Psychology of Work', did so initially because he was not happy with the essays they had written on earlier topics. He realized that the poor essays resulted from his students not having anything to write about. He had assumed they could analyze the text. Realizing that they needed help, he demonstrated a structure, so that they had the pertinent information at their fingertips. Their essays improved because they could extract information and therefore had something meaningful to write about.

Graphic Outlines are a good way of introducing students to the concept of outlining. The box system, used in the Stage 1 Graphic Outline model, can be converted to a letter and number system when students are familiar with the technique. Eventually, students can create these letter and number coded outlines for themselves. Once they are able to do this, they can analyze a text globally in terms of its main sections and headings.

When this stage is reached, the teacher can move on to showing students how diagrams, such as that given for the different types of rocks, can be converted to conventional outline form.

Example 2.21. Converting a Graphic Outline Into a Skeleton Outline. Imagine a Graphic Outline which looked like this.

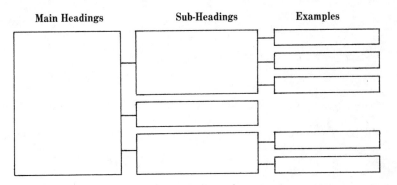

Once students are familiar with this format the teacher can begin to add a letter and number coding system so that the Graphic Outline now appears like this.

Main Headings	Sub-Headings	Examples
A.	1.	(a)
		(b)
		(c)
	2.	
	3.	(a)
		(b)

Eventually the boxes can be taken away and students left with just the letters and numbers to form a Skeleton Outline.

A   1.

                        (a)

                        (b)

                        (c)

        2.

        3.   (a)

                        (b)

Similarly, the flow-diagram on different rock types can be converted into a Skeleton Outline.

TYPES OF ROCK
A. Sedementary Rocks
   1. Formed by: _____
   2. Types   (a) _____
                  (b) _____

   3. Type A: Sedementary Rocks
      (a) Name   _____
      (b) How formed   _____
      (c) Where formed   _____
      (d) Time to form   _____
      (e) Features   _____
                 _____
      (f) Examples   _____
                 _____

   4. Type B: Sedementary Rocks
      (a) Name   _____
      (b) How formed   _____
      (c) Where formed   _____
      (d) Time to form   _____
      (e) Features   _____
      (f) Examples   _____

B. Igneous Rocks
   1. Formed by: _____
   2. Types   (a) _____
                  (b) _____

   3. Types A: Igneous Rocks
      (a) Name   _____
      (b) How formed   _____
      (c) Where formed   _____
      (d) Time to form   _____
      (e) Features   _____
      (f) Examples   _____
   4. Type B: Igneous Rocks
      (a) Name   _____
      (b) How formed   _____
      (c) Where formed   _____
      (d) Time to form   _____
      (e) Features   _____
                 _____
      (f) Examples   _____
                 _____

CONCLUSION

1. In the ERICA Model, Extracting and Organizing information is a natural link between 'understanding' and 'translating into one's own words'. Before readers can start to use the information provided in the text, they must first *understand* it and then must be able to *select and order* those parts which are necessary for the assigned task.

2. Four aspects of Extracting and Organizing information have been considered.

- Seeing the Overall Plan.
- Seeing Main Ideas and Supporting Details.
- Using Diagrams as Aids to Understanding.
- Outlining.

Each aspect has required the teacher to lead students through the means of analyzing and organizing textual information. However, each approach can ultimately be applied by students on their own. This leads to more effective and more independent reading. The four aspects have been described as 'keys' which, once understood, provide readers with a means of unlocking the meaning embedded in a text.

3. The different kinds of diagrams produced when extracting and organizing information, serve different purposes. They can function as ends in themselves where the diagram produced actually completes the set task. Examples of this type of transformation of prose into diagrams are:

- Maps.
- Mathematical graphs.
- Signs.
- Display charts.

Diagrams can also serve as a means to an end. This end can include:

- Improved understanding.
- More precise answers to questions.
- Carrying out instructions.
- Improved essay writing.
- Increased knowledge of a subject.

In these cases, diagrams help readers pick out important points and organize them into a structure which displays relationships not obvious in the original prose.

4. Extracting and Organizing information activities have long-term benefits for both teachers and students. Because the activities are based on the *processes* of how to obtain and structure information, students are provided with skills which can be applied when required. They are able to function more independently of the teacher and are better equipped to meet assessment criteria.

From the teacher's point of view the students are closely involved in *thinking processes*, which encourage not only better performance, but also more-active learning situations. This increased success for both teacher and students creates a more positive learning environment.

Reading to Learn: the ERICA Model

Activities

1. To show that you understand and can carry out extracting and organizing activities, turn the following examples into diagrams.
   Compare your products with those of your colleagues and see if you can devise diagrams which are mutually acceptable.

   (a) The MacDonnell Ranges in the Northern Territory of Australia are surrounded by a vast area of near desert lands. There are rugged mountain ranges running east-west with wide gently-sloped valleys between. North and south of the mountains are broad and undulating lands covered with spinifex and mulga.

   (b) The textile industry was revolutionized during the eighteenth century, when several inventions made it possible for more and more yarn to be spun and more cloth to be made in less and less time. In 1733 Kay's Flying Shuttle enabled a weaver to quadruple her output and by 1767, when Hargreaves invented the Spinning Jenny, yarn could be spun in greater quantity, because more threads could be used simultaneously. Thinner, yet stronger thread could be spun using a water powered spinning wheel, invented by Arkwright in 1769, while a more efficient, steam-engine powered spinning machine perfected by Crompton ten years later increased production again.

   (c) A student's allowance is spent in the following way: forty per cent rent and electricity, twenty per cent on food and fares, ten per cent on books and stationery and five per cent each on clothes and miscellaneous items.

2. Examine the diagrams produced in the above activities.
   What information, if any, has been omitted?
   What new information has been revealed by the diagram?

3. Produce examples, based on a print resource of your own choice, to illustrate:

   - An overall plan of a piece of text.
   - A flow-diagram to lead the reader through a particular section.
   - A diagram which can serve as a final product illustrating some aspect of the material.
   - A skeleton outline analyzing the structure of the passage.

Stage 4. Translating Information from Reading to Writing

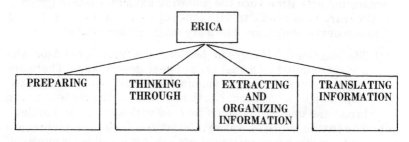

Teacher concerns:
- 'My students can't write essays.'
- 'My students don't seem to be able to write connected passages that are logically sequenced and which hang together.'

INTRODUCTION

Reading, writing and talking are aspects of interrelated language/thinking processes through which we learn more about the world around us. The preceding chapters of this text have focused on strategies to develop reading-to-learn competencies. At the same time, small mixed-ability group discussion has been suggested as one means of thinking-through ideas to clarify and negotiate meaning in text. Many of the suggested strategies rely, for their learning impact, on the exchange of ideas and the comparison of reading outcomes through talk. *Talking about reading then, is accepted as an essential part of the reading-to-learn process.*

Expressing one's understanding about information gleaned from text can also take the form of written response. In school learning situations, we often require students to respond to questions about reading in written form. These forms are many and varied, but they include:

- Prose summaries.
- Note-form outlines.
- Answers (both short and long) to assignment questions.
- Reports.
- Letters.
- Descriptions of processes and methods.
- Essays.

'Retelling' Experience
The value of acquiring information lies in a learner's ability to understand and express it as personal knowledge. Such expression can take various forms. For example, it may be:

- In either oral or written form.
- A personal or a public statement.
- Formally expressed, as in an essay.
- Informally expressed in a retelling to share in an event or a discovery with a friend.
- A piece of gossip.
- An interpretation of some item in the newspaper that has captured our attention.
- An exchange of 'what we did'.
- The passing on of a joke.

Retelling stories and reporting events to other people in other situations is an age-old tradition and we owe much of our knowledge of culture to such a transmission process.

In most encounters in our everyday lives, we pass on or receive information. When we pass on information we rarely 'tell it as it was'. We tell it in our own way, possibly embellishing details or leaving out what we think is not relevant. No matter the 'purity' of our telling, we use our own words. Our purpose is to recapture a *sense* of the original event or experience and to *communicate* that sense to our audience.

How Does This Relate to School Learning?

Much of school learning demands that students 'retell' what they have learnt, either to aid a teacher in developing a lesson or to demonstrate mastery of content through assignment work or testing. In the first instance, retelling information frequently involves responding to questions, often in just a few words. For example, from a Year 8 Geography lesson:

Teacher: 'Could somebody tell me the name of this line around here?'
Student: 'The Equator.'
Teacher: 'Right. What's the latitude of that line around there?'
Student: 'Zero degrees.'
Teacher: 'Right. What's the other name for that line?'
Student: 'The Great Circle.'

Of course, pupils are also given the chance to retell what they know in connected discourse and are encouraged to expand their efforts. For example, from a Year 8 English lesson:

Teacher: 'Do you think it's fair that people who sell goods should make a big profit?'
Student One: 'Not a big profit.'
Student Two: 'What about the man on the news the other day? Because he was making a big enough profit, as much as he needed and yet they wanted him to put it up to the proper price because he was selling them six dollars below all the others.'
Student One: 'Yes, and they wouldn't supply him, the wholesaler you

know, because he was selling them for less and they made him put it up to even more.

Teacher: 'And that's not fair?'

Student Two: 'No, that's not fair. They wouldn't supply him, and all the people that wanted to buy it cheaper, they had to pay an extra six dollars because of the orders.'

Mostly, however, students' efforts at expressing information gleaned from direct teaching or from independent research, take the form of written exercises or reports. Hence they respond to written assignment questions. For example, from Year 8 History assignment responses:

Question: What is a ziggurat? — one paragraph.

Answer 1: A ziggurat is a temple in which people used to make sacrifices and pray to their gods. It was found in most of their cities, it is also very tall and wide.

Answer Two: A ziggurat is a huge building about 60 metres in length, 45 in width, and 15 metres in height. Among other things it was a burial tomb for kings. Everything that the king owned would be put in the tomb including servants and relatives. Ziggurat means mountain. Originally the Sumerians came from the mountains so they built their own 'mountains' to be close to the gods.

Or they copy large chunks of information from resource material in response to open-ended research topics. For example, from a Year 8 History contract:

Question: Research and write about the Sumerian's religion.

Answer: In Sumerian belief, there were many gods. Anu, the supreme lord of the world ruled over all. Below him came a god of Air and Earth, again, gods of the Moon (Nannar), of the Sun, and of the planet Venus . . .

The latter example is an inaccurate transcription, demonstrating that the student was not interacting with the text as he or she prepared the response, omitting a line of text in the process.

In classrooms, students are rarely encouraged to use the same devices that they use in recreating and communicating their experiences in everyday discourse among their peers. They are rarely permitted to use their appropriate words to recapture the flavour of the learning experience, to interpret or to use analogy to help them make sense of the knowledge embodied in their experience. Mostly they are constrained to express in concise and teacher-acceptable terminology, ideas that are only partially understood, let alone articulated and given full-bodied expression and communicative effectiveness.

The combined result of situations such as these is that students' experiences of 'retelling' in school does not mirror their experiences of 'retelling' in real life. That is, in school, they often do not interpret events and experiences meaningfully *in their own way*.

144

TRANSLATING INFORMATION: WHAT IS IT?

Translating information occurs when students change ideas expressed in print materials and resources into their own words. It is very much a *process strategy* and teachers need to exercise patience in listening to, and reading about, yet unformed ideas — ideas that are in the making and which require clarification, refinement and good articulation.

In this text, the authors are very much concerned with expressing and translating ideas into a form which is readily accessible to you, the reader. In developing the ERICA Model we have had many talking sessions to clarify our ideas, to express them, refine them and to communicate them to each other. Our subsequent notes, drafts and amendments after discussion and many redrafts, have shown numerous re-arrangements of ideas and re-focusing of emphases. The very process of communicating our ideas, which have been discussed and criticized at innumerable inservice seminars and courses, has been lengthy and, at times, difficult, as we have shaped language which gives expression to our thoughts. If you write, you will appreciate that giving expression to ideas is not easy and that it takes time.

It is the same for students who are required by teachers to write in up to six or seven different subjects each day. Mostly, the form of such writing is predictable — summaries, a few notes, a paragraph, a short answer, a composition or an essay. Yet the content varies considerably and the structure or ordering of ideas is necessarily different as each subject, topic and purpose dictates adherence to particular sets of conventions — a comparison/contrast between similarities and differences, a cause-effect relationship, a logical conclusion, a reasoned judgement or a justified opinion.

When students fail to fully understand the nature of the relationships between ideas or the special requirements of the writing task, it is little wonder that they resort to 'copying out'.

Perhaps the tendency of some teachers to value quantity over quality only serves to reinforce the habit for many students, who sit and stare at blank paper wondering what they ought to write, if only they had something to write about!

How then, do we help students to get to the stage of having something to write about and communicate in subject areas? The section on Extracting and Organizing Ideas, especially, has been designed to aid in the process of getting information off the page, into students' heads, and reorganized in other forms to show relationships between ideas. This process is supplemented by activities aimed at prompting pupils to think through ideas and to discuss, clarify and negotiate their own meanings and interpretations, as preparation for using the information gleaned to serve their own purposes. Simply recording information is not sufficient. It must be puzzled about and assimilated, within the learner's own frame of reference, if it is going to make sense to him or her and then be reorganized.

Recording information orally and in writing does have its usefulness, but it should not always be an end in itself, as it would appear much transcription is. Recording does not necessarily demonstrate to anyone, let alone the learner, that the ideas talked about or written down are either understood or reflect a thought process that has been worked through. Recited or copied material usually reveals that the student has been unable to extract ideas relevant to the task, and has been unable to analyze and synthesize them into a meaningful form which exhibits *personal understanding or authorship*.

WHY TRANSLATE IDEAS THROUGH WRITING?

Overcoming Verbatim 'Copying Out'

Principally, students should be encouraged to write-to-learn, as an integral part of the process of untangling strands of information, which hopefully will become part of their working store of knowledge. It is suggested, that through a variety of different kinds of writing experiences, students will be prompted to tease out ideas, clarify, rework, expand on and develop them.

Verbatim copying does not take account of the value of 'working-writing', which demands a thinking out of ideas, the organizing of them into a cohesive and purposeful whole, and the presentation of them in a written work, through which the writer's voice may be heard.

For authors, writing is a process of coming to 'own' both the interpretation and the arrangement of ideas, as well as the way they are expressed. It includes shaping ideas to meet their needs in situations which create new demands. Authors also have to satisfy purposes for writing. Purposes which have relevance and meaning and which prompt them to take up the pen, spontaneously, excitedly and determinedly to discover where the writing journey may end. Authors, in their writing, consciously take into account the audience, which will read and respond in some way.

Unfortunately, many students fail to experience the purposeful 'need' or 'want' to write as an integral part of the learning process. They may well ask, 'What's the point?', when confronted with unimaginative and unstimulating writing assignments, which they see as requiring them only to repeat what they have read or heard.

In discussing a 'process approach' to school writing, Graves (1981) suggests that:

> Writing is a marvellous unifier. We teachers have yet to make proper use of its power in securing the deepest kinds of learning, in improving children's critical thinking, and in integrating the curriculum.   (p. 15)

Opportunities for writing in subject areas should be seen as an integral part of the learning process, which is a means of helping students to express and thereby 'see' what they know and understand. The motivation to *want to write* is embodied in the students' acceptance of the real purposes for writing, over and above assessment criteria. To this end, we recommend that teachers accept responsibility for receiving and responding to students' writing empathetically and sincerely, and not merely with a grading or a curt remark.

'Copying out' becomes a ploy for many students who fail to see the purpose and relevance of the writing tasks they are assigned, who do not understand the nature of the information they are dealing with, and who derive little enjoyment and satisfaction from writing. They become transcribers: transporters of blocks of information from one source to another. Undoubtedly they sense too, that school writing is a requirement and an imposition, which is divorced from meaningful dialogue about things which interest them. Perhaps, too, they recognize that their products, restricted in content and form, are unlikely to be valued by the teacher/reader except as an object of assessment.

When one Year 10 student was questioned about why he habitually copied material, he gave this reason. 'The book says it better than I can. I don't have the words. The book does.' While this sounds plausible, it shows that the student missed the point. If he is to really 'know' the content we wish him to learn, he has to be able to explain it in his own words, however immature that expression is. True, he may quote a few times (as we have done above) to support a point, but copying in a broader sense will only prevent internalizing the information. It will remain the author's knowledge. It will not become the student's personal knowledge.

One aim of translating information is to give that type of student access to making sense of and using 'the words' so that he, too, can express content thoughtfully and coherently. Translating information through writing, can help bridge the gap which some students feel exists between book knowledge and their expression of it.

Making Use of Information

To reiterate, the value of information to a learner lies in his or her ability to understand and express it as personal knowledge. To this can now be added the notion of using that personal knowledge meaningfully for real purposes.

When teachers plan units of work, they establish aims and objectives. They may be stated in various ways. The *Report on School Based Assessment*, Scott *et al*, Board of Secondary School Studies, Queensland, (1978), for example, recommended four kinds of objectives:

1. *Cognitive objectives* — focusing on thought processes involved in understanding particular topics and the ways in which ideas relate to each other.
2. *Content objectives* — having to do with the knowledge base of a unit.
3. *Skill objectives* — or the abilities necessary to perform various tasks demanded by the topic.
4. *Affective objectives* — embracing aspects to do with personal response and judgment.

We need to frame learning objectives so that students can, and do, do something meaningful with information extracted from text. Let's say a Year 10 class is engaged in learning about skin cancer. The knowledge base is derived from a variety of sources, including a pamphlet description of the causes and effects of skin cancer, together with procedures for protecting the skin against the harmful effects of the sun. Sunscreens are recommended as one protective measure.

The following newspaper report prompts some suggestions about the kinds of writing activities which could make use of the information about skin cancer. It involves translating information and applying it to new situations.

One in four get skin cancer

One in every four Queenslanders will develop skin cancer during their life-time, according to the Health Department's Health Education and Information division.

The most common form of skin cancer was usually the result of years of exposure to strong sunshine.

To help guard against skin cancer the division has produced two pamphlets with helpful advice for summer.

"Sunscreens '81-'82" and "Skin Cancer" discuss moles, symptoms to watch, causes of skin cancer and treatment, and lists sun protection and tanning products according to their effectiveness.

"Skin Cancer" says the common tan moles almost never become cancerous, but dark brown or bluish-black moles may be responsible for the malignant melanoma—the most dangerous type of skin cancer.

A dull brownish zone which appears around a mole and spreads from it, is one of the most probable signs of danger.

Tanning does not prevent skin damage, it says.

Fair skinned prople are particularly prone to skin cancer caused by prolonged exposure to strong sunshine.

Tips for guarding against skin cancer are:

● Restricted sun-bathing, not sun-baking.
● Wear sun-shades and sensible clothes on the beach.
● Wear a wide brimmed hat and use sunburn protectives.

"Sunscreens '81-'82" lists sun tanning and protection lotions in maximum, high, moderate and minimal protection categories.

It also warns that sunscreens can only protect if they are applied before exposure to the sun and on a clean, dry skin.

Both pamphlets are available from the Health Education and Information division, 5-9 Costin Street, Fortitude Valley.

(a) Composing a letter to the Health Education and Information Division of the State Health Department requesting class copies of pamphlets. The letter would describe the current study to provide a context for the request. A request may also be made for an officer of the Department to visit the class to elaborate on the information contained in the pamphlets, thereby offering the opportunity to participate in a discussion of the information.

(b) Preparing a series of posters for display in all classrooms, warning of the hazards of over-exposure to the sun.

(c) Designing and printing a simplified pamphlet for younger children and distributing it, with cover notes, to parents.

(d) Conducting a survey among local chemist shops to determine which sun-screen lotions are most frequently bought, comparing the data with the information supplied in the pamphlets, and reporting on the results.

(e) Examining the advertisments for sun-screen products in popular magazines to see whether advertising is consistent with scientific data. Writing a review of such advertisements for publication in a class or school newspaper.

(f) Writing an imaginative story about the need for protection from the sun for publication as a library book for peers or younger children.

To engage in the above projects requires students to *read* and *analyze* information, *extract* aspects relevant to their task, *negotiate* and *decide* upon the nature of the final product, and go *through* a process of *organizing* ideas.

To make choices about how best to express selected information demands trial and error, drafting and re-reading, reviewing and re-drafting and finally, editing and publishing.

This process is time-consuming and the antithesis of the 'once-off' first draft to be handed in for teacher assessment after a forty minute sprint effort. Those teachers who protest, 'But, I've a syllabus to cover', may need to review the nature of their objectives. Certainly a transmission-of-information model of teaching doesn't take account of the students' need to sort through to make sense of ideas for themselves in their own way. Students also need to be aware of the purposes of learning and of the potential uses of their understandings, in this instance, by writing.

Promoting the Writing Habit

The adage 'we learn to write by writing' is well worn, but true. Too frequently, however, we tend to deny students opportunities to write in a sustained way in subject areas. We impose restrictions on them, structuring their written responses by our questioning and our worksheet formats. We undervalue writing as a learning process, preferring to focus on what is produced as a result of engaging in the process. We rarely, if ever, write *with* our students, to demonstrate how *we* go about shaping ideas, reworking phrases and sentences, rear-

ranging the order of our paragraphs and trialling our compositions.
*How often do we actively assist students, through talking with
them about their problems with writing, and supporting them in their
efforts to clarify and elaborate on their ideas?*

It is not too harsh a judgement to suggest that we *assign* writing
tasks and then withdraw from the writing situation, handing over the
struggle for students to wallow in within classroom constraints. We
then re-enter the situation as judges, either accepting or rejecting
their efforts.

It is fact that many students are 'turned off' writing — that they
are reluctant to write. Who wouldn't be when the task has been
imposed without consultation, and little attention is paid to what the
students themselves want to write about? Who wouldn't be when end
products are returned mutilated beyond recognition by teacher suggestions for 'improvement', or bearing only an impersonal, numerical
response? It is too easy for teachers to unwittingly reject students'
writing, because it doesn't meet the *teacher's* expectations!

In one Year 8 General Science class, students had been studying
vertebrates and classifying them according to various criteria. Some
degree of personal involvement had been encouraged by suggesting
that students research sharks. Busily, they consulted specialist
books, magazines and an encyclopaedia to locate information relevant
to their task. One boy, a fisherman's son, who often accompanied his
father on fishing expeditions, became engrossed in his writing. Occa-
sionally he checked a resource to verify his working knowledge of
sharks, but mostly he wrote, uninterrupted.

However, *his* intentions — to recount an experience on his father's
fishing vessel and the subsequent capture of a shark — did not match
those of the teacher: to compare different kinds of sharks. No criteria
for comparisons were given. The student was making sense of the
topic in his own terms, through writing, and providing a vivid description of a particular shark's features in the process. He normally didn't
like to write, but here was a topic which engaged him, so he decided to
risk interpreting the assigned task to suit his *need* to write on this
occasion, informatively and in narrative form.

In such a situation, what takes precedence? Student intent and pro-
lific writing, or teacher intent and meaningless plagiarism? How
would *you* respond on receipt of this boy's writing? Has such writing
from a personal perspective, revealing sophisticated understanding, a
placed in the Science classroom? What will be the effect of rejecting
the writing as being inappropriate to the assigned task?

Here, we need to decide on our priorities about school writing objectives. Do we expect students to make the leap from personal and spontaneously produced writing, to controlled, precise writing in an appropriate register and shaped into a particular genre, without trial,
tentativeness and exploration? How do students make the transition

from the 'expressive' to the 'transactional' modes which Britton (1970) defines? The simplest answers to these questions only come through long and wide-ranging experiences in writing for different purposes and audiences, and in different situations.

Britton talks of the central role of expressive writing — that which is personal and spontaneous — in learning how to shape and arrange ideas prior to coming to master the finer, more controlled conventions of what he terms 'transactional' written forms: those which are more formal and concerned with the transmission of information. Undoubtedly, he would approve of the shark narrative as a means of entry into the transactional mode.

Graves (1981) values the effects of students choosing their own writing topics. He uses an 'ownership' metaphor to elaborate:

> When people own a place, they look after it; but when it belongs to someone else, they couldn't care less. It's that way with writing. From the first day of school we must leave control of the writing with the child — the choice of topic and the writing itself. Then children write and care more . . . Nothing influences a child's attitude to writing more than the choice of topic . . . (in Walshe, R.D. (Ed.) *Donald Graves in Australia*. P.E.T.A. Sydney, p. 9, 1981.)

Although Graves' studies concern primary students' writing, he is talking about an important principle which spans *all* school years.

As teachers, we need to offer writing options to students, rather than rigidly dictating these parameters:

- Form (an essay or summary).
- Content (a specific topic).
- Audience (teacher, usually).
- Purpose (to report, record, persuade).
- Length (usually imposed).

If we value writing as a means of understanding and of expression, we need to provide ample opportunities for students to write. This may mean re-thinking our priorities and restructuring the way in which information is handled in our classrooms. We may need to establish writing workshops in which, *together with our students*, we explore the possibilities of writing and discuss the satisfactions and difficulties of the composing process. We may also need to review our perceptions of the role of writing: as an active learning tool or as an assessment device.

To master various forms of writing, we need experience in composing different forms. To foster the writing habit so that it becomes an adjunct to, and means of learning content, we need to make writing an integral part of the curriculum. We learn to write by writing.

Spasmodic writing assignments are meaningless, except perhaps for assessment. Even then, they are of limited value. Writing needs to be continuous. *Writing ought to be frequent and habitual.*

**Showing How Reading and Writing Are Interrelated
Language/Learning Activities.**
Concern over the reading abilities of students probably far outweighs
expressed concern over students' capacities to use writing for learning purposes. Yet, teachers have continually complained that
students have difficulty in making their meaning clear, through
writing.

- 'My kids can't write!'
- 'They don't say what they mean.'
- 'They don't know how to put sentences together.'

Such complaints are all myths. Children *can* write, given
encouragement, purpose and time. They say what they mean per-
fectly well when they recognize that they have control over what they
want to say orally or in writing. They've had years of practice in using
the grammar of their native tongue. Perhaps this is what teachers
ought to be saying:

- 'My kids have problems in realizing my expectations.'
- 'They ignore, or have yet to master, the conventions that govern
  writing in my subject.'
- 'I don't really help them master writing because I use writing to
  test knowledge, rather than to promote learning.'
- 'Because I use writing to test what they know, I restrict their
  written work to answering questions that I think are important.'
- 'I don't always let them write their way into understanding and I
  usually want the writing done quickly.'
- 'They need to write in my subject, but writing's not my field, so I
  leave them to do it for homework.'

When does writing occur in subject classes? At what point in the
learning process does writing assume importance? Of course,
teachers will protest that writing occurs at all points in the study of
topics. Students, after all, will take notes from their books, record
information that has been written on the blackboard, take dictation,
and perhaps transfer important points made in resources into their
note books. They may also answer questions in written form.

Such writing is recording and not the kind of exploratory writing
we want to foster as a means of coming to understanding. Nor is it the
kind of sustained writing used to communicate that understanding.

Translating information through writing is intimately related to
reading. When we write, we also read. That is, if we are writing about
something that interests us, and if we feel we have command over the
information, in the very act of shaping our thoughts and putting them
on paper, we write and read together. As we make decisions about
how ideas might best be expressed, we review what we have already
written, perhaps altering a word or two or rephrasing a section. But,
constantly, we backtrack in order to go forward. Just as we don't read

word for word, neither do we compose one word at a time (although we physically record one word at a time). Thus, the task of writing is also a reading task, giving practice in thinking about and reworking ideas related to a topic. Writing is essentially a *reflective process* which helps us to clarify our thinking as we try out combinations of words, phrases and clauses, constantly reviewing the word choices available to us.

Writing is also *for* reading. When we know that what we write will be read by others, we take more care in expressing ourselves accurately, so providing our readers with a context which allows them to make sense of what it is we want to say.

In school, however, the most regular reader of student writing is the teacher, mostly for assessing 'how well' transmitted information is understood or expressed, within the constraints of the form required: essay, paragraph and so on. There isn't the sense of a real audience; one which is akin to readers in the world beyond the classroom and the subject objectives. A desire to communicate isn't instilled in students as they seek to complete the assigned writing task, with little attention to anything, save task completion.

If the intention in writing is that the product be read, then we need to provide students with real audiences, not just the teacher. In one school where a work experience program was undertaken in conjunction with Careers Education, students were responsible for writing letters to employers prior to and after the experience, writing letters to 'The Editor' of the local newspaper commenting on the value of the program, diary writing, report writing, form filling in, poster design, and imaginative writing. Apart from the external audiences for whom they wrote, the students also collated their collected experiences into a book for peers to read. The purposefulness of the various writing activities is reflected in their writing as shown in the following examples.

NEWSPAPER REPORT

ROCKHAMPTON — OVER 5000 STUDENTS FROM VARIOUS SECONDARY SCHOOLS THROUGHOUT CENTRAL QUEENSLAND, YESTERDAY ATTENDED A CAREERS MARKET HELD AT THE ROCKHAMPTON SHOWGROUNDS. MR JONES, THE PRESIDENT OF ROTARY, WHO ORGANIZED THE EVENT, SAID HE WAS DELIGHTED BY THE ENTHUSIASM SHOWN BY THE PUBLIC.

The Careers Market was organized in an effort to educate local school leavers about the many options available to them after leaving school. Over three hundred booths were set up to display various job and career opportunities, and any questions or difficulties the students may have had were expertly handled by the many experienced people operating the booths. The students took full advantage of their knowledge, none being fearful to seek advice.

Booths were also set up by various Colleges and Universities of Queensland, so that those students interested in gaining further education could also gain valuable information in their interested field of study.

Some of the more popular booths included were those of Nursing and Bricklaying. A general concensus proved that the most frequented booths were those whose display included practical examples of the type of work involved in the occupation.

Students also used the opportunity of attending the Careers Market to talk with students from other schools, because after all, these students are those with whom school leavers will be competing for positions of employment.

Perhaps the only fault one could make with the day was that the number of students visiting the booths far out-reached the availability of room at each booth. The going was slow as large crowds milled around the more popular booths.

It is hoped that next year, schools will be allocated set times to attend the Market so that congestion of traffic will be minimal and the attendants will have more time to advise properly and help all those interested students in their chosen interest of occupation.

The Editor,
'The Morning Bulletin',
ROCKHAMPTON. 4700.
Dear Sir,

I recently attended the Careers Market at the Rockhampton Showgrounds.

I found the display areas particularly interesting. The people concerned with their arrangement are to be congratulated.

My thanks goes to the Q.E.G.B. (Queensland Electricity Generating Board) whom I found very helpful.

Their follow-up attention in the form of extra brochures and application literature was received by mail.

It is a great incentive to students to know that Employers and Education Centres are interested in our future.

Yours faithfully,

Judy and Judy (1979) focus on the interaction between writer, subject and reader, both in reading and in writing. They assert that if writing in school is restricted to the teacher's eyes, then 'the interaction between reader and writer will remain constant, perhaps even stagnant' (p. 228). They add:

Changing the audience, however, creates new ways of conceiving the subject. On the basis of the type of audience for which they are writing, students have to make decisions about the kinds of information they must include or exclude, depending on what the audience knows or needs to know about the subject.

(*The English Teachers' Handbook*, p. 228)

By challenging students to take account of different audiences for whom they can write, new purposes for writing emerge and writing takes on a different complexion. It becomes purposeful, responsible and self-motivating. As students receive different kinds of feedback for their efforts, the desire to write is increased and, hence, attempts more frequent. Frequent writing leads to promoting a writing habit which is free from the traditional constraints of both limited and limiting school writing.

WHAT AUDIENCES ARE THERE FOR STUDENT WRITING?

In-Class Audience
Every classroom has a self-made audience — other students. But, while audiences for school writing have traditionally performed an editing and corrective role, peer audiences can also perform the role of partners in a written conversation, by responding honestly and inquisitively, and reacting to ideas in it. Peer writing is for sharing, enjoying and clarifying ideas that each writer has, prompting discussion and further exploration of numerous concepts. It might be published in booklets or pamphlets, displayed on bulletin boards, overhead transparencies, or duplicated sheets or simply exchanged among small groups. It may be read orally by the author or another reader.

In-School Audience
Beyond the classroom in which the writing occurred, there are other classes at the same year level as well as older or younger classes who can be audiences. If student authors are aware that their audience extends beyond their own class, they will quickly realize that there is a need to become more explicit in presenting ideas. Also if there is a genuine attempt to cross-exchange written work within a school, their experience of reading a range of writing from other classes will assist them in understanding the problems of writing for others.

Audiences in Other Schools
As with in-school exchanges, writing may be intended to be read and responded to beyond the school. Exchanges between schools become particularly valuable in subjects like Geography, where weather, climate or urban patterns are topics of study. The content focus, being particular to a given area, can be exchanged through written reports. Students from a dry, rural region, such as Alice Springs, could exchange the results of their local area study with those of students living in a wetter, coastal, urban settlement, such as the Gold Coast. Thus contributing to each others' understanding and appreciation of climatic diversity.

Adult Audiences
Known adults form another audience for student writers. These may be teachers, parents, adult friends or relatives. The object of writing for such people is mainly to seek reactions to ideas and the way they

are expressed, to explore the possibilities within a topic, and to clarify concepts through sounding out ideas with another person. Of course, the class teacher can assume this role too, provided he or she understands that such writing is still being crafted.

Graves (1981) would recommend a conference approach, whereby students share perceptions and explain what it is they are wanting to express in writing. The teacher, far from being a judge, at this point becomes a partner in the writing act, helping to expand and extend ideas, and helping students to seek alternative ways of making thoughts clear for their readers.

Judy and Judy (1979) provide an extensive list of unknown audiences for whom students can write. It's certainly not exhaustive, and students themselves will be able to suggest other people for whom they can write, depending on the subject matter. Among those audiences suggested by the Judys are:

Local and National Politicians	Editors
Inventors	Athletes
Industrial Leaders	Journalists
Scientists	Lawyers
Musicians and other artists	Doctors

One needs only to browse through newspapers to generate a comprehensive list of people, companies and agencies to whom students can write: for information, to gauge opinion, to outline a project and invite reaction and comment, to express their own reaction to a particular issue that's pertinent to their study of a topic, to ask questions, to suggest solutions, and so on. There are many instances of student letters to the Editor being published in the daily press on a wide range of concerns.

Often, when members of the public write to agencies, they do not receive personal responses, but rather pre-packaged information brochures, along with a covering letter, often prepared by a clerk or a secretary. Such a situation can be turned into a discussion on the role and effectiveness of information services in public relations and in disseminating information.

A role play, where students offer alternative kinds of responses incorporating the agency's response, can be a valuable learning experience in itself, leading to further opportunities for writing.

Sharing One's Writing with Others
The school environment provides a multitude of opportunities for sharing writing with others. Some of these have already been mentioned in the preceding section on extending the range of audience for students' writing. However, while individual teachers may act on some of the suggestions made, there are more public opportunities for sharing one's written outcomes.

Class and school newspapers and magazines are popular media for publishing student writing, but often the need for editorial selection results in only a sample of writing being printed.

Topic books, written for peer or junior classes can be prepared as a class project. Work on collating a class resource library can be semester or year-long project. Students might pursue aspects of topics which particularly interest them, and organize their understanding of content into subject encyclopaedias, topic glossaries (with illustrations), 'how-to' books, or guides to laboratory experiments. Students may record excursions in the form of travel brochures, or compile a *Did You Know?* book.

Numerous organizations and groups celebrate particular events: Book Week, International Literacy Day, Health Week, National Mathematics Week and so on. Students could proclaim their own special day or week and write a range of materials to advertise and encourage other classes to join in to share their writing on the special focus subject. Birthdays of scientists, artists, poets, authors, composers or the people who make history can prompt reasons for writing to share information and understanding through publishing students' writing.

Making a Book: Considerations
1. What will the cover include?
   * Title, author, illustration.
2. What preliminary pages will be included?
   * Half title page.
   * Title page.
   * Copyright page.
   * Table of contents.
   * Foreword.
3. What procedures will you follow to create a book?
Consider processes for:
   * Writing the text.
   * Determining the shape and size of the book.
   * Having the text typed or typeset.
   * Working out the amount of text for each page, allowing space for any required illustrations.
   * Working out where illustrations should go.
   * Preparing the illustrations.
   * Cutting, drawing up and folding the cover, e.g. by covering cardboard with cloth.
   * Adding decorations.
   * Working out the number of pages allowing for facing pages and end blanks.
   * Numbering and collating the pages.
   * Printing the book.

- Stapling or sewing the spine of the book.
- Taping the book pages to the cover. You can glue down the first and last book pages to the inside cover or use adhesive tape.
- Trimming the pages.

In a great number of secondary schools, many teachers feel restricted in publicly displaying students' writing in specialist classrooms, yet, if school policy were to encourage the practice of displaying students' efforts, the arguments offered against the practice would soon be dispelled.

This could be done by adopting a 'Writing-to-Read' school project, or by planning a History Book Week, or an authors' fair. One section of the school library could be used to display student work published as books, or topic books could be catalogued alongside commercially published materials.

DEVELOPING FLEXIBILITY IN COMMUNICATING WHAT HAS BEEN LEARNED

In everyday life, various demands are made on individuals to express their understandings in writing. While schools may not necessarily be able to provide students with experience in writing in all the available forms found in the world, they can go a long way towards extending the traditional writing options open to students.

Some of these have already been mentioned. Other forms might include:

- Articles for newspapers, magazines and journals.
- Reports to different kinds of groups.
- Radio and television scripts and documentaries.
- Puppet plays.
- News stories and reports.
- Research reports.
- Short stories, poems and plays.
- Press releases.
- Bulletins and newsletters.
- Editorials.
- Progress reports and plans for future development.
- Publicity brochures and posters.
- Instructions and handbooks.
- Recipes.
- Minutes of meetings.
- Scripts of group negotiations.
- Replies to letters and other forms of correspondence.
- Slide/tape presentations.
- Caption books to accompany a visual record of an experience.
- Comic strips for entertainment and information sharing.

In each instance, students will need to consider their intended audience, the purpose of their communication, the selection of necessary content, and the language style or register appropriate to the task.

HOW IS TRANSLATING INFORMATION ACHIEVED?

Most successful authors *enjoy* writing because it satisfies a range of needs, and is a natural response to a situation which compels them to write. To initiate a need to write in subject classrooms, it's necessary to establish conditions conducive to writing and to promote writing as a natural response.

The Writing Environment: RSVP.

The writing environment should be motivating, non-threatening and co-operative. It should be one where the teacher acts as a partner, discussing individually or with groups of students, ways in which the writing may take shape, how ideas may be extended, elaborated or refined, how ideas may be linked and emphasized, and how chosen words can produce various effects.

Students should be supported in their efforts to *draft* and *review* their writing. They need to understand that first attempts may be *changed, reworked* and *edited* into a polished product. To this end, it's imperative that teachers do not set time limits on students' writing sessions. Students can be encouraged to maintain a file of written drafts and final versions as a folio of writing, which demonstrates to them the variety of writing and its development over time.

While the constraints of class time are appreciated, it needs to be recognized that writing coherent, well-formed texts requires time for:

- Thinking.
- Pre-writing.
- Draft writing.
- Reviewing.
- Redrafting.
- Editing.
- Proof reading.
- Publishing.
- Responding.

The rewards for making time available for writing are many. Students will come to value their efforts as they see them published, displayed and praised. There is no short-cut to gain these rewards. It takes concentrated effort over periods of time. In turn, as the students value the results of their efforts, their 'want' to write will become self-motivating.

Teachers need to be constructively responsive, by helping students to search their experience of language and content knowledge, rather than merely to exercise a red pen on finished products. By experimenting and exploring, teachers need to learn to put aside overriding concerns for accuracy and to respond interestedly to what students are wanting to express. Teachers need to *accept* students' writing initially as attempts to work with new ideas and the ways of expressing them.

Students well regard a sincere response from a teacher. If teachers engage in correspondence with students, reacting to ideas, opening up different ways of viewing an issue, and endorsing students' interpretations, they can increase students' motivation to write. In response to one teacher's dialogue on his writing about the treatment of convicts of Colonial Australia, one Year 9 student wrote a covering letter to his teacher:

> Dear Mrs K...
> No teacher ever wrote a page to me before. When I saw all your writing on my project I thought it must of been all wrong and I put it away. But then I read what you said. So here is another assignment about convicts. I've made a diary. It's about how the convict felt he was treated. You said the book told only one story, well, I've written the other side of the story.

Neither the original assignment, nor the unsolicited revision and extension, was specifically for assessment purposes. Rather, they were part of folio work, a record of students' writing in History over a term. The student, accepting that there were views other than that which he originally produced, was prompted by the teacher's interest to extend his understanding through another piece of writing.

So, the first maxim for establishing a writing environment has to do with accepting and responding to student effort. It's rather like inviting your students to write ... RSVP being unstated.

Reasons for Writing

When we write, we have a reason for doing so. That reason is inextricably bound up in the context of the situation that we are in at the time. Thus, when we write a letter, we want to share our experiences or exchange information with friends, family, authority or public services. We have something to say to someone!

In school, students' reasons for writing traditionally revolve around teacher expectations and a benign acceptance of writing being a school-related task. Mostly, students write to gain marks through demonstrating their grasp of information, transmitted during lesson after lesson. This need not be the sole reason for writing. However, some ingenuity on the part of the teacher may be required to incorporate real-world writing demands in their subject teaching.

Conditions for purposeful writing are numerous. Time, place, state of mind of the author, and his or her role and purpose all bear on the writing act. As well, account needs to be taken of the audience for whom the writing is being done.

Role, particularly, is important. Traditionally, students write as students. Rarely are they invited to project themselves into the shoes of another, despite teachers' efforts to foster role by assigning tasks requiring students to imagine they are a scientist, a mathematician, a personality in history or a literary character. Projecting oneself into a role, other than that which one plays in real life, requires considerable background knowledge and understanding of the person (albeit fictional), his or her life-style, ambitions, tasks, attitudes, feelings and relationships with others, as well as having the capacity to use that knowledge to create a convincing personality in their own right.

Thus, students need to identify who they are, the social role of the person whose character they are assuming, and the situation they are in, before writing. This can be decided upon individually or in a group.

For example, in an urban settlement study in Geography, students might assume different roles within a family, discussing the pro's and con's of settling in Beneen, a new suburb on the outskirts of a large city. The following map has been provided.

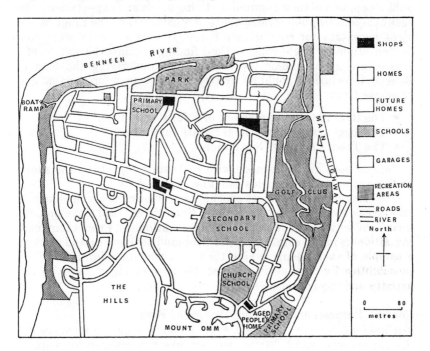

A group of five or six students might negotiate roles within the family. For example:

Father: a city businessman whose hobbies include golfing and fishing.
Step-mother: a saleswoman in a bakery.
An elderly grandmother: who prefers to live with other people her own age.
Children: all of school age.

The sociology provides a context for writing, as each family member composes his or her part of a joint letter to relatives overseas, telling of their plans to buy a house in Beneen.

Another group could be engaged in taking on the role of an estate agent responsible for promoting land sales in Beneen. His publicity campaign includes the preparation of a brochure, a window display and a one-page advertisement in the newspaper.

Yet another group might explore the planning that went on to establish Beneen as an urban community. Preparation for such planning may include the development of a questionnaire seeking the public's opinion of their community living needs and expectations, the ease of access by public transport to new estates, and the range of services necessary for comfortable living. If such a survey were conducted, students might confirm their findings against the opinion of a real estate agent and/or the assumptions underlying the plan of Beneen. Conclusions could be written up as a report for reaction and response from:

• The Real Estate Supplement of a daily newspaper.
• The local branch of the Real Estate Institute.
• The Town Planning Department.

Comparisons might be made with real estate reports by the above bodies and any discrepancies could be explored.

The class could also collect brochures promoting the sale of land in new areas from real estate agents. Sometimes, land development incurs the wrath of groups such as conservationists. From their reading, students might establish criteria for land developers, and write to a sample of such people asking them to exchange information. The possibilities for writing in context, thereby giving purpose to the activity and incorporating an audience, are endless.

Context, Purpose, and Audience Determine Form

For too long, we have imposed writing forms or genres on students. We have instructed 'write me an essay/poem/description/play/report/review', and have often been disappointed by the outcomes.

When students have established their context for writing, have determined their purpose for writing, and have identified the audience they wish to read and respond to their writing, the form or genre, register or style fit into place. The context, purpose and audience form a baseline for considering what form of writing is appropriate.

Thus, in a unit about Roman 'Bread and Circuses', students have read text material describing the events surrounding public holidays in Ancient Rome, and have sorted out the views of members of different social sectors towards festival days. They are asked to choose a role from a list:

- A slave-gladiator.
- The Emperor, Caesar.
- A worker-spectator.
- A condemned criminal.
- A straight-laced citizen.

Students are then invited to write in role about their attitudes and feelings towards the Roman circus. Will they:

- Petition their employer begging not to have a fight?
- Prepare a public notice to encourage citizens to attend?
- Write a scroll-letter to a friend who didn't attend the show?
- Maintain a secret diary from the depths of the catacombs?
- Write to *Actu Diurna* — a Roman 'newspaper' — to demand that circuses be stopped?

The audience, in this situation, are peers who swap each other's writing or display it on classroom walls.

Some students feel more comfortable with one form of writing in preference to another. While it is our job to develop students' strengths, it is also our responsibility to extend the range of forms with which a student is familiar, and will openly attempt to use. At the same time, we should never cause students to be apologetic about their writing, but be open to the range of possible forms and directions that writing may take.

GOING ABOUT WRITING

Having established the topic and context for writing and having identified purpose and audience, the task of writing begins.

It may be individual, personal and private, or it may be group negotiated and scribed. Whatever the method of writing adopted, students should not be pressured to complete a final draft at one sitting.

Pre-Writing
It is imperative that students become involved in talking among themselves about the direction their writing might take. This procedure

enables group consideration of possibilities, of leads and of the shaping and clarifying of ideas. Perhaps they'll need to research, to read or to consult resources.

What kinds of questions will they need to explore? Where will they locate information? How will they record answers to their questions so that retrieval of information will be efficient?

Hoffman (1976) describes a number of class projects which students, at different levels, shaped for themselves through small-group negotiation. A model for project organization which aims at a class publication is detailed in *The Reporter*, a Level 5 text in the Mount Gravatt Developmental Language Reading Program (Addison-Wesley, Sydney, 1981).

Rough Drafts

Having prepared for and organized the writing task, students now need to draft their rough copy. The first draft is an attempt to get ideas down on paper, to select and organize information, and to trial ways of articulating thoughts. Many writers find it easier to write their first draft in pencil; the words on the page are less 'permanent' that way, and erasures enable the writer to rephrase or re-order as he or she creates the piece of writing.

First draft writing may stop and start or may display bursts of fluency. It may be messy, with additions, deletions, arrows indicating the replacement of phrases or words, words misspelled, punctuation missing and sentences imperfectly formed. *These faults do not matter, because the object is to record ideas for later review.*

The Conference Approach

Conferencing, which is a conversation between students and teacher (Graves, 1981), may be helpful during the drafting to help clarify ideas and to talk through ways of expressing them. The concept of conferencing during subject writing is challenging, for it suggests a *workshop approach* to writing which may be vastly different from the conditions under which students traditionally write in class. It suggests also, that classroom organization needs to be such that it enables the teacher to move freely, systematically and interestedly among students. It implies intervention in the writing process, not in a censorious way, but rather in a consultative capacity, with the teacher seeking to be informed by the student, and not the other way around.

Graves thinks that:

> At the core of the conference is a teacher asking a child to teach her about the subject. The aim is to foster a bursting desire to inform. So the teacher never implies a greater knowledge of this topic than the child possesses, nor treats the child as an inferior learner. We are in the business of helping children to value what they know. Ideally, the

poorer the writing the greater the interest the teacher will show in it — or rather what it might become.

(Walshe [ed.], 1981, p. 125)

While Graves here is referring to very young writers, it's our belief that the principles apply equally in secondary schools. For too long, teachers have believed that they are the subject experts, failing to acknowledge that there are other ways of seeing things and that students may have access to information which they (the teachers) have edited out of their didactic presentations. Teachers have been content (perhaps even prompted) to demand only that students regurgitate information they have transmitted, rarely providing them with the chance to become experts. They undervalue *students'* knowledge of the world. The conference approach to writing, which operates throughout the entire writing act, in a sense reverses the roles of teacher and student and places responsibility for the control and presentation of knowledge on students.

Reading to Review

Once rough copies have been drafted, *reading-to-review* sessions are held. These may be informal within groups, whereby students swap their writing and discuss content, arrangement of ideas, expression and surface mechanics among themselves. The object is to improve on individual pieces of writing, by clarifying what was intended to be conveyed to the reader, expanding on incomplete ideas and suggesting where changes might be made. It is aimed at assisting individual writers express more clearly and precisely *their* views on a subject.

If teachers feel that such sharing of writing at this stage may lead to unfair copying of other students' ideas, then they need to reconsider their objective in subject writing. Co-operative learning is an efficient means of gaining mastery over key concepts. The tendency to unconsciously foster competition between students for the acquisition of knowledge, has no place in this approach.

What we want is for *all* students to gain mastery over the subject matter, together with the means of expressing it to inform others, and to make use of it to satisfy a range of purposes.

The review stage can be completed individually, but you know from your own writing experiences that what is clear to you may not be clear to an outside reader. Thus, co-operative, shared reviewing is recommended. As teacher, you too, should participate in the reviewing of draft scripts, suggesting alternatives upon which the student may or may not act.

Redrafting

Following comprehensive reviews, students are now in the position to be able to rework their rough drafts. Redrafting may be lengthy. It may involve:

- Rethinking ideas on the basis of review comments.
- Reshaping ideas to express them more precisely.
- The re-ordering, editing out or addition of information.

While many students may initially feel ill-at-ease or impatient with redrafting their writing, the satisfaction and pride in 'owning' a carefully written work at the end will more than compensate for the urge to be satisfied with a first draft.

Editing
When students feel that they have reworked their ideas and form of expression into a cohesive and communicative whole, editing takes place. This process takes the wrinkles out of the writing by attending to the surface features of spelling, punctuation and grammar. Again, teachers should use the editing stage as an opportunity to discuss problems associated with the mechanics of writing and help students to use aids, such as dictionaries and a thesaurus, to check their own and other students' writing.

Final Copy
The final copy results in the production of a piece of writing that can be published, displayed and/or assessed. It may become part of a folio of work which is gradually built up over a semester or term, or it may be combined with other students' work to form a class publication. Where necessary, it may be elaborated with an appropriate set of graphics.

Publishing Students' Writing
Publishing can take several forms. It may be the sending of a letter, the duplicating of copies for sharing, the display of writing on a bulletin board, or the compiling of a book, class journal or diary.

Response to Writing
The audience for whom the writing was created is now given a reading task and is invited to respond in some form: orally or in writing. Response to writing should combine sensitivity and genuine interest.

HOW IS SUCH WRITING ASSESSED?

The answer to this question is in two parts. Firstly, the very process which asks students to *review, share, redraft, publish* and *invite reactions* to their writing is a means of *self-evaluating* the communicative success of their writing. *And it is important to stress student participation in this process.* Students become their own critics and make suggestions for altering aspects of each others' writing.

Secondly, the final product can be taken as that to be assessed just as other *written outcomes* are assessed. The difference lies in the approach and possibly the *wider range of products* which emerge as a result.

BUT IT MUST TAKE UP A LOT OF TIME!

This heading is certainly true, writing *is* a lengthy task. We really need to examine our beliefs about the value and use of writing in learning to adequately address the stock, 'I can't afford the time to do it' protest.

Consider first, the following *principles* which guide *content area writing*:

* Writing involves *thinking through* and *clarifying* ideas; talking helps this process.
* *Writing as an aid to learning* involves translating subject language into your own words.
* Writing is addressed to many audiences, the teacher being just one.
* Writing can be improved by sharing ideas in a writing group.
* Writing is a learning tool as well as a testing device.
* Writing can be prompted by reading.
* Writing should be used as a reading resource.

If you agree with some of these principles, at least you'll be seeking ways to improve the quality of students' learning, so that they can become independent in their search for knowledge. Writing-to-learn as outlined above is one means of helping students towards independent learning. When subject matter writing is shared, it can become important reading resource material. Also, of course, when students are drafting, reworking and reshaping their writing, they are reading for meaning and to clarify their interpretation of ideas.

PART 3
Background to the ERICA Model

Existing Models

[handwritten annotation: habitual thoughts]

The ERICA Model was developed as a framework to guide content-area teachers in helping their students become more effective readers and consequently, more effective learners. Although content-area teachers have frequently attempted to help their students read more efficiently, it has been shown that many need help and guidance if they are to succeed in this venture (Morris and Cope, 1976). The development of the ERICA Model should be seen in this context.

In the past, several procedures have been devised for helping teachers plan reading experiences. The most widely adopted model is known as the Directed Reading Activity (DRA). Although there are variations of the DRA Model basically they all involve four stages.

1. *A preparation stage* in which the teacher reviews the necessary background and skills, introduces new vocabulary, sets purposes for reading, and generally motivates students to read objectively.
2. *A silent reading stage* in which the readers seek out the desired information.
3. *A discussion stage* in which the teacher questions the students to ensure that they have located and understood the desired information.
4. *An extension stage* in which skills are developed and/or enrichment activities are undertaken.

A number of authors have criticized the DRA approach. Stauffer (1969) suggests that it is stereotyped and fails to develop thinking skills.

In contrast Stauffer developed the Directed Reading Thinking Activity. (DRTA., 1969) which stressed these four phases.

1. Declaration of purpose.
2. Reasoning.
3. Judging.
4. Refining and extending ideas.

Stauffer's DRTA is a much more dynamic approach than the DRA. Whereas the DRA simply asks students to 'Read' (Stage 2), the DRTA provides structured activities which encourage reasoning which Stauffer says, 'is productive thinking and is to be contrasted to previously learned stimuli, or reproductive thinking.' (1969, p. 24).

Judging is described by Stauffer as:

... an evaluative process by which the reader draws conclusions. The

171

judgments made must be relevant to the purposes declared, and they must be fair and verifiable. In order to judge, the reader must select and weigh facts and make decisions that are pertinent and discriminate.

(Stauffer, 1969, p. 24)

Herber (1970, 1978) also criticizes the DRA. He notes that, 'the DRA assumes that a level of independence has already been attained by the readers.' (1978, p. 226).

Herber's model, the Instructional Framework, provides a lesson structure not available in the DRA. Although both models involve a preparation stage, the Instructional Framework is much more highly structured at the point at which students are asked to read. While the DRA assumes that students can read (Stage 2), Herber introduces activities which *guide* reading. It is this aspect which distinguishes Herber's model from the DRA.

The Instructional Framework consists of three stages:

- Preparation.
- Guidance.
- Independence.

The Guidance stage uses specially prepared reading-guides to lead students through a piece of text. Herber bases these guides on three levels of comprehension and organizational patterns, and provides a series of activities which closely resemble Stauffer's reasoning and judgement stages. Thus the DRTA and the Instructional Framework concern themselves with the active development of reading as a thinking process.

SQ3R

Robinson (1967) proposes an approach to effective reading which has been widely used and reported. The anacronym SQ3R, standing for Survey, Question, Read, Recite and Review and derivatives of it, is probably the most widely recommended study approach found in reading research literature. The stages require that the reader first:

1. *Survey* the text looking for headings, general organization, study aids provided and illustrations. It is suggested that these features provide the reader with a conceptual framework of the material to be studied.
2. The reader next frames appropriate *Questions* which will direct purposeful reading.

   - What do I think the text will be about?
   - Is it broken up into sections?
   - What is the relationship of the sections to each other?
   - What am I expected to do with the information?
   - What aids are provided to assist me?

Background to the ERICA Model

The aim of the questions is to direct the reading so that it is purposeful and not haphazard.

3. Having developed some relevant questions, the piece is then *Read* to find answers to these questions.
4. The answers are then *Recited* to clarify and understand them.
5. Finally, the text is *Reviewed* to ensure that no misunderstandings or omissions have occurred.

Development of the ERICA Model

Use of the existing approaches already discussed, showed that none was able to help teachers cater satisfactorily for the range of reading needs they encountered in their classrooms.

The Directed Reading Activity offered insufficient help to students when they undertook the silent reading phase. The Directed Reading Thinking Activity was difficult to adapt to content-area class situations where the teacher was under pressure to deal with large volumes of factual knowledge. The Instructional Framework, although more easily applied in functional content-area situations and of value in developing comprehension, did not provide strategies which would help readers analyze and record the arguments developed in text. SQ3R placed too much responsibility on the reader and was not adopted by the students to whom it was introduced.

Experimentation with these models over a five year period showed disappointing results. Teachers still complained about students' poor vocabulary, lack of comprehension, poor note-taking skills, copying and inability to convert print information into words of their own, expressed either orally or in writing. Readability formulae were warmly received, but were soon seen as empty panaceas when few alternative texts were available. In short, content area reading appeared to be going backwards. A visit to the United States of America allowed one of the authors to observe Herber's Instructional Framework at work in schools in New York State. These observations showed that teachers were comfortably using Herber's Instructional Framework, although with local modifications. Thus, in Jefferson Junior High School, Adams, NY, work was carried out with teachers to develop note-taking and flow-charting activities. These teachers had, with the help of monthly after-school meetings, maintained a content-area reading program for five years and were firmly committed to its continuation.

Observation of this and other similar programs, convinced the authors that development of an improved model, which would aid teachers plan the integration of reading-to-learn activities into their regular subject area classes, was a feasible proposition. The work on note-taking and flow-charting seen at Jefferson Junior High, was related to John Merritt's work in England and was seen to open up an entirely new dimension: that of showing students how to extract and organize information.

One final dimension which the authors felt needed to be more strongly developed, was the use of small group discussion. Barnes (1976) and Richards (1978) had drawn attention to the value of well-structured discussions, a view which had been strongly reinforced by the authors' own experiences with cloze activities and Herber's Three-Level Guides.

In order to develop a model which would prove useful to *teachers*, it was decided to start with the concerns which teachers tended to express most frequently. Several hundred teachers in upper primary and secondary schools were asked to list the problems which their students most commonly exhibited in content-area reading situations. Collection of these opinions over a one year period showed that five difficulties were continually listed. These have been referred to throughout this text, and are:

1. That students copy 'out' sections of text rather than attempt to translate them into their own words.
2. That students can read but do not understand what they read.
3. That the available textbooks are too difficult and teachers, therefore, have to tell students the relevant information.
4. That students have poor vocabularies.
5. That students are able to comprehend reading exercises which their English teachers set them, but do not seem able to transfer this skill into content-area reading situations.

In addition, many teachers referred to their students' inability to write clearly and logically about what they had read. On the basis of these concerns it was decided that the ERICA Model should include the following stages:

1. *A preparation stage* which could provide students with a logical framework into which they could fit the information they were about to read. This stage would be similar to the DRA and the Instructional Framework.
2. *A reflective or thinking through stage* which would require students to interact closely with print and would cause them to make a number of judgements. This stage would be similar to stage 2 of the Instructional Framework (Guidance), and to phases 2 and 3 of the DRTA (Reasoning and Judgement).
3. A third stage which would show students *how to recognize, extract and organize the information* which the author provided. This would be a new stage and would distinguish the ERICA Model from those previously referred to. It was decided to call this type of activity, *Extracting and Organizing Information*.
4. Although the model was originally conceived as a reading model, the authors' conviction that reading, writing, listening and speaking are mutually supportive aspects of the larger concept of language, led inevitably to the inclusion of a *writing stage — translating*.

It was also decided that whenever possible, strategies to be included in the final model would include small, mixed-ability group discussions. Use of these discussions as part of Herber's reading-guide technique, had shown them to be highly motivating encounters, which allowed students to use oral language to exchange ideas, clarify their thinking and improve their ability to use the language registers of different subjects. Oral language was therefore built into the total model so that the translating staged could be addressed directly towards writing.

The first ERICA Model had five stages:

1. Preparation
2. Thinking Through
3. Visual Transformation
4. Verbal Transformation
5. Consolidation

Visual Transformation and Verbal Transformation were synonymous with the present Extracting, Organizing and Translating stages. The earlier terms, whilst satisfactory to the authors, were not liked by teachers who thought them too 'jargony'. The present terms are more appropriate, perhaps because they have more action oriented connotations.

The fifth stage, Consolidation, was dropped not because the authors found it to be redundant, but because teachers felt it added too much of a burden and so was rarely used. In this stage, games were utilized to encourage review and consolidation of important vocabulary. The authors still regard this as an extremely worthwhile activity, but have found that its inclusion led to misunderstandings and sometimes rejection of the model. Readers interested in following up this stage are directed to Morris B., and Stewart-Dore, N., *Assigning Reading as a Teaching Strategy*, Kelvin Grove College Press, 1981.

SMALL-GROUP DISCUSSIONS

The use of small-group discussion with the various strategies suggested, generates such intense on-task activity that the authors and teachers who use the technique (Berget, 1973), intuitively recognize them as useful learning and socializing activities. As yet, these perceptions are not supported by conclusive research (Jongsma, 1980), although several positive findings have been reported (Gunn and Elkins, 1976; Grant, 1976; Shablack and Dixon, 1979).

Small-group discussion allows students to become closely and thoughtfully involved in using the language register of a particular subject (Rosen, 1972) and to reflect upon the content of the subject, which Lunzer and Gardner (1978) found was not encouraged in secondary schools. Dixon (1975) asks:

How did classroom dialogue, a central method — the general

mode — of teaching and learning, come to be so largely neglected? Why is there still so little published discussion among teachers and research workers on dialogue between *pupils* as a mode of learning?

(p. 28)

Dixon suggests that teachers have to work on developing a *classroom atmosphere* which is conducive to students verbally exploring the nature of an idea and which is 'socially relaxed and supporting'. The authors' experience confirms this and shows that some teachers using the ERICA Model do have to adjust to the use of small-group discussions. Students are encouraged to do the talking and some teachers find it very difficult to 'control their tongues' to permit this to occur. Some noise is generated and some teachers need reassurance that this is not a loss of control, but an indication of the success of the activity. However, the use of Three-Level Guides and cloze activities provides for much more structured and objective discussions than teachers are used to, and most find them a pleasant surprise. Students remain on task for longer periods, have more successful experiences, and receive more immediate feedback for their suggestions; all factors which Berliner (1981) identifies as necessary components of successful classroom environments. The atmosphere, therefore, becomes one which Dixon would recognize as socially relaxed and supporting.

In supporting each other, students provide guidance which could not possibly be offered by a class teacher in a classroom situation. Meyer (1975) found that more-able readers could identify logical propositions more completely than average and below-average readers. In small group discussion, more-able readers demonstrate the missing elements of the less-able readers' incomplete propositions and thus help shape their processing towards a meaning-getting solution (Jenkins and Pany, 1981).

CONTENT OF THE ERICA STAGES

McConkie (1977) in reviewing the literature on 'Learning from Text' comments that:

> No book, let alone a single chapter, could adequately review all the research related to learning from text. Any comprehensive attempt would include research in many fields, including rhetoric, communication, education, artificial intelligence, and areas of linguistics and psychology as well as branches of philosophy and neurology.
>
> (McConkie, 1977, p. 3)

This present summary of research literature to underpin the ERICA Model must necessarily be extremely selective and readers should note that the authors are aware of this. In deciding upon which research evidence to take particular note of, the authors had to draw upon their own experiences and intuitions, together with practising teachers' responses to a variety of trial models. The resulting combination of stages and strategies finally included in the ERICA Model is the result of much reading, teaching and debating.

PREPARATION STAGE

Reading readiness is a term well-known to primary school teachers, particularly those who teach children who are at the beginning reading stage. Unfortunately, the concept is not as well-known to teachers of children who are beyond the beginning reading stage. Herber (1978) suggest that many secondary teachers assume that their students are able to effectively use a print resource without prior preparation. Why else would so many teachers set their students the task of summarizing a chapter or article without any preparation?

When considering what strategies to include in a preparatory stage, one is faced with a mass of inconclusive research information. In addition, much of this research is not relevant to school classroom situations. It has been conducted with adult subjects, on short pieces of text, which bear very little resemblance to the long pieces of connected discourse found in conventional textbooks (McConkie, 1977). The task of selecting teaching strategies, which have a strong empirical basis, is therefore not an easy one, and means that the suggestions made here should be treated as ones which appear justified on the basis of existing research evidence and experience in a classroom setting. Levin and Pressley (1981) suggest that

> ...a vast number of prose-processing activities have the *potential* to be effective strategies for children. Whether or not a particular strategy realizes its potential depends on a host of situational factors ...
>
> (p. 68)

That being the case, teachers and their students cannot wait for a 'best' strategy to be developed and tested. Their problem is to find techniques which they can integrate into regular class activities. Glaser (1977) describes the new challenge for education as being one in which we need to:

> ...teach comprehension skills that enable individuals to use advanced comprehension skills to read unfamiliar text in order to gain new information, to draw inferential judgments from text rather than accept directly stated information, and to interpret complex text so that it can be related to knowledge already acquired.
>
> (p. x)

It is in this spirit that the authors selected the strategies for inclusion in the ERICA Model, suggesting that teachers, in a constructive, positive manner, might try these ideas for themselves.

Much research has focused on ways in which learners can be better prepared for a reading task. This work has gathered momentum since the mid-1960s as many experimental psychologists have moved from a behaviourist to a cognitive perspective (Rickards and Danner, 1978).

In reading, this shift has been mirrored by the writings of Goodman (1967) and Smith (1973). Reviewers of the research, whilst revealing the as yet inconclusive nature of our present knowledge, *do* identify several directions which seem to hold great promise. (Faw and Waller, 1976; Hartley and Davies, 1976; McConkie, 1977; Gagne, 1978; Jenkins and Pany, 1981.)

Advance Organizers

The term *advance organizer* is usually related to the work of Ausubel (1960). Ausubel found that learning was facilitated by the provision of an introductory prose paragraph written at a higher level of generalization than the text to be read. Much interest was generated by this finding, but other workers have rarely been able to reproduce Ausubel's results (Faw and Waller, 1976; Jenkins and Pany, 1981). Earle (1973) commented that if it worked, it was an advance organizer and if it didn't, then it wasn't. For these reasons the technique has not been included in the model. However, the term advance organizer can be used in a wider sense to suggest any pre-reading activity introduced to facilitate learning and so, in this sense, can be applied to all preparatory activities.

Purpose-Setting Questions

Following the work of Rothkopf (1976), a large number of researchers have looked at the role of purpose-setting questions. Interest in this area is based on the thesis that reading which is more purposeful will be more objective and more productive of understanding than indiscriminate reading. Although some research has shown that such focusing questions do improve recall (Frase, 1967), typical findings are that this recall is only related to the matters directly questioned. Little incidental learning of material not directly questioned seems to take place (McConkie, 1977; Rickards, 1979). More value seems to accrue when such adjunct questions are placed after a reading rather than before it. Post-questions also have a specific learning effect, but, in addition, tend to produce more incidental learning of non-questioned material than that which results from pre-questions (Faw and Waller, 1976).

Researchers have also considered the effects of the *type of question* asked. Studies have repeatedly shown that higher-level questions which require analysis and synthesis of material, produce more and better-organized recalls of passage information than do low-level questions, which only test verbatim recall. (Watts and Anderson, 1971; Rickards and Denner, 1978; Rickards and Hatcher, 1978; Rickards, 1979.) Getting readers to generate their own questions has been shown to be an even more powerful way of improving recall

(Frase and Schwartz, 1975; Owens, 1980).

While the evidence supporting pre-questioning is positive, it is not as favourable as that for post-questions. Nevertheless, the evidence that content focus, regardless of its source, is likely to be associated with positive learning outcomes (Frase, 1977), means that it cannot be ignored. Ideally, such pre-questions should be reader generated and should demand meaningful interpretation, rather than verbatim identification of specific facts (Hartley and Davies, 1976).

The ERICA Model attempts to obtain the benefits of pre-reading questions by including opportunities for them. However, the finding that their effects are narrowly directed and do not encourage wider, incidental learning persuaded the authors to try to tie these effects to other strategies which might have a broader influence.

Descriptions of how Structured Overviews and Stage 2 Graphic Outlines might be used, therefore include interpretive, pre-questioning activities. The benefits of post-questions are provided for and discussed in the later Thinking Through and Extracting and Organizing stages.

Structured Overviews

Another advance organizer which has become widely recommended is the Structured Overview (Barron, 1978). In this technique, a list of key words relevant to a topic is prepared. These words are then arranged to show the development of the topic and relationships which exist between ideas. The resulting layout provides a visual representation of the topic being considered. Use of Structured Overviews has generally been favoured over the use of Ausubelian prose passages. (Estes, Mills and Barron, 1969; Earle, 1969, 1973; Walker, 1974; Snouffer and Thistlethwaite, 1979.) However, Snouffer and Thistlethwaite (1979) cite Readence and Moore (1979) as conducting a detailed analysis of research on Structured Overviews which found that the results obtained to date are far from conclusive.

The decision to include Structured Overviews was made because teacher response to them was very favourable and because they provided a link with Schema theory. Rumelhart (1981) describes schema (plural schemata) as the 'building blocks of cognition' and says they are the 'fundamental elements upon which all information processing depends'. Schemata are the units of memory which record our perceptions and understandings of objects, situations, actions and events.

When we receive information it is matched against existing schemata to see into which slot it can be fitted. Through schemata, we identify and categorize information and also recognize the various relationships that prevail between it and existing knowledge. Estes, Mills and Barron (1969) found that Structured Overviews worked when students had an existing background schemata which provided a meaningful framework to which new knowledge could be tied. This explanation is also the basis of modern schema theory and it thus provided a classroom technique which could be used to show how this theory could be brought into a classroom context. Work has now shown that readers with appropriate background schemata:

- Are more effective comprehenders (Pearson *et al*, 1979).
- Use schema to organize recall of information (Anderson *et al*, 1978(a), 1978(b)).
- Find familiar ideas easier to recall than new ones (Kintsch *et al*, 1975).
- Organize ideas into superordinate and subordinate relationships (Kintsch *et al*, 1973, 1975).

Schema theory is thus at the heart of current interpretations of the reading process (Milligan, 1979). Readers can now be seen to interpret prose in terms of their existing schemata (Anderson *et al*, 1977, 1978), and to lack understanding where appropriate schemata are lacking or are not activated (Rumelhart, 1981).

The Structured Overview is seen as a way in which new information can be related to old (Herber, 1978), that is, it can be integrated into a schema network. The integration of subordinate ideas into a superordinate network is likely to result in better recall over time, since memory for subordinate information decays more quickly. (Kintsch, 1973, 1975; Meyer, 1975; Miller *et al*, 1977.) Waters (1978) has also shown that superior recall of superordinate propositions holds good across a wide range of ages and materials. Rumelhart (1981) suggests that there are at least three reasons in schema theory which might explain why a reader fails to understand a written message:

1. The reader does not have the appropriate schema.
2. The reader has the appropriate schema but the available clues fail to activate them.
3. The reader fits the incoming information to a meaningful schema which, however, does not match the author's.

(p. 22)

The question of how schemata are activated, is an intriguing one. Prior to the work of Goodman (1968) and Smith (1972), much emphasis in reading focused on the word. Arguments raged as to whether it was better to teach reading through a whole-word or phonic (sound/symbol) approach. However, Goodman and Smith stressed the *meaningful nature of reading*. They suggested that the reader need not read every word, but rather, need only read until sufficient clues have been gathered to enable an intelligent interpretation to be made.

Therefore, reading was seen as a series of hypothesis-testing activities, with the reader attempting to predict what was to come. Knibe *et al* (1979) suggest that the older word-by-word methods can be viewed as *bottom-up* approaches in which information is gathered piece by piece. Krulee *et al* (1979) propose an alternative *top-down* approach in which the reader works from a conceptual overview position. Rumelhart (1981) describes a further integrated approach in which the reader switches from *top-down* to *bottom-up* working and *vice-versa* as necessary.

The advance organizer concept can easily be related to this view of how information is processed. Meaningful-reception learning (Hartley and Davies, 1976) can be seen as an information processing activity, in which higher-order conceptualizations are used to review and categorize incoming low-level information, as a series of sentences are linked into a meaningful chain (Trabasso, 1981).

Texts on content area reading (Aukerman, 1972; Shepherd, 1973; Robinson, 1975; Karlin, 1977; Herber, 1978) make much of the ways in which subject-area teachers find it difficult to understand why primary school teachers and secondary English teachers do not teach students how to read subject-area texts.

Work on schema theory has pointed out that we develop schemata for different forms of writing and reading, and that since narrative forms are far more frequently encountered, our schemata for narrative are far richer than those for expository material. (Van Dijk, 1972; Rumelhart, 1976, 1977; Thorndyke, 1977; Baker and Stein, 1981.) Not only are we more experienced in reading narrative forms, but these forms *per se* tend to have functional structures (story grammars) which are far more familiar, more concrete and hence more predictable than expository text. The ERICA Model emphasizes much in-class reading in content areas and thus seeks to redress this imbalance by greatly increasing the reader's familiarity with the nature of expository texts. This increased exposure to expository text will, it is hypothesized, increase the reader's intuitive awareness of expository forms, thus enhancing the potential for accurate prediction.

Text Structures
Apart from the reader's lack of experience with them, expository materials are also difficult to predict, because of an apparent lack of consistent top-level structure or text grammar. However, some promising efforts are being made to identify consistent top-level structures. Authors of texts on content area reading have, for some time, recognized the existence of organizational patterns and have drawn the readers attention to these (Herber, 1970, 1978). During the 1970s, experimental psychologists took this work further and showed that expository text materials could be analyzed to reveal the organizational structure used by the author. Meyer (1975) has provided a method of text analysis based on Fillmore's case grammar (1968) and Grimes' semantic grammar (1975). Using her text analysis

technique, researchers have now demonstrated that ideas or propositions high in the text structure are better remembered than those placed low in the text; that some top-level structures are more facilitating for students' comprehension than others; and that similar structures produce similar recall protocols, irrespective of content. (Meyer, 1975; Thorndyke, 1977; Meyer, Brandt and Bluth, 1978; Marshall and Glock, 1978; Meyer and Freedle, 1979.) Bartlett (1978) has also demonstrated that readers can be taught to recognize top-level structures and to use this knowledge to improve their comprehension when processing expository texts.

While the ERICA Model does not specifically use the notion of top-level structure as a preparatory device, teachers, who have become familiar with the concepts of the Graphic Outline, the Structured Overview and Extracting and Organizing information, have been able to integrate the principle into these areas. Extracting and Organizing activities have been found to be the best way to introduce students to various top-level structures, such as cause-effect and comparison-contrast, which can be identified and readily diagrammed. Having familiarized students with typical structures used by authors, the teacher is then in a better position to introduce students to them as preparatory, predictive activities. This is congruent with the evidence so far presented on focusing questions and schemata. Once students have developed appropriate top-level structure schemata, these can then be used as the basis of higher-order, pre-questioning exercises (Krulee, Fairweather and Berquist, 1979).

Surveying
The Structured Overview has been presented as a means of 'activating' existing schemata and displaying relationships between them, so that new information can more readily be slotted into place. In contrast, the Graphic Outline has been presented as a means of introducing readers to the organization and content of the text to be studied. Because of many students' relative inexperience with expository texts and thus their relative lack of expository schemata, the Graphic Outline is seen as a particularly useful strategy. Traditional study techniques, such as the SQ3R method (Robinson, 1967), include a survey stage which requires the reader to skim through the section of text to be studied in order to identify such things as headings and illustrations. This process can now be explained in terms of schema theory. The surveying process activates the reader's existing schemata for expository content and allows meaningful predictions to be generated about what is likely to be encountered (Meyer and Freedle, 1979). However, the survey technique can be seen to be weak where the reader lacks appropriate schemata for:

• Expository text structures.
• Generating predictive hypotheses about text content.

In these cases, the Graphic Outline allows the reader to build up the necessary schemata until such time as the process becomes internalized as a schema for approaching new expository material. Since texts vary considerably (Jackson, 1980), the extent of the task should not be minimized. Teachers need to recognize that considerable practice may be required (Thorndyke, 1977).

Very little research appears to have been done on the effects of diagramming text structures, although Walker (1979) has shown that Graphic Organizers based on text content, were superior to conventional SQ3R techniques as a means of improving the recall of content in less-able Junior High School Social Studies students. The decision to include the Graphic Outline in the ERICA Model is, therefore, based on hypothesis rather than on research evidence on content-clarifying strategies (Levin and Pressley, 1981).

Pre-Teaching Vocabulary

Unfamiliar vocabulary has long been recognized as a source of difficulty in reading. Most beginning reading schemes work on the basis of controlling the introduction of new vocabulary; informal reading inventories predict the suitability of particular materials; intelligence and reading tests include vocabulary sections; and readability formulae invariably have some measure of word difficulty built into them. Reading-to-learn activities quickly bring students into touch with new vocabulary, as different subjects introduce new concepts and areas of knowledge.

Lack of familiarity with vocabulary is a difficulty which we intuitively recognize as a factor which reduces a reader's ability to comprehend a written message (Guthrie and Tyler, 1978). In 1974, La Berge and Samuels suggested a Theory of Automaticity, in which they proposed that comprehension was enhanced or inhibited by the amount of attention the reader had to give to the processing of the words they encountered in reading. Unfamiliar words require more processing and so reduce the amount of attention which the reader can give to comprehending. This view has been supported by Perfetti (1977).

It seems that there is general agreement that, 'vocabulary knowledge is a crucial pre-condition to comprehension' (Pearson and Johnson, 1978), since 'without understanding the basic concepts in the text or question, one cannot make inferential links' (Trabasso, 1981).

Research on the pre-teaching of vocabulary is, however, not as clear-cut as the foregoing might have us hope. Wittrock, Marks and Doctorow (1975) have shown that changing 'hard' words to 'easy' words did facilitate understanding, and also helped in the understanding of the hard words when they were later encountered. Pearson (1981) reports research which shows that intensive pre-teaching of vocabulary was useful for below average readers on familiar material

(Swaby, 1977), and for above average readers on unfamiliar material (Schachter, 1978).

Anderson and Freebody (1981), in reviewing research on vocabulary knowledge, suggest that three differing views might be recognized:

1. An *Instrumentalist view* which proposes that vocabulary knowledge permits comprehension to take place. The more words one knows, the better one's comprehension will be. While no-one would argue with this proposition, Anderson and Freebody see the implication as being the systematic, but isolated teaching of vocabulary, as in a typical workbook vocabulary exercise.
2. The second position sees vocabulary in terms of *Verbal Aptitude*; a skill which one either has or hasn't, to a greater or lesser degree.
3. The third view is based on schema theory and represents what Anderson calls a *Knowledge Hypothesis*. This view suggests that vocabulary should be taught in meaningful contexts, so that words can be integrated into a schema framework. In this approach new words are related to other words in existing schemata.

The third view, Knowledge Hypothesis, is the position recommended in the ERICA Model. Pre-teaching of vocabulary is seen as vitally important and is tied to the use of context clues and glossary, dictionary and index usage, in order that processing schema for finding out the meanings of words can be developed.

THINKING THROUGH

The ERICA stage of Thinking Through is designed to help students to better understand a particular piece of text, and also to teach students to search for and synthesize clues which exist in the prose. Because of this, the stage has short-term and long-term objectives. Two processing strategies are used.

1. Three-Level Reading Guides (Herber, 1970, 1978).
2. Selective Deletion Cloze Activities.

In addition, both strategies employ small-group discussion as an integral part of their design.

Herber's Instructional Framework (1970, 1978) includes a heavy emphasis on teaching students how to comprehend prose material, and offers the Three-Level Guide strategy which is recommended in the ERICA Model. Herber (1970) and Doake (1976) have long claimed that too many teachers assume that students know how to comprehend, and have called for well-structured activities which lead students through the processes of gathering and synthesizing information. Herber's claims have now been fully justified, as research in both primary schools (Durkin, 1978) and secondary schools (Lunzer and Gardner, 1979) clearly shows that very little is actually done to teach students how to comprehend prose information.

Three-Level Reading Guides

One problem with trying to teach comprehension is that no-one really knows what comprehension is. The foregoing discussion of pre-reading strategies has already pointed out some of the many theories which seek to explain the process, and which give some idea of its complexity.

Although some debate exists as to the validity of the concept of levels of comprehension (Tierney and Bridge, 1978), it is accepted that class teachers need a framework within which to work. Consequently, ERICA adopts the view of three levels of comprehension, as articulated in Herber (1970, 1978), Ruddell (1974), Perfetti (1977) and Pearson and Johnson (1978), and includes Herber's Three-Level Guide, as a principal strategy. Research has shown that use of the guides, with discussion, has led to improved comprehension (Estes, 1969; Berget, 1973) and suggests that they have much to offer teachers in subjects as diverse as Mathematics (Riley, 1978) and Social Science (Estes, 1969).

The guides appear to tap several areas which have been considerably researched. Use of the guides appears equivalent to the use of generative post-questions (Watts and Anderson, 1971; Rickards, 1979; Owens, 1980), in that students respond to the guides after reading, and, through discussion, generate justifications for their decisions. The guides encourage *inferences* to be drawn (Trabasso, 1981); the *chunking of ideas* (Miller, 1956; Stevens, 1981); *paraphrasing* (Doctorow, Wittrock and Marks, 1978); *identification of more-important* from less-important information (Baker and Stein, 1981); and *identification of phrase boundaries* (Rode, 1974).

Selective Deletion Cloze Activities

As with other research already reviewed, that on cloze appears poorly executed and equally inconclusive.

Jongsma (1980), in a comprehensive review of research on the use of cloze, concluded that it is effective in developing comprehension, but is no more or less effective than many conventional methods. The literature also suggests that cloze may be effectively used with all ages and ability groups and with narrative or expository materials. The research is encouraging and suggests that it is worthwhile to persist with the technique.

As used in the ERICA Model, cloze activities require the teacher to make selective deletions rather than semi-random deletions, a practice which Jongsma recommends. Use of selective deletions means that the teacher can focus attention on connectives which indicate top-level structures (Jongsma, 1980; Pearson and Camperell, 1981), and on context clues which remain in the text (Marino, 1981). The use of the technique is related to meaningful situations and involves practices which would appear to be strongly supported by schema theories already discussed.

EXTRACTING AND ORGANIZING INFORMATION

Teachers frequently show concern about their students' inability to make notes or summaries. These concerns usually manifest themselves most strongly when the work of students in Years 11 and 12 is being discussed. This is understandable, because these students have a great deal of independent reading, note-making and summarization to carry out, consequently any weaknesses are quickly revealed. Many teachers have only themselves to blame if students are weak in these areas, because very few schools appear to work consciously and consistently towards developing these independent study skills (Johnson and Barrett, 1981).

Attention to the pre-reading and comprehending stages, already discussed, should improve students' ability to conceptualize the content of prose passages, thus leading to an improvement in their ability to first analyze and then synthesize the content of a passage in their own words. However, it appears that no research has attempted to demonstrate these links, hence the inclusion of this section on Extracting and Organizing Information so that this particular need is not overlooked. Indeed, this is what Glaser (1977) was suggesting in his comments on the new challenge to education.

Baker and Stein (1981) point out that *Metacognition*, the knowledge or awareness people have about their methods of congitive processing in such areas as memory, comprehension or communication, is rarely taught. What evidence there is, suggests that teachers do most of the thinking about how ideas are to be organized for students, rather than teaching them how to set about organizing information for themselves (Wertsch, 1978; Tierney and Bridge, 1978). Pearson and Camperell (1981) suggest that students need to learn that there are many ways to express an idea and that they should be taught general frameworks and structures so that they can find the author's message for themselves.

Bartlett (1978, 1981) has shown that a wide range of students can be provided with insights into text structures, which allow them to analyze the content of passages far more efficiently than control groups. Krulee, Fairweather and Berquist (1979) suggest that students need a frame of reference against which they can make judgements. Unfortunately, few systems for categorizing expository text have yet been developed, and it is not possible to provide teachers with simple methods of text analysis which are easily applicable.

The work of Meyer (1975, 1979) and Bartlett (1978, 1981) on prose analysis is promising, as is that of Fry (1981) on graphical analysis; this suggests that it should be possible to develop techniques for teaching most students to recognize and evaluate structures commonly found in expository text.

In the long term, it may be that we need ways of dealing with poorly-constructed texts, as well as better ways of preparing texts. Obviously, this is a problem which faces researchers and publishers rather than teachers. However, since we now know of several features which contribute to text difficulty, we can hope for better texts to be produced in the long term. Amongst these difficult features we might note the following:

Conceptual Overload
Kintsch *et al* (1975) have shown that texts containing many concepts, very densely compressed into short passages, are harder to understand and are not as well recalled as texts which repeat a few concepts several times.

Cohesion
In striving for low scores on readability formulae, many writers and publishers have been encouraged to cut long sentences into two or more shorter fragments. However, Pearson and Camperell (1981) suggest that this technique usually removes the connectives which give cohesion to text, and which draw attention to the relationships which exist within it. Fragmented text of this type, therefore, imposes a heavy inferential burden on the reader, who has to mentally replace all the connectives, which have been deleted in an attempt to re-establish meaningful reasoned relationships.

Poor Paragraph Structures
Kieras (1978) has demonstrated that 'well-structured' paragraphs — defined as those having a topic-sentence beginning — are better recalled, require less reading time and are more likely to facilitate choice of theme than are paragraphs which are 'badly' structured. Kieras concluded that an opening topic-sentence provides a *top-down structure* which gives the reader a cognitive reference, against which further information can be related and so chunked into meaningful units.

The above features are all subject to development, which seems to justify Pearson's optimism for long-term improvements to occur. *However, what of the present? How can we help students to extract and organize information?*

Present teaching seems to focus on finding the main idea in a passage of text, but, for a number of reasons, not least those discussed above, this has not proved successful (Baker and Stein, 1981). Picking out the main idea is difficult task, even where different readers approach it with similar background schemata. Where backgrounds or expectations vary, different readers can legitimately recognize alternative *main ideas* within the same text (Anderson *et al*, 1977).

Two approaches have been built into the ERICA Model. One approach calls for the reader to produce diagrams to represent the content of the text. This approach actually requires much reflective reading and was originally included in the Thinking Through activities. It has now been placed within the Extracting and Organizing section, because it was felt that these processes more accurately reflect what the reader is required to do when making up a diagram to represent a text passage. In order to make a visual representation of a prose passage, the reader must first search the passage to determine the author's message(s). The message(s) then have to be categorized so that a suitable diagram can be developed.

A number of studies have shown that diagramming is a most promising learning technique, and the authors' experiences also support this contention. Among those who have discussed the effectiveness of diagramming are Lesgold, McCormick and Golinkoff (1976), Merritt, White and Moore (1978), Fry (1981) and Geva (1981). These studies have demonstrated the usefulness of diagramming with a wide range of readers from Year 4 to College level, using both expository and narrative prose. Merritt and Fry, have tried to develop categories into which prose can be diagrammed and Fry (1981) has published a textbook, *Graphical Comprehension: How to Read and Make Graphs*, showing how this can be done.

The technique appears to have much in common with generative post-reading activities (Doctorow *et al*, 1978; Rickards, 1979) and the provison of a pictorial organizer which aids recall (Bransford and Johnson, 1972).

The second approach which has been used in this section is a variation of the flow chart. This involves breaking the text down into a series of main points and representing these in diagrammatic form. Merritt's term, *modelling*, has been employed to identify the use of this approach. As yet no empirical evidence is available to demonstrate the efficacy of the technique. However, classroom trials over a two-year period indicate that average, and below average students enjoy the exercises produced, and show that they can break text down into meaningful pieces. Berliner's finding, that students respond positively to work which provides a high rate of success, seems partly to explain why students respond in this way (Berliner, 1981).

TRANSLATING INFORMATION

The inclusion of a writing component in the ERICA Model resulted from the authors' belief that reading and writing are complementary language processes, and that both need to be regarded as functional tools through which meaning and learning can be effected. The framework, within which the writing component fits, derives in the first instance from language and learning theory.

The Role of Language in Learning

Britton (1970) reviewed and developed notions of the role of language in learning. Drawing on the work of Cassirer (1944), Piaget (1951, 1959), Bruner *et al* (1956), Luria (1959), Langer (1960), Sapir (1961), Vygotsky (1962) and others, he formulated a persuasive theory of how language in classrooms can be used as a means of organizing our respective views of the world. Using Kelly's personal construct theory (1963) as a basis, Britton (1977) argued that every new teaching situation demands that teachers ask the question: 'Given that I interpret my experiences this way or that, what do I now do about it in the classroom?'

At the heart of such a pragmatic problem is Kelly's idea that humans do not merely respond to the environment, but actively engage in its representation. That representation comprises language; it is formulated by and through it. Thus, Britton's language and learning theory (1977) has to do with seeing students and teachers as creatures who take up enterprises that embody intentions and set up expectations.

Learning with and through language in school then, has to do with a partnership between teacher and student. This partnership engages in various teaching/learning enterprises aimed at acquiring knowledge and understanding experience. In ideal situations, this enterprising partnership has the potential to realize mutual intentions which evolve from shared experiences. Expectations, derived from, and consistent with, past experiences and ways of representing that experience, are drawn up as a consequence. *Expectations are established with reference to what we consider to be possible.* The theory suggests that at that point, students and teachers engage in hypothesising, testing and confirming or not confirming. Britton (1970) suggests:

> In the experience of any given moment — in any confrontation with the world — what we make of the occasion will depend a good deal upon the appropriateness and subtlety and complexity of the expectations we bring to it. These in turn, for most of us, are very largely the fruits of past thinking, reading, writing and talking — in other words they reflect the degree to which we have been able to use language as an organizing principle in our accumulated picture of the experienced world.

Background to the ERICA Model

Barnes (1969) in studying classroom language interactions drew attention to learning *processes*, which in part was a response to Rosen's (1967) observation that school language 'looks at children across a chasm', and that its conventions 'are not taken over as are the conventions of other uses of language, at first experimentally and then with growing confidence, but unthinkingly, lock, stock and barrel language and experience have been torn asunder.' (p. 107).

Barnes *et al* (1969), considering another aspect of language in learning, namely writing, suggested that:

> ... young writers are frequently at a loss when confronted with a typical school assignment or they are reduced to summaries and paraphrases from the textbooks and notes ...
>
> Much they are asked to write is broadly speaking informative; yet no genuine informative act is taking place, i.e. no-one is being informed. The tasks frequently seem to lack a clear function, nor do they seem to leave room for the expression of the writer's own ideas and his way of seeing things. All too rarely in school writing assignments is the writer expressing something he wants to say ...

The question was asked: *How could this situation and condition be changed?*

The Bullock Report (1975) gave credence to such rightful concerns when it recommended that:

> In the secondary school, all subject teachers need to be aware of the linguistic processes by which their pupils acquire information and understanding (Rec. 138), and that progress in writing throughout the school years should be marked by an increasing differentiation in the kinds of writing ... for a variety of readers and audiences (Rec. 126 and 127).

Subsequently, a spate of publications: Martin *et al*, 1976(a), 1976(b); Stubbs, 1976; Harpin, 1976; Barnes 1976; Mallett and Newsome, 1977; Davis and Parker, 1978, Hunter-Grundin and Grundin (eds.), 1977; Marland, 1977; Richards, 1978; Torbe, 1976; Lunzer and Gardner, 1979 and others, all concerned themselves with aspects of language and learning. Some concentrated on writing (Harpin, 1976; Martin *et al*, 1976), some focused on talking to learn (Barnes, 1976; Stubbs, 1976), some concerned themselves exclusively with reading (Hunter-Grundin and Grundin, 1977; Cashdan, 1979), and others referred to interrelationships of various kinds (Mallett and Newsome, 1977; Richards, 1978; Barnes, 1976; Lunzer and Gardner, 1979). While some reported the findings of research projects (Harpin, 1976; Mallett and Newsome, 1977), others explored the reflected wisdom of far reaching experience in classrooms (Carre, 1981). Whatever the forms, the central concern had to do with exploring how language might be used as an effective tool for learning.

Reading and Writing: Interrelationships

While content-area reading instruction has been given increased attention by reading specialists in the last decade, studies to improve reading performance across curriculum areas have rarely incorporated a writing component as an integral part of systematic teaching procedures. Studies by Evanechko, Ollila, and Armstrong (1974); Hughes (1975); Klein (1980); and Smelstor (1979) established varying kinds and degrees of relationships between reading and writing growth. Carroll (1971) found that the 'integrated' language skills of reading and writing tend not to be separable statistically from general verbal ability, although measures of these skills tend to be highly interrelated. Loban's longitudinal study (1976) yielded data which similarly demonstrated positive correlations between general language ability as rated by teachers, and performance in reading and writing. In addition language facility in the early years proved to be a reliable predictor of superior performance in later years. Lazdowski (1976) focused on the features of high school and college students' writing samples to predict reading achievement. On the basis of a formula derived from mean sentence length, syllables per thought unit, and polysyllabic words per sentence, Lazdowski predicted reading achievement to within one grade level. Reliability was 0.88.

Takahashi (1975) used syntactic knowledge as a link between reading and writing skills. The result of her study demonstrated a stronger relationship between reading and syntax at Year 6 level than at Year 9 level. Likewise Kuntz (1975) reported 'a close and reliable' relationship between reading and written syntactic attainments in Year 7 students.

Applebee (1977) suggests in his review of related literature that there is 'solid evidence' that 'reading and writing skills are closely related'. He asks however, whether these relationships imply that writing can be used as a means of improving reading and conversely, whether reading instruction can be used to promote growth in writing. Braddock *et al* (1963) suggest there is merit in exploring: 'the effects of various kinds and amounts of reading on the quality and kinds of writing a person does'.

Squire and Applebee (1968) found that there was an increase in the amount of time students claimed they spent on reading when their teachers reported composition to be the primary reason for student successes. This apparent anomaly was interpreted as being the result of students needing to read widely to search out ideas for writing, so that they could successfully formulate and communicate ideas. Wolfe (1975) concluded that, among community college freshers in a remedial reading course, vocabulary skills practised through words in sentences and through words in multiple choice exercises generalized to later composition activities. While Wolfe's study drew on aspects of semantic cueing, Hughes (1975) focused on syntactic cueing in a study concerned with correlations among various language skills which emanate from their mutual dependence on syntactic maturity. Experimental pairs were exposed to writing exercises, based on transformational sentence combining. This led to gains in writing fluency over control pairs, as well as leading to significant improvement in the ability to use syntactic and semantic cueing strategies in reading.

Empirical evidence concerning the relationship between reading and writing is inconclusive, but warrants further study. A pedogogical concern of high school teachers relates to how, through their subject teaching, they might facilitate the development of those language skills necessary to understand, assimilate and use information. Since there is some evidence to support the thesis that reading and writing skills are in some way integrated (Carrol, 1971; Loban, 1976), a teaching model designed to address the pedagogical concerns of teachers and to integrate reading and writing processes as means of learning was required.

Integrated Reading and Writing Models

Lehr (1980), reporting theory on methods of content-area reading instruction, suggests it is necessary to identify those skills needed to complete a given assignment and to incorporate them into subject instruction. Aspects of writing are incorporated into a reading teaching model proposed by Ribovich (1977). Among the approaches he suggests is one whereby the teacher provides sentence models to demonstrate the means of creating relationships among ideas. This is allowed by the construction of sentences, paragraphs and the staging of information into superordinate and subordinate ideas. The final stage in generating text, which reflects organizational features of the text to be read, is that of constructing longer passages incorporating logical connectives and summary statements.

Singer and Donlan (1980) suggest that writing as a means of response to textbook information is more frequently assigned than taught. They address ways of prompting students to 'write clearly and effectively'. Drawing on Moffett's (1968) notion of composition as transaction, Emig's (1971) conclusion that students put more effort into reflexive than extensive writing, Kirby and Liner's (1980) thesis that journal writing is a productive means of extending fluency, O'Hare's (1973) notions of composition as language structure, and composition as process (Britton, 1975), it can be concluded that, 'instruction in learning from text and instruction in writing are closely connected' and 'that teachers need to teach students the writing requirements of their subject.'

Other reading models which incorporate a writing component include that of Cassidy (1977) who, during inservice programs, aims to produce support materials to reinforce and develop skills appropriate to a given content area. However, Cassidy's (1982) presentation of two models of reading and of writing, as discrete entities, need not rely on each other's interdependence in practice.

Gray and Keech (1980) used materials derived from 'given information' — defined as 'collections of data from ... curriculum areas ... (which) have been transformed into charts, lists, maps, illustrations' — as prompts for students at Year 9 and 11 to convey the given information in clear prose. Results of the study, conducted over a ten week instructional period, showed dramatic improvement by Year 11 students in organizing comparison/contrast essays. The writing performance, as measured by holistic scores and stylistic analysis, of Year 9 students on the other hand, showed a decline in holistic scores in a post-test, although there was evidence of increasing mastery of register. This study involved students in moving from print information (albeit *not* prose) to expressing their understanding in structured, extended prose forms. It reflects some aspects of ERICA strategies and can be regarded as one study which attempts to measure gains in writing from reading.

Writing Processes

The study of students' writing development in general and the art of writing in particular has frequently been undertaken by means of the case study approach. Emig (1971) examined how Year 12 students went about composing, while more recently, Graves (1975); Nolan (1979); Calkins (1980); and Kamler (1980), have tracked how children develop control over learning to write in Years 1-4. Shafer (1982), in an ethnographic study of the effect of group interactions on sustained writing in family groupings in a British classroom, focused on contextual variables and their influence on what and how children write.

Kress (1982) takes 6-14 year olds as subjects for a study of what children learn when they learn to write. He focuses on 'the linguistic process and substance of writing'. At a more general level, Smith (1982) analyzes 'the act of writing' and suggests implications for classroom practice.

These and other studies suggest frameworks within which teachers may review much classroom practice relating to writing teaching. Recent research particularly focuses on writing *process* rather than product, and implies, when not explicitly stated, that the need for time, experimentation and interaction are the conditions of learning to master and control written language in its various forms. As well, attention to contexts within which school writing occurs and the ways in which these affect how and what students write (Bennett and Walker, 1978; Shafer, 1982) are helpful in defining the kinds of situations and conditions which best promote writing development.

Background to the ERICA Model

Translating activities included in the ERICA Model exphasize writing processes rather than products, and draw on a range of theory, research and current practice to provide a means of learning and a much needed link between reading and writing in content areas.

PART 4
Appendix

Sample Curriculum Units of Work Incorporating ERICA Strategies

Units	Prepared by
UNIT 1: Science	A. Morris
UNIT 2: History	A. Morris
UNIT 3: Geography	A. Morris
UNIT 4: Mathematics	B. Bopf
UNIT 5: Home Economics	N. Stewart-Dore
UNIT 6: English	S. Innes

Each of the ERICA Stages incorporates a series of learning objectives which have been described in these terms.

(a) **Content Objectives** — having to do with the knowledge base of a unit.

(b) **Cognitive (or Process) Objectives** — focusing on thought processes involved in understanding particular topics and the ways in which ideas relate to each other.

(c) **Skill Objectives** — the abilities necessary to perform various tasks demanded by the topic.

(d) **Affective Objectives** — embracing aspects to do with personal response and judgment.

Because the ERICA model is made up of a range of strategies designed to teach students how to learn-to-learn from print resources, the following sample curriculum units clearly demonstrate the application of this generalized model to all content areas. This is possible because the model describes stages which are common to most classroom situations in which readers attempt to process and learn from print.

For each ERICA strategy the following *process objectives* may be specified.

STAGE 1: PREPARING FOR READING

Strategy: Structured Overview

Process Objectives: to *marshall* students' prior knowledge as an introduction to the study of a given topic in order to *organize* that knowledge into a conceptual "map" which *shows relationships* between ideas.

Strategy: Graphic Outline

Process Objectives: to *survey* a text to *identify* the organizational layout and to make *predictions* about its likely content as preparation for critical reading.

Strategy: Vocabulary — Context Clues
Process Objectives: to *search* text for *explicit* or *implied clues* to the meaning of subject vocabulary items and to *identify, interpret,* and *use* these clues to *express meanings* in the students' own words.

STAGE 2: THINKING THROUGH READING
Strategy: Three-Level Guide
Process Objectives: to *examine* text to determine information which is literally stated and then to *reflect* on this information to *make inferences* and *generalizations* to justify individual responses to text and so negotiate a concensus of opinion in group discussion.

Strategy: Group Cloze
Process Objectives: to *reflect* on the meaning of text within and across sentences by making use of *context clues* to predict possible solutions to deleted words, and then to *justify individual choices* of words to group members in terms of the context clues available.

STAGE 3: EXTRACTING AND ORGANIZING INFORMATION
Strategy: Outlining
Process Objectives: to *distinguish* between *main ideas* and *supporting details* and to present these in a *summary outline* format.

Strategy: Diagramming
Process Objectives: to *identify* key information and interrelationships between ideas and to *transform* these into suitable graphic forms for display and easy retrieval.

STAGE 4: TRANSLATING INFORMATION
Strategy: Writing from Given Information
Process Objectives: to *express* interpreted text meanings in a range of cohesive written forms and to *communicate* these meanings to various audiences.

UNIT 1: Science

SUBJECT : Science
YEAR : 8
TOPIC : Forces: Moving and Stopping
SOURCE : Stannard and Williamson, *Exploring Science*, Chapter 5, pp. 60-77

WEEK	TOPIC	DAY 1	DAY 2	DAY 3	DAY 4	DAY 5
1	Friction Forces	Ex.1. Structured Overview Ex.2. Graphic Outline: Chapter 5 Independent Study Ex.3. Vocabulary 1, pp. 62-65	Investigation 1	Ex.4. Cloze Exercise, p. 62 Explaining Friction Investigation 2: Predictions	Investigation 2	Ex.5. Categorizing Exercise, pp. 64-66 Ex.6. Vocabulary 2, pp. 67-69
2	Gravitational Forces	Ex.7. Three-Level Guide, pp. 67-69 Gravitational Forces	Ex.8. Structured Overview Balanced and Unbalanced Forces Ex.9. Vocabulary 3, pp. 70-74	Investigation 3	Ex.10. Three-Level Guide Balanced and Unbalanced Forces, pp. 70-74	Ex.11. Translating

Friction Forces: Pages 60–66

TEACHER NOTES

Lesson 1

Exercise 1: Structured Overview: Friction Forces

To be developed by teacher and students prior to encountering the text.

1. List words which you think are key words related to the topic.
2. Arrange these in a diagram to show how you think the topic develops logically.
3. Draw lines between words to indicate relationships.
   The resulting diagram is a *Structured Overview* in reading terms but is variously described as a 'concept map', 'word map', or 'semantic web' by other disciplines.
4. The Structured Overview is best built-up with students rather than simply being presented to them. What they build-up by themselves, they think through and internalize. Giving them a complete model takes away this thinking activity and is less productive.
5. In some cases, you may feel that students do not have enough background knowledge to work with you in creating a Structured Over-

view. In these cases you need to remember that the more you do, the less they do, so your input should be limited to the amount of help, guidance, and structure *they need*.

6. The design and implementation of the Structured Overview has not been developed. You need to decide on how to go about it.

Exercise 2: Graphic Outline

Exercise to be done in class. Some clues have been built into the outline to help students complete this first one.

Exercise 3: Vocabulary 1, pp. 62-65: Using Context Clues
This is an independent exercise. Explain the setting out and requirements before students begin.

Lesson 2

Investigation 1
Experiment specified in the text

Lesson 3

Exercise 4: Cloze Exercise
This exercise is to be completed *after* Investigation 1 is done. *Students are not to use their texts* as they do this cloze exercise.

Step 1: Have them work independently to complete the exercise.
Step 2: Have them compare their ideas with a partner to determine the 'best' words.
Step 3: Pull the activity together by having students point out the context clues they used.

N.B. You only need to go over a sample of words, not all of them.

Lesson 4

Investigation 2: Predictions
Experiment specified in the text

Lesson 5

Exercise 5: Categorizing Exercise, pp. 64-66
To follow Investigation 2.

Exercise 6: Vocabulary 2, pp. 67-69: Using Context Clues
Set for independent study before doing the Three-Level Guide on Gravitational Force.

Gravitational Force: Pages 67-77

Lesson 6

Exercise 7: Three-Level Guide: Gravitational Force, pp. 67-69
To be completed in class after Exercise 6.

Appendix

Exercise to be used as a teaching exercise, and teacher to review main points afterwards.

Lesson 7

Exercise 8: Structured Overview: Balanced and Unbalanced Forces
To be developed as per Exercise 1.

Exercise 9: Vocabulary 3, pp. 70-74: Using Context Clues
To be done as independent study and then discussed in pairs or threes in class.

Lesson 8

Investigation 3
Experiment specified in the text.

Lesson 9

Exercise 10: Three-Level Guide: Balanced and Unbalanced Forces,
         pp. 70-74
To be used after completion of Investigation 3.

Lesson 10

Exercise 11: Translating Information
To follow Exercise 10.

CLASS EXERCISES

Exercise 2: Graphic Outline, Forces: Moving and Stopping

Survey Chapter 5 then complete the Graphic Outline below to show the content and organization of the text.

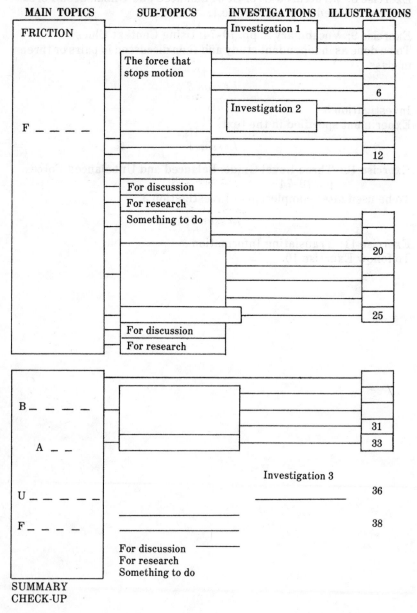

MAIN TOPICS	SUB-TOPICS	INVESTIGATIONS	ILLUSTRATIONS

FRICTION — Investigation 1

The force that stops motion

6

Investigation 2

12

For discussion
For research
Something to do

F _ _ _ _

20

25

For discussion
For research

B _ _ _ _

A _ _

31
33

Investigation 3

U _ _ _ _ _   36

F _ _ _ _   38

For discussion
For research
Something to do

SUMMARY
CHECK-UP

Appendix

Exercise 3: Vocabulary 1: Using Context Clues

Each of the following words is used and explained in your textbook. Look up the words below on the page indicated and then find the given explanation. Write this explanation in your book and then write another explanation in your own words.

Example: Set out your work like this.

> Word: friction   Page: 62
> 1. Book Explanation   The force that stops the block moving is due to the two sur-
>   faces rubbing together. This force is called *friction.*
> 2. My Explanation   Friction is caused when two surfaces rub together.

Now look up the following words. Set out the book explanation and your explanation for each word, as shown in the example above.

Words	Page
interlock	62
frictional force	62
lubricants	64
hovercraft	65

Exercise 4: Cloze Exercise

Fill in each blank in the following exercise with a word which you think makes the best sense. Work by yourself and try to remember why you chose each word.

The Force That Stops Motion

Investigation 1 showed three things.

1. To .... a rubber band, you use a force.
        (1)
2. A stretched rubber band can .... movement.
                                       (2)
   In .... words, it can exert a ....
          (3)   (4)
3. The bigger the stretch, the .... the force.
                                  (5)

The force of a stretched rubber band can move a block of wood. ...., the block does
                                                         (6)
.... move far across the table. It soon .... down and stops. Why does it ....?
(7)   (8)   (9)
If you want to stop anything, you have to exert a force .... to the way it is moving.
                                               (10)
With the .... block, it seems that the .... force acting is the force exerted by the
        (11)   (12)
.... rubber band. .... there must be .... force. The block is touching the
(13)   (14)   (15)
table top. The .... that .... the block moving must be caused by the ....
           (16)   (17)   (18)
surfaces .... together. This .... is called friction.
         (19)   (20)

Exercise 5: Categorizing Exercise

On page 62 we looked at friction and learned about the *frictional force* which is caused by two surfaces rubbing together. In Investigation 2 we found that different amounts of frictional force were caused as the wood block moved across different surfaces. Pages 64 and 65 explained that a frictional force can be an advantage or a disadvantage.

In this exercise we are going to work out some ways in which frictional forces can be an advantage or a disadvantage.

Work with your partners to think of as many examples as you can in which frictional forces are involved. As you think of examples, decide whether they have a *high* or a *low* frictional force and whether this is of advantage or disadvantage to us.

The list of discussion questions on page 66 will help you get started. An example of each kind has already been put into the chart for you. Make sure you can explain your choices when you discuss them.

Learning to Learn from Text

	High Frictional Force	Low Frictional Force
Advantages	Car tyres against bitumen road	Skis on snow
Disadvantages	Car engine needs oil	Car skidding on ice

Exercise 6: Vocabulary 2: Using Context Clues

Each of the following words is used and explained in your textbook. Look up the words below and find the explanations. After writing the explanation given in the book, give an explanation in your own words.

Example: Set out your work like this

    Word: gravity   *Page*: 67
    1. Book Explanation Gravity is the force pulling the block down towards the earth.
    2. My Explanation   Gravity is the force that holds us down on the earth and stops us floating off into space.

Look up the following words and set out the explanations as shown above.

Words	Page
motion	67
suspend	67
weight	68
Newtons	68
mass	68
gravitational force	68
perpetual motion	69

Exercise 7: Three-Level Guide: Gravitational Force

LEVEL 1: LITERAL LEVEL

Read the section on 'Gravitational Force', pages 67-69. When you have done this, read the following statements and *tick those which mean exactly what the book says*. The words may be different but they must have the same meaning. Be ready to explain the reasons for your choices.

_____ 1. Gravity is the force which holds us down on the earth.
_____ 2. A spring balance is used to measure the force of gravity on an object.
_____ 3. Weight is caused by gravity.
_____ 4. Some forces are measured in Newtons.
_____ 5. Gravitational forces only occur between planets.
_____ 6. The moon has the same mass as the earth.

Appendix

LEVEL 2: INTERPRETIVE LEVEL

Tick those statements which you think mean what the author meant us to understand. Be ready to explain the reasons for your choices.

_____ 1. There was no gravity until Sir Isaac Newton invented it.
_____ 2. Big people are more attracted to each other than little people.
_____ 3. Very thin people make the best high jumpers.
_____ 4. The moon has a stronger gravitational force than the earth.
_____ 5. Weight can only be correctly measured by a spring balance.

LEVEL 3: APPLIED LEVEL

Tick those statements which you think the author would agree with.

_____ Gravity is more important to us than the sun's heat.
_____ Gravitational force and gravity are two different things.

Exercise 9: Vocabulary 3: Using Context Clues

The following words are introduced in the section of your text on Balanced and Unbalanced Forces, pages 70-74. Find the meaning of the words given in the text and record this in your Science notebook. Now, give your meaning in your own words.
Set your work out as you did in Exercises 3 and 6.

Words	Page
Balanced forces	70,71
Unbalanced forces	70,71
Action	73
Reaction	73
Turbine	74
Air compressor	74
Exhaust gases	74
Combustion chamber	74

If you wish, you may use a dictionary for this exercise.

Exercise 10: Three-Level Guide: Balanced and Unbalanced Forces

Read pages 70 to 74, 'Balanced and Unbalanced Forces', before completing the following reading guide.

LEVEL 1: LITERAL LEVEL

Tick those statements which can be found in the textbook. If the words are different, the statement must mean exactly the same as the textbook. Be ready to justify your choices.

_____ 1. Forces that cause changes in motion are called unbalanced forces.
_____ 2. Balanced forces leave things as they are.
_____ 3. Forces seem to come in twos.
_____ 4. Each action has an equal and opposite reaction.
_____ 5. If the same force is applied to a small and a large object they will both move at the same speed.

LEVEL 2: INTERPRETIVE LEVEL

Tick those statements which you think can be inferred from what you have been told in the text. Be ready to explain your reasons.

_____ 1. Swimming in togs is more efficient than swimming in clothes.
_____ 2. Smooth-shaped cars use less petrol than rough-shaped cars.

_____ 3. It pays to keep your bicycle tyres pumped up and your chain and wheels oiled.

_____ 4. Rockets travel faster than jets because there is no air outside the earth's atmosphere to slow them down.

LEVEL 3: APPLIED LEVEL

Tick those statements which you think the authors would agree with. Be ready to explain your reasoning.

_____ 1. Tyres which grip the road very well have both advantages and disadvantages.

_____ 2. Standing behind a jet engine would be very dangerous.

_____ 3. Jet engines are probably more efficient at very high altitudes where the air is very thin.

_____ 4. The idea of equal and opposite reactions is probably very important to scientists.

Exercise 11: Translating Information

1. You work for the government and have the job of trying to get people to use less petrol in their cars. Using ideas from this chapter, write a short message telling them what they can do to help.

2. If you were the coach of a tug-of-war team which was very evenly matched with another team, how could you use your knowledge of friction and forces to help your team win?

3. Your best friend is going to enter a bike race and wants to do his best to win. Write him a letter telling him what he can do. Use the information from this chapter.

UNIT 2: History

SUBJECT : History
YEAR : 8
TOPIC : Ancient Festivals
SOURCE : Hendy *et al*, *Foundations*, pp. 32-37

WEEK	TOPIC	DAY 1	DAY 2	DAY 3
1	Ancient Festivals	Ex. 1. Structured Overview	Ex. 2. Graphic Outline	Ex. 3. Vocabulary
2		Ex. 4. Three-Level Guide	Ex. 5. Extracting and Organizing	Ex. 6. Graphic Outline
3	Further Research	Ex. 7. Consolidation		

Exercise 1: Structured Overview: Ancient Festivals

1. Have the students work in small groups of four or five to list words which they can think of that are related to festivals. Remind them that the topic they are to study is Ancient Festivals so that their words should be related if possible. Allow about 4-5 minutes for groups to list say 8-12 words.
2. Find which group has the largest list.
3. Have them read their words out for you to write up and display.
4. Ask other groups if they have any extra words and include these until all words are listed. If you are short of words you can accept new suggestions at this time.
5. Ask the class if any words have the same meaning. If so, decide which ones subsume the others. Delete those subsumed. For example, retain *massacre* and delete *killings*.
6. Ask the students whether the remaining words can be grouped into sets (they will know about sets from Mathematics). Give them an example — say a set of words to do with school. Cluster the words in sets and use symbols to identify each one.
7. Have the students work in their groups to try to arrange these word-clusters into a diagram to show how festivals have developed.
8. Pick out the one you think is most appropriate and draw it on the board. Have the students comment and make any changes which you and they agree on.
9. This should now be a Structured Overview which represents what they already collectively know about festivals, and which is organized, with your help, into a meaningful diagram. Here is one possible example.

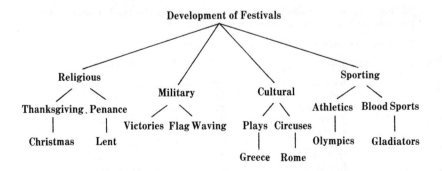

Learning to Learn from Text

Exercise 2: Graphic Outline

1. First, take the class through the text to show them the difference between topic headings (in italics) and sub-topic headings (in bold type). Show them that the captions next to the illustrations have to be read to find out where each illustration relates. (The book does not number pictures so short titles will have to be made up.)
2. Hand out a Graphic Outline sheet to each student, *but* let them work in two's or three's to fill it in. *Each* student should complete his or her own Graphic Outline and retain it. Check on what the various groups expect to find in each section.

Make sure they *predict* from the headings.

DO NOT LET THEM READ THE SUB-SECTIONS.

The idea is to build-up survey and prediction skills so that they come to anticipate what will be explained. One way is to fill in the headings and illustration details first and then get students to close their books before doing the predictions. This may be too hard for some, so use your own judgment.

NOTE: Check Exercise 6 before you use this exercise.

Topic Heading	A	B	C ....
Sub-Topic Headings	1.	1.	1.
		2.	2.
Illustrations	(a)	(a)	(a)
	(b)	(b)	(b)
	I expect this section will tell me about	(c)	Sub-topic 1 will probably tell me about ....
	....	(d)	
	....	(e)	
	....	(f)	....
	....	I think sub-topic 1 will be about	....
	....	....	Sub-topic 2 will most likely be about ....
	....	....	
	....	And I think sub-topic 2 will be about	
	....	....	....
	....	....	....
		....	....
		....	

Exercise 3: Vocabulary: Context Clues

The following words can be found on pages 32-37 of your textbook. Look each one up, then work in twos or threes to complete this exercise.

Write out an explanation for each one in your own words.

Word	Page	Your Explanation
festival	32	....
deities	32	....
processional way	32	....
divine	32	....
sanctuary	32	....
comedy	33	....
tragedy	33	....
free-born	34	....

Appendix

unity   35   ....
circular arena   37   ....
mock   37   ....

When you have finished, compare your answers with the group next to you. See if you agree on the meaning of each word.

Exercise 4: Three Level Guide

LEVEL 1: LITERAL LEVEL

Tick those statements which have the same meaning as the text. The words may be different but the information must be the same. Be ready to explain the reasons for your decisions.

_____ 1. Festivals have a very ancient history.
_____ 2. The main Babylonian festival was a religious one.
_____ 3. Several gods attended the Babylonian festival.
_____ 4. The Greek festivals were religious festivals.
_____ 5. Greek festivals were only sporting occasions.
_____ 6. The Greeks invented drama.
_____ 7. Everybody in Greece attended the plays.
_____ 8. Greek theatres were very large.
_____ 9. The Olympic Games began as a public holiday.
_____ 10. The Greeks gave valuable prizes to the winners of races.
_____ 11. The Romans held more festivals than the Greeks.
_____ 12. Roman Festivals were religious festivals.

LEVEL 2: INTERPRETIVE LEVEL

Tick those statements which can be inferred from the text. Be ready to explain the reasons for your decisions.

_____ 1. Nebuchadnezzar was afraid of dying.
_____ 2. The Greeks had many gods.
_____ 3. The feast of Dionysus must have been extremely important.
_____ 4. Greece must have been a very violent country when the Olympic Games were first held.
_____ 5. The Romans were extremely proud and cruel people.
_____ 6. The Romans thought more of festivals than either the Babylonians or Greeks.

LEVEL 3: APPLIED LEVEL

Tick those statements which the author would probably support. Be ready to justify your decisions.

_____ 1. Festivals are an essential part of human society.
_____ 2. All festivals are religious in origin.
_____ 3. Although the present-day Olympic Games get more publicity they probably meant more to the Greeks than they do to us.
_____ 4. Festivals are a bad thing. They waste money which could be better spent in other ways.
_____ 5. The Greek festivals were probably the best ever held.

Exercise 5: Extracting and Organizing Information

Your text provides a lot of information about festivals. Now, try to put this together on a chart to see how the festivals compared. Some side headings have been put in for you, but see if you can think of any more to add. You may go on to an extra sheet if you wish.

About Festivals	Babylon	Greece	Rome	Other festivals to be researched
Reasons for holding festivals				
Different festivals which were held, together with their purpose				
People involved				
Effect on the community				

Exercise 6: Translating Information

Look back at your Graphic Outline (Exercise 2) to see what you predicted you would find in each section. Compare your predictions with those of your neighbours.

Now work together to make up a new set of headings for pages 32-37. You may add extra headings if you think they are needed to help readers predict what they are likely to read about.

Compare your set of headings with those of another group. See if you can agree on a set of headings which would improve the passage.

Exercise 7: Consolidation

1. Which of the three civilizations described would you like to have lived in? Explain why.
2. Further Research:

   Either (a) Find other books related to the civilization you chose in the first part of this exercise and do a project on it. Arrange your work in sub-topics such as Festivals, Houses, Equality, and so on.
   You should aim to cover at least five sub-topics.

   Or (b) Find out about festivals in another civilization and compare your findings with the civilizations you have studied. Add the new information you find to the chart you completed for Exercise 5.

UNIT 3: Geography

SUBJECT : Geography
YEAR : 8
TOPIC : Weather and Climate
SOURCE : Swan, *Living Geography*, Chapter 4, pp. 53-67

WEEK	TOPIC	DAY 1	DAY 2	DAY 3
1	Weather Instruments	Ex.1. Structured Overview Ex.2. Graphic Outline	Ex.3. Vocabulary: Group Discussions. Then class lesson on Weather Instruments	Ex.4. Three-Level Guide: Weather Instruments Ex.5.1. Independent Study: Vocabulary
2	Clouds and Precipitation	Ex.5.2. Vocabulary: Group Discussions. Then class lesson on Cloud Forms.	Ex.6. Three-Level Guide: Clouds and Rainfall	Ex.7. Extracting and Organizing Information. Stages in the production of rain. Ex.8.1. Independent Study: Vocabulary
3	Pressure Belts and Wind Systems	Ex.8.2. Vocabulary: Group Discussion. Class lesson		

Weather and Climate: Pages 53-67

TEACHER NOTES

Exercise 1: Structured Overview

1. See handout on developing a Structured Overview in class.
2. Work out your Geography aims and terms for this unit, and develop your own Structured Overview.
3. Keep your model in mind as you work with the students to get them to list words which they think are related to weather and climate.
4. Guide the students through the exercise of clustering words into sets and finding more general words to label these sets.
5. Make up a class Structured Overview on the blackboard.
6. If this is radically different from yours, present yours either on an overhead transparency or as a handout and ask students to point out how yours differs from theirs. They should record both overviews in their exercise books.

Exercise 2: Graphic Outline

You will need to guide students at first. Start in class and either finish as independent study, *or if this isn't possible*, complete it in class next lesson.

Exercise 3: Vocabulary

To be completed in class.
    Teacher to add any further information or practice required after the exercise.

Exercise 4: Three-Level Guide

To follow teacher's input after Exercise 3.

Exercise 5: Vocabulary

Independent study exercise.
Ensure that the discussion group part of the exercise follows in class.

Exercise 6: Three-Level Guide

Use in class *after* normal class lesson on Cloud Forms.

Exercise 7: Extracting and Organizing Information

To follow Exercise 6 in the next lesson.
In the class exercise, the initial reading and development of a diagram could be done as independent study with follow-up comparisons and discussions held in class.

Exercise 8: Vocabulary

May be used as a class exercise or an independent study activity. Ensure that the discussions in the second part of the lesson lead to acceptable explanations. Class lessons to follow as necessary.

Exercise 1: Structured Overview

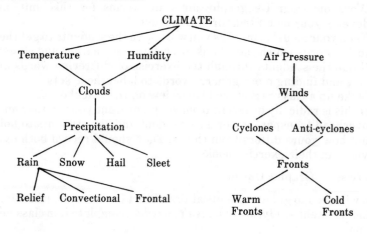

Appendix

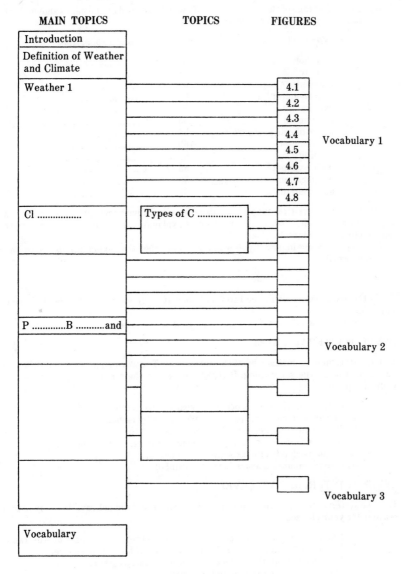

MAIN TOPICS   **TOPICS**   **FIGURES**

Introduction

Definition of Weather and Climate

Weather 1

4.1
4.2
4.3
4.4
4.5
4.6
4.7
4.8

Vocabulary 1

Cl ....   Types of C ....

P ....B ....and

Vocabulary 2

Vocabulary 3

Vocabulary

Learning to Learn from Text

Exercise 3: Vocabulary, pp. 53-57: Using Context Clues

Look up the meanings of the following words which are used on the pages shown. Write out an explanation for each one in your own words.

Word	Page	Your Explanation
weather	53	....
climate	53	....
elements	53	....
thermometer	53	....
rain gauge	55	....
barometer	55	....
atmospheric pressure	55	....
hygrometer	55	....
humidity	55	....
water vapour	55	....
evaporation	56	....
anemometer	57	....

When you have written out your explanations, work with your group to agree on an explanation for each word. Write the group's explanation again if it is better than the one you made up yourself.

You may use a dictionary if you wish, but remember that explanations are to be in your own words.

Exercise 4: Three-Level Guide

To do this exercise, you will need to find information given in your textbook between pages 52-56.
Don't forget to study the illustrations as well as the print.

LEVEL 1: LITERAL LEVEL

Tick the statements which say what the author said. The wording may be a bit different, but it must mean the same thing. Be ready to explain the reasons for your choices to your group.

_____ 1. Cold Polar air masses occur in areas of high latitude.
_____ 2. Places with equal air pressure are shown by isobars.
_____ 3. Thermometers measure the temperature of the air.
_____ 4. A Stevenson Screen protects thermometers from too much sun.
_____ 5. Cumulus clouds always signal fine weather.
_____ 6. Coastal mountain areas have low rainfall.

LEVEL 2: INTERPRETIVE LEVEL

Tick the statements which you think the author meant but did not say. Be ready to give reasons for your choices.

_____ 1. Tropical maritime air masses bring rain to the eastern coast of Australia.
_____ 2. An isobar "reading" of 1026 shows an area of high air pressure.
_____ 3. A keen eye is all that's needed to observe the weather.
_____ 4. Stormy weather is predicted by a barometer.
_____ 5. Low humidity means it's going to rain.
_____ 6. Coastal mountains prevent rain from falling inland.

LEVEL 3: APPLIED LEVEL

Tick those statements which you think can be concluded from the text. Be ready to say why you think the author would agree.

Appendix

_____ 1. "Make hay while the sun shines" is good advice to farmers.
_____ 2. It's easy to set up a backyard weather station.
_____ 3. Weather records must be based on very accurate records.
_____ 4. You can't read the weather by the clouds.
_____ 5. "Fine with showers" is a reasonable weather forecast.

Exercise 5: Vocabulary, pp. 57-59: Using Context Clues

Look up the following words which are used in your textbook on the pages shown. Write out an explanation for each one in your own words.

Word	Page	Your Explanation
accumulation	57	....
stratiform	57	....
cumuliform	57	....
cirriform	57	....
condensation	58	....
precipitation	58	....
initial	59	....

When you have written out your own explanations, work with your group to agree on an explanation for each word. Write this explanation again if it is better than the one you made up yourself.

Exercise 6: Three-Level Guide: Clouds and Rainfall, pp. 57-59

LEVEL 1: LITERAL LEVEL

Tick those statements which give information that is given in your text. The information in your text may be in words or in the diagrams. Be ready to give the reasons for your choices.

_____ 1. The text describes three forms of cloud.
_____ 2. Rainfall is caused by air rising and being cooled.
_____ 3. Precipitation means rainfall.
_____ 4. Relief rainfall only occurs near hills.
_____ 5. Convectional rain occurs over land.
_____ 6. The first stage in the creation of all rainfall is the rising of warm, humid air.

LEVEL 2: INTERPRETIVE LEVEL

Tick those statements which can be inferred from the information given in the text. Be ready to explain the reasons for your choices.

_____ 1. Cold air can hold as much moisture as warm air.
_____ 2. Convectional rainfall, shown in Figure 4.13, probably falls during thunderstorms.
_____ 3. More rain is associated with a warm front than with a cold front.
_____ 4. Steady rain is more likely with the conditions shown in Figure 4.13 than with those shown in Figure 4.14.

LEVEL 3: APPLIED LEVEL

Tick those statements which can be supported by information in the text. Have your reasons ready for a discussion.

_____ 1. Charleville is likely to only ever have two of the three kinds of rainfall shown.
_____ 2. Cirrus clouds are common over Charleville.

217

Learning to Learn from Text

Exercise 7: Extracting and Organizing Information

Read pages 58 and 59 of your text to find out what happens when it rains. Draw a diagram which shows the three stages in the production of rain. Try to get as much information on your diagram as you can, to show what happens.

When you have finished, compare your diagram with those of the other students in your group. See if they have:

(a) Missed out any important information.
(b) Put in information which is not concerned with how rain is produced.

Decide which diagram is the best, and be ready to explain your reasons.

Exercise 8: Vocabulary, pp. 60-62: Using Context Clues

Look up the following words in your textbook.
Write out an explanation for each in your own words.

Word	Page	Your Explanation
ascending	60	....
descending	60	....
low pressure	60	....
high pressure	60	....
trough	60	....
cyclone	60	....
anticyclone	60	....
warm front	62	....
cold front	62	....
isobar	63	....

Work with your group to develop a group explanation for each word. Write this explanation again if it is better than your first effort.

UNIT 4: Mathematics

SUBJECT : Mathematics
YEAR : 8
TOPIC : Integers with Distributive Law and Inequations
SOURCE : McMullen and Williams, *On Course Mathematics 1*, (New Ed.), Chapter 15

WEEK	TOPIC	DAY 1	DAY 2	DAY 3	DAY 4	DAY 5
1	Integers	Preparation Ex.1. Graphic Outline	Thinking Through Ex.4. Three-Level Guide	Ex.5. Thinking Through Three-Level Guide	Ex.6. Translating	
			Cloze Activity	Cloze Activity	Ex.7. Consolidation	
		Ex.2. Structured Overview	Extracting and Organizing	Extracting and Organizing		
		Ex.3. Vocabulary p. 223, Table of Integers	(Addition of Integers)	(x & ÷ of Integers)	Text exercises on p. 224	
	Laws Particularly Distributive Law					Ex.8. Preparation: Laws — Vocabulary Group A: pp. 226-8 Group B: Distributive Law Preparation: Vocabulary and Thinking Through
2		Continue Distributive Law with Group B Group A complete pp. 226-228.				

TEACHER NOTES AND EXPLANATIONS FOR PROGRAM AND EXERCISES

It is anticipated that there would be too many problems with integers if a separate unit was not given on this concept to emphasize addition, multiplication and division laws with integers.

Day 1: This would involve Preparation Exercises 1, 2, and 3 as well as teacher introductions to integers and the notion of *positive* and *negative* numbers. There should be discussion of their use in practical situations.

Day 2: Exercise 4 is a *link* between Three-Level Guide, Cloze, and Organization and Extraction of Information exercises — the Thinking Through stage.

The concept being taught is that of *addition of integers* of the rule, which is important to future success in equations and in any *accurate* work. A set of simple exercises could be given on the blackboard.

Day 3: Exercise 5 follows the same approach as Exercise 4 but with an emphasis on *multiplication and division of integers.*

N.B.: In Level 2 (applied) a useful discussion exercise would be to find the *reason* why some students choose *wrong* answers.

Before working through the division problem, it is sufficient to show that division and multiplication, as for addition and subtraction, use the same rules.

For example:

$$-6 \div 3 \quad = \quad -6 \times \tfrac{1}{3}$$
$$\text{and} \quad -6 + -3 \quad = \quad -6 - 3$$

∴ the same rule applies

These exercises could be followed by further class or independent exercises.

Day 4: Exercises 6 and 7 should be followed by numerous exercises on basic operations, using integers and frequent verbalizing of rules, particularly the addition rule which is always a problem.

Day 5: Since a Graphic Outline and Structured Overview for the chapter have been completed, this unit on laws — mainly the distributive law — would begin with a vocabulary preparation. You could then break the class into two groups, allowing the more capable students to proceed to pp. 226, 227, 228, while weaker students revise distributive law and its use with integers.

Appendix

Exercise 1: Graphic Outline

Read Chapter 15 and complete this Graphic Outline.

CHAPTER HEADING

(Large, heavy block print)

(Look for the long pink boxes)

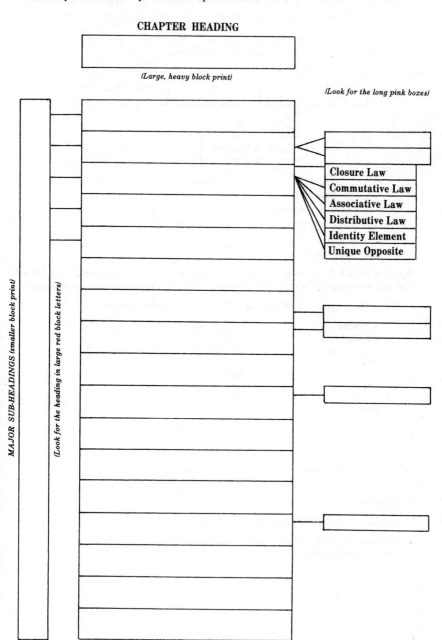

MAJOR SUB-HEADINGS *(smaller block print)*

(Look for the heading in large red block letters)

Closure Law
Commutative Law
Associative Law
Distributive Law
Identity Element
Unique Opposite

Exercise 2: Structured Overview

Discuss what you have read in Chapter 15 and complete this Structured Overview.

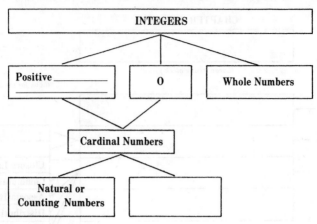

Exercise 3: Vocabulary

Integers are *whole numbers* and their *opposites*. Each integer can be matched by one and only one *opposite* integer. For example, 7 and – 7. This is called a *unique* opposite.

1. Match these opposites by writing in the correct word or number.

addition	*subtraction*
....	credit
....	white
girl	....
....	man
positive	....
....	south
east	....
12	....
– 7	....
....	– 4
True	....
above sea level	.... sea level
....	deposit

2. Complete this statement.

.... is neither negative or positive.

3. The opposite of 9km south would be ....
Show this on a number line.

Appendix

Exercise 4: Thinking Through: Addition of Integers

1. *Three-Level Guide*
   Simplify this expression: $6 + {}^-9$

Literal	Applied	Interpretive	
Add $6 + {}^-9$	(a) 15	Start at 6.	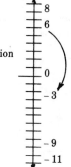
	(b) ${}^-3$	Take 9	
	(c) ${}^-15$	steps in a	
	(d) 3	negative direction	

Answer: $6 + {}^-9$
$= {}^-3$

2. *Cloze Exercise*
   Arno had $6 but he wanted to buy a record worth $9. He decided to .... some money from his mother, which meant that he .... her $3. In other words, he was in debt for ....

3. *Extracting and Organizing Information*

Arno has   Arno wants

Positive		Negative
6	+	${}^-9$

MAIN IDEA: Arno will have a debt of $3.
That is ${}^-3$
$6 + {}^-9 = {}^-3$

RULE:

Given		$6 + {}^-9$
Forget signs		6 9
Take smaller number from larger number		3
Put sign from in front of larger number in front of answer		${}^-3$

4. *Three-Level Guide*
   Simplify this expression: ${}^-8 + 3$

Literal	Applied	Interpretive
(Facts)	*(Answer)*	*(Number Line)*

5. *Cloze Exercise*

Arno had $ ...., but he wanted to buy a .... worth $ ....,
(1)   (2)   (3)
so he decided to .... some .... from ...., which meant
(4)   (5)   (6)
that he .... her .... In other words, he was in debt for ....
(7)   (8)   (9)

6. *Extracting and Organizing Information*

Arno has   **Arno wants**

....

MAIN IDEA: Arno will have a debt of ....

That is [ ]   integer

[ ] + ⬠ = ◺

RULE: Adding Integers

Given ⟶ [ ]

Forget .... ⟶ [ ][ ]

Put sign from in front of .... ⟶ [ ]

number in front of .... ⟶

7. *Three-Level Guide*

Simplify this expression: $-4 + 9$

Literal   **Applied**   **Interpretive**

8. *Cloze Exercise*

Arno had ...., and went out to buy a .... worth .... This
(1)   (2)   (3)
meant that he only had .... left. At least he wasn't in ....
(4)   (5)

9. *Extracting and Organizing Information*

Arno has   **Arno wants**

....

MAIN IDEA: Arno will have a credit of ....

That is ☐ integer

☐ + ◇ = △

RULE:

Given ——► ☐

Forget .... ——► ☐   ☐

Put sign from in front of
.... number in front of
.... ——► ☐

Exercise 5: Thinking Through: Multiplication and Division of Integers

1. *Three-Level Guide:* Simplify 4×-2

Literal	Applied	Interpretive
(Facts)	*(Answer)*	*(Working)*
Multiply -2 by 4	(a) -8	
	(b) 8	
	(c) 2	
	(d) -2	

$-8 -6 -4 -2 \quad 0$

Taking 2 steps at a time in a negative direction, make 4 loops. That is 4 lots of -2.

2. *Cloze Exercise*

Ben had a hole in his pocket, and his loose change fell out. First he lost 2 cents, then another .... (1), then another 2 cents, then another .... (2) Altogether he lost .... (3) lots of .... (4) This meant that he was short of .... (5)

3. *Extracting and Organizing Information*

LOST

4 lots of ☐

$= 4 \times$ ☐ integer

$=$ ☐ integer answer

MAIN IDEA: Ben lost 2c.
or .... integer

That is $4 \times -2 =$ ☐

RULE: *Unlike* integers give a *negative answer*.

$+$ ☐ $\times -$ ☐ $= -$ ☐

4. *Three-Level Guide*: Simplify -4×-2

Literal	Applied	Interpretive

Multiply -2 by -4

(a)   6
(b)   8
(c) -8
(d) -6

Positive 4 by Negative 2 means you take 2 steps at a time in a negative direction and make 4 loops. That is, 4 lots of -2.

$-8 -6 -4 -2 \quad 0$

THEREFORE
Negative 4 by Negative 2 means that your loops are *reversed*. That is, go in the opposite direction.

$0 \quad 2 \quad 4 \quad 6 \quad 8$

That is, -4 lots of -2 equals 8
Remember "negative" means "the opposite of" here.

5. *Cloze Exercise*

$4 \times -2 = \boxed{}$ and $a \times -b = \boxed{}$

$-2 \times \boxed{} = -8$ $\qquad -a \times b = \boxed{}$

$-2 \times -4 = \boxed{}$ $\qquad -a \times -\boxed{} = ab$

$2 + -4 = \boxed{}$

$-2 + -4 = \triangle$

$-4 + 2 = \triangle$

6. *Extracting and Organizing Information*

Complete this multiplication table.

$\times$	-5	-4	-3	-2	-1	0	1	2
-5								
-4								
-3		A				B		
-2								
-1								
0								
1								
2				C				D

Appendix

Now complete these exercises.

BOX A = ▭ × △ = ⬠

That is, 2 .... give a ....

BOX B = ▭ × ⬠ = △

That is, an integer multiplied by zero gives ....

BOX C = ▭ × ⬠ = △

That is, a negative by a .... gives a ....

BOX D = ▭ × ▭ = △

That is, a .... by a .... gives a ....

RULE: .... gives .... ($-a \times b = -ab$)
.... gives .... ($-a \times -b = ab$)

(unlike, like, positive, negative)

7. *Three-Level Guide*: Simplify $-6 - 3$

Literal	Applied *(possibilities)*	Interpretive
	(a)	
	(b)	
	(c)	
	(d)	

8. *Cloze Exercise*

Arno owed $ ....(1)............. He decided to pay back equal amounts over a period of 3 weeks. The first week he paid ....(2)............., the second ....(3)............., and the third ....(4)............. That is, each week his ....(5)............. was ....(6)............., shown by the integer ....(7).............

9. *Extracting and Organizing Information*

DEBT

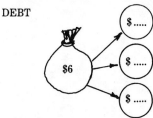

$3 \times$ ▭
Debt

RULE: Unlike gives .... ($-6 \div 3 = -2$)
$$-a \div b = \frac{-a}{b}$$

227

Exercise 6: Translating

Write a story about Arno's finances (his money) assuming that he started off with
nothing (at zero). Use the number of jumps on the number line as a guide.

Write a number sentence to match this diagram also.

Now do the same for Ben, but note that Ben starts off with $3.

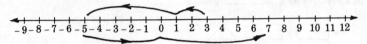

Who ended up with more money, Arno or Ben?
What was the difference?
Who showed he was in debt?

Exercise 7: Consolidation

Fill in the spaces.

(a) a + –b .... (same integers, different integers)

(b) 6 + –7 =   1

(c) –6 + –5 $\boxed{}$ 6 + 5   (<, >)

(d) 14 + 0 $\boxed{}$ – 14 + 0   (= , ≠)

(e) –a × –b = $\boxed{}$
like gives ....

(f) $\boxed{}$ × –2 = 6

(g) –4 × 4 = $\boxed{}$

(h) 16 + –16 = $\boxed{}$

(i) $\boxed{}$ × $\boxed{}$ = 6

(j) +7 – 6 = $\boxed{}$

(k) –3 + 4 = $\boxed{}$ + △

(l) Which of the following are integers?
$2\frac{1}{4}$, –2, 0, 4, –3, $\frac{1}{3}$, 119

(m) The opposite of 19 is ....
The opposite of – 2 is ....
The opposite of – 9 is ....

(n) 16 + $\boxed{}$ = △

(o) 0 × –1 = –1 × $\boxed{}$

Appendix

Exercise 8: Preparation Vocabulary

Match these laws to the given expressions.

Associative, Commutative, Distributive, Closure, identity element, unique opposite, multiplying by zero.

$2(6+3) = (2 \times 6) + (2 \times 3)$	....
$4 + {-4} = 0$	....
$4 + 2 + 2 + 4$	....
$a \times 1 = a$	....
$0 + 7 = 13$	....
$b + 0 = b$	....
$16 \times 0 = 116$	....
$(3 + 16) + 9 = 3 + (16 + 9)$	....
$19 \times {-16} = {-16} \times 19$	....

Exercise 9: Thinking Through: Distributive Law (Group B)

Vocabulary

No. of apples = ...   No. of apples = ...

That is, 3 apples   + 2 apples   = ⬚ apples

3 common factor + 2 common factor = ⬚ common factor

That is,
3 a	+ 2 a	= 5a
3a	+ 2a	= (3 + 2)a
3 lots of apples	+ 2 lots of apples	= (3 + 2) lots of apples

This is the *Distributive Law*, and in it the apples make the *common factor*.

Let's try this in another way.
Using b(2 + 4) where b can be bananas.   b(2 + 4)

or (2 + 4)b

(2 + 4) lots of bananas

Break up the boxes.

Draw in the *common factor*.

That is, 2 b + 4 b = (2 + 4)b
In the side 2b + 4b the .... is the common factor, spread out over the 2 and the 4. That is, it is distributed.
Try this.
3   + 3   = (3 + 3)
Write in your own *common factor*.
This can be written as:

3 + 3 = (3 + 3)
or (3 + 3) = 3 + 3

This is the *Distributive Law*.

UNIT 5: Home Economics

SUBJECT : Home Economics
YEAR : 10
TOPIC A : Consumer Affairs
SOURCE : Maclean and Lawrence, *You the Consumer*

WEEK	TOPIC	DAY 1	DAY 2	DAY 3	DAY 4	DAY 5
1	Consumer Affairs	Present Structured Overview class discussion. Ex.1, Ex.2. Vocabulary	Ex.3. Graphic Outline	Ex. 4. Thinking Through Information: Three-Level Guide	Ex.5. Cloze Exercise Ex.6. Extracting and Organizing Information: Cash and Credit (as independent study)	Discuss Ex.6.
2	Consumer Affairs	Ex.8. Extracting and Organizing Information: Hire Purchase. Ex.9. Independent Study Exercise: Surveying Credit Services	Ex.10. Translating Information: Kinds of Credit Facilities	Continue Ex.10.	Review, Reporting on, and Discussion of Ex.9.	
3	Buying and Selling: Selling Techniques.	Ex.11. Structured Overview introduction. Ex.12. Vocabulary	Ex.13. Thinking Through Information: Three-Level Guide	Continue Ex.13.	Ex.14. Extracting and Organizing Information: Advertising	Continue Ex.14: Discussion.
4	Consumer Rights and Responsibilities	Ex.15. Extracting and Organizing Information: Handling Complaints	Ex.16. Translating Information: Handling Complaints	Continue Ex.16.	Ex.17. Translating Information: Consumer Protection Campaign	Continue Ex.17.

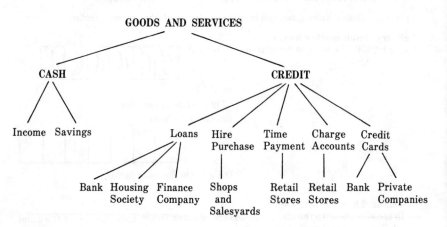

Exercise 1: Vocabulary

Initially, this is an independent study exercise.
Some new words for this topic appear in dark print.
To find their meanings, read around the following words or phrases as they appear in the text.

In your own words, write down what you think their meanings are. Compare your answers with those of a partner, and also with a dictionary meaning. In pairs or small groups, try to work out the wording for your definition so that everyone is satisfied.

Appendix

Word/Phrase	Page	Your Meaning	Negotiated, Agreed Meaning
exchange	41	....	....
medium of exchange	41	....	....
barter	42	....	....
money	43	....	....
cash	44	....	....
credit	45	....	....
hire purchase	46	....	....
charge account	46	....	....
credit rating	47	....	....

Enter your agreed meanings into a glossary or wordbank.

Exercise 2: Vocabulary

The word "consumer" is used quite often in this chapter. Here are some of the sentences in which it appears.

- "When a *consumer* pays for an article purchased, he normally has the choice of either paying for it out of his savings and immediate income or paying for it through the use of credit." (p. 44)
- ". . . the *consumer* pays for the goods when he obtains them. . . ." (p. 44)
- "*Consumers* who purchase goods on credit usually have to pay some form of interest payment. . . ." (p. 44)
- ". . . all the goods and services purchased by *consumers* were paid for in cash." (p. 45)

From the clues in the above sentences, write a definition of a *consumer*.

Learning to Learn from Text

Exercise 3: Graphic Outline

Complete the chart below by filling in the boxes according to the type of headings and features used in the text.

Chapter 6: Paying.

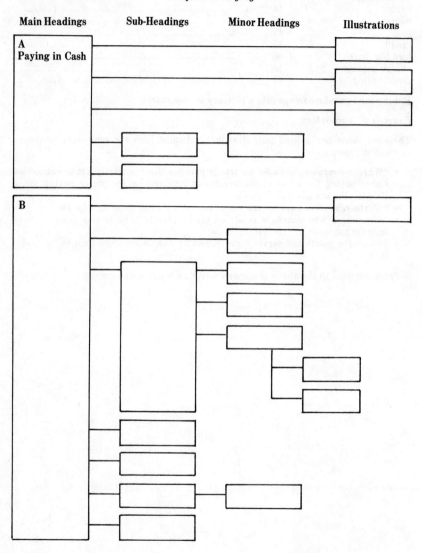

Learning to Learn from Text

Exercise 4: Thinking Through Information

Read through the section "Paying through the Use of Credit", pp. 45-46, then read the statements below. You may refer back to the text as many times as you like to check what is said.

Tick those statements which you think mean what the authors have said. The wording may be different, but decide whether the information is the same as what the authors wrote. Think of reasons to support your choices.

LEVEL 1: LITERAL LEVEL

_____ 1. In past times, people always paid cash for goods and services.

_____ 2. A credit purchase means you agree to pay for goods at a later, or by a particular date.

_____ 3. Credit is convenient, costly, and helps you balance your budget.

_____ 4. People save for goods so they can live within their budget.

_____ 5. Credit is of great use to the average family.

Now compare your responses with a partner. Do you agree with each other? *Discuss why or why not.*

LEVEL 2: INTERPRETIVE LEVEL

Tick those statements which match with what you think the authors meant, but did not say. What reasons can you give for your answers?

_____ 1. People who use credit are impatient because they don't earn enough money to buy goods they need.

_____ 2. Twentieth century consumers live beyond their means.

_____ 3. Interest charges increase the value of goods bought on credit.

_____ 4. Why save for an item when you can buy it now, on credit?

_____ 5. You must be cautious when deciding to use credit.

LEVEL 3: APPLIED LEVEL

Tick those statements which you think sum up or can be concluded from the text. Why would the authors agree with your choices?

_____ 1. "Buy now, pay later" is an alternative heading for this section.

_____ 2. You can't have your cake and eat it too.

_____ 3. "Charge it" is the modern way of spending.

_____ 4. It would be easy for people who don't budget well to get into debt when buying on credit.

_____ 5. "Penny wise, pound foolish" is a motto for people who use credit rather than their savings to buy luxuries.

Compare your responses with those of your partner. Did you agree or disagree? *Discuss why or why not.* What reasons do you have for your choices?

Exercise 5: Thinking Through Information

Read the passage below and fill in the missing words by reading around the blanks. For every blank, there are clues in the passage to help you. Circle the clues in red pen and link them to the relevant blanks. The first one is done for you.

Credit is very common today and it's easy to get! But you don't get credit just by (1) asking for it. Before you qualify for credit, you need to be able to prove that you can pay for it. This is called having the "........... to ....". If you earn $210 per week, pay out (2)   (3) $160 on expenses (rent, food, clothing, petrol, household bills) and want to buy a house

233

which costs $38,000, you have only $50 per week to .... a loan. That's $200 per month.
If repayments are $240 per month, you don't have the ability to meet them. The ability
to pay is very important when asking for credit.

People who have a record of not meeting their .... are called "bad risks". Firms,
banks, and companies which let purchasers use credit can check on debtors through a
list of consumers who in the past have not kept up repayments. A car buyer, who used
hire purchase facilities and did not maintain payments so that his car was repossessed
by the finance company who lent him the money to buy the car, would have his name
listed as a .... If that purchaser at a later date asked for credit to buy a refrigerator,
he may find that he is .... credit.

Your .... is important when asking for credit. If you are unemployed, and
unreliable and have a history of untrustworthiness, you are more likely to be refused
credit than if you have steady employment, and are reliable and trustworthy. .... is
the basis for giving credit, and if there is doubt about how trustworthy you are, a company may ask for a character reference before giving you credit.

'Secured loans' are those which require you to "hand over" to the finance company
or bank something of value that you own. It might be the title to your house or some
land. Secured loans show that you are willing to meet the company's loan .... to pay
it back. It is a sign of the purchaser's .... and .... credit
obligations.

Now give the passage a heading, and explain why you chose that particular one. In
small groups, discuss and compare your responses.

Exercise 6: Extracting and Organizing Information

Re-read the sections on "Advantages of Paying for Goods in Cash", pp. 44-45, and
"Advantages of Using Credit", p. 47. See if you can counter the advantages of each with
some disadvantages. The text will help you. In groups and using your own words, complete the chart below in numbered point form.

SYSTEM	ADVANTAGES	DISADVANTAGES
Cash	1. .... 2. .... 3. .... 4. .... 5.	1. .... 2. .... 3. .... 4. .... 5. ....
Credit	1. .... 2. .... 3. .... 4. .... 5.	1. .... 2. .... 3. .... 4. .... 5. ....

Exercise 7: Extracting and Organizing Information

Read pp. 46-7, "What Are the Different Types of Credit Available to the consumer?"
Using the headings in the text as a guide, complete the following flow chart.

Appendix

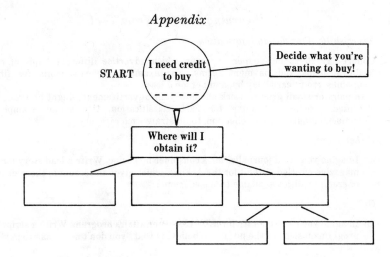

Exercise 8: Extracting and Organizing Information

Focus on the passage headed HIRE PURCHASE on p. 46. Read the passage carefully, reading for the detail of how to go about purchasing goods using the hire purchase method. Complete the flow chart below to clearly show the steps involved.

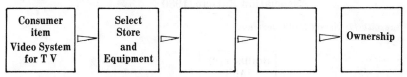

Exercise 9: Organizing Information

Conduct a survey of your family, friends, and newspaper and magazine advertisements to find out what credit services — other than those mentioned in the text — are available to consumers.

Maintain a file of information, and enter your findings on the chart below.

TYPE OF CREDIT	JOINING FEE	INTEREST RATE p.a.	RESTRICTIONS ON USE	WHERE HONOURED
Bankcard				
American Express				
Diners Club				
Store Account				
Other				

Exercise 10: Translating Information

Collect say 10-12 newspaper clippings which advertise different kinds of credit facilities, loans and payment terms. For example, advertisements for finance companies, credit cards, lay-by, and personal loans.

In pairs or small groups, work out how your advertisements might be grouped or classified. Create a heading for each classification. Use actual examples of advertisements from your collection, to illustrate each category.

Either

(a) Imagine you are a journalist for a consumer magazine. Write a lead story for your magazine entitled "Credit for the Asking" which gives an account of the wide range of credit facilities available to the consumer.

Or

(b) Imagine you're a reporter for a TV consumer affairs program. Write a script for a program on some of the pitfalls of believing that "you don't need cash to pay".

TOPIC B : Buying and Selling
SOURCES : • *This Is No Way to Handle a Complaint*
     • *Take One ... It's Free*, Queensland Consumer Association Bureau, 1980

Exercise 11: Structured Overview

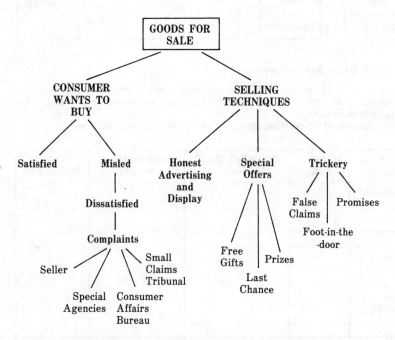

As you progress through this unit, add to this overview of the topic.

236

Exercise 12: — Vocabulary Preparation

The two pamphlets use the words listed below. Find them in the text. If there is a clue to their meaning in the text, tick the word and write out the text clue. Remember to read around the word. If there is no text clue, use a dictionary to check the meaning of the word and then write your own definition.

SOURCE: *This Is No Way to Handle a Complaint*

WORD	CLUE IN TEXT	YOUR MEANING
contractor liability claim rectified transaction		

SOURCE: *Take One ... It's Free*

WORD	CLUE IN TEXT	YOUR MEANING
bonus manufacturer guarantee pyramid selling		

TOPIC C: Consumerism — Selling Techniques

Exercise 13: Thinking Through

Read the pamphlet *Take One ... It's Free*. Now read the statements below.

LEVEL 1: LITERAL LEVEL

Tick the statements which appear in the text. Although the wording may be different, it must mean the same thing as is said in the pamphlet. Be ready, to defend your choices by quoting from the text.

_____ 1. Car dealers are unethical.
_____ 2. Don't post money to a mail order firm.
_____ 3. Before you sign or buy something, find out how much it's all going to cost you.
_____ 4. For every buyer, there's someone making a profit.

LEVEL 2: INTERPRETIVE LEVEL

Tick those statements which mean the same as what the author wrote but did not actually say. Be ready to justify your choices.

_____ 1. Dealers advertise falsely to get you interested.
_____ 2. Mail order firms hide their true identity behind a post office box.
_____ 3. It's up to you as to whether or not you buy because of a free gift offer.
_____ 4. Selling is a profitable business.

LEVEL 3: APPLIED LEVEL

Tick those statements which can be concluded from a reading of the pamphlet. You can draw on information in the text and your own experience to provide reasons for your choices.

_____ 1. Behind every good deal there's a catch.
_____ 2. Mail order firms take your money and run.
_____ 3. Nothing of value is free.
_____ 4. A fool and his money are soon parted.

Exercise 14: Extracting and Organizing Information

SOURCES: • *Take One ... It's Free*
         • Student collected advertisements.

Collect a range of newspaper advertisements which use *gimmicks* to promote goods or services. For example, something offered free as a bonus, or the product offered at a discount or on special terms.

Read your collected advertisements to *compare* them with the examples used in the pamphlet. Using the pamphlet headings, *classify* examples from your own collection.

Now re-read each newspaper advertisement for small print *details*. Make notes under the following headings. Some points will be made in the text, but you'll need to work out other points for yourself.

Advertisement	"Eyecatcher" offer	Details of offer	Small print conditions	What a buyer needs to ask before buying
Buy a colour T V on terms and receive a bonus backgammon set				• Do I need the bonus? • What's the bonus worth? • How long will it take me to own the T V?

TOPIC D: Consumer Rights and Responsibilities

Exercise 15: Extracting and Organizing Information

SOURCE: *This Is No Way to Handle a Complaint*

Appendix

Read the pamphlet to find out what steps you, the consumer, can take to complain about faulty goods or services.

Using the information in the pamphlet, complete the following flow chart.

LODGING A COMPLAINT

START

PROBLEM: Your newly painted house has cracks appearing in the paintwork. There is a 5 year guarantee on paint and workmanship.

Personal or phone complaint

NO

NO — Action refused — NO — OR

Small Claims Tribunal

This diagram shows one way of displaying the steps to take if you want to lodge a complaint. Try to improve upon its clarity by drawing a flow chart of your own. Remember that you need to show all steps and any alternative actions that you can take.

TOPIC E: Consumer be Wary

Exercise 16: Translating Information

I am 75 and I sent away for an ornament for a gift for my daughter. I have been waiting for this parcel since February last year. I know quite a few people have received the same ornaments. Perhaps they have been delayed because of a heavy demand — Mrs N, Brisbane

Sadly for you the firm is in liquidation and your money has gone. Write to Mr D. Johnson, Johnson, Porter and Co, 99A Pitt St., Sydney, and he will list your name. You may receive some compensation after all outstanding debts have been paid.

I sent away for some goods last May but did not receive them. I wrote and the firm promised me a refund. I am still waiting for it. What are my chances? — Mrs J, Sydney.

Your chances are non-existent as the firm has no listing. It could be one of those companies using the same telephone numbers as those firms that have gone into liquidation. There is no way of finding out. I'm afraid your $40 is well and truly down the plughole.

There are many ways you can complain about bad goods and services. These consumers wrote to a weekly newspaper column for advice.

Complaints may be made to a number of different organizations. Some of these are listed under Consumer Protection Agencies in the pamphlet *This Is No Way to Handle a Complaint.*

Learning to Learn from Text

1. Choose a consumer role for yourself.

   - A child who's bought a 500g packet of potato crips and found it to be only half full.
   - A home owner whose new verandah has 'sunk'.
   - A doctor whose patients are suffering food poisoning following the purchase of tinned salmon.
   - A householder whose gas bill is twice as high as that of last quarter.
   - A secondhand car buyer who finds the vehicle's roadworthiness certificate is a fake.
   - A secretary whose uniform is returned uncleaned from the drycleaners.
   - A buyer of a secondhand TV set who gets electric shocks everytime she turns to a particular channel.
   - A hire-purchaser of a refrigerator who thinks he's being charged too much interest.
   - A housewife who claims her delivered bread is always stale.
   - A person who bought a motorcycle on hire purchase, missed a few payments because he was sick, has received a repossession notice, and can't afford to pay for legal advice.

2. From the list of consumer agencies provided in the pamphlet, select the most appropriate one to contact to complain about your situation.

3. Write a letter of complaint, setting out the following information.

   (a) Your address and date of correspondence.
   (b) Details of purchase or service, including name and address of proprietor, date of service, and cost if applicable.
   (c) Nature of the complaint.
   (d) Action you've taken to resolve the problem.
   (e) Advice or action you would like from the agency.

4. Send your letter to a classmate who plays the role of Officer-in-Charge of the relevant agency. Have him or her draft a reply, commenting on your complaint. For example, he or she might ask for more details about one aspect of your complaint, or for evidence that you have tried to gain satisfaction from the company concerned.

5. Discuss letters and replies in small groups. How effective is the letter of complaint? How helpful is the reply?

6. Invite a representative of one of the agencies to talk to your class. Ask him or her to react to your letters.

Exercise 17: Translating Information

SOURCES: • *What's the Catch?* handout from Exercise 14.
           • Student collected advertisements

As preparation, students will need to have collected a series of advertisements making "good offers" from newspapers, magazines and the like. These should be mounted on suitable paper to be included as illustrative material in a class publication.

Work in pairs or small groups, so that you can discuss and exchange information and ideas, and can negotiate and plan an appropriate format for your end product.

WHAT TO DO

1. Use *What's the Catch?*, your notes, and collected advertisements as your main sources of information to conduct a consumer protection campaign against doubtful advertising claims. You might also conduct some interviews to add to your store of information.

2. Think and talk about the following before you begin to plan your campaign.

   (a) What will be the campaign's message?

Appendix

(b) Who will it be addressed to — housewives, children, or business people?

(c) What forms will it take — poster, handbill, letters to the editor/householder, newspaper reports, TV news item, documentary or current affairs segment, full page advertisement in daily newspaper or weekly magazine, or a jingle for a "commercial"?

(d) What information will you include — reproductions of actual advertisements, records of interview with advertisers, your own opinions, the opinions of others, or consumers who might have been "taken in"?

(e) Remember too, that you'll need to plan how you will organize your materials into a campaign kit, so that you end up with a package which can be distributed for others to read, listen to, or watch.

3. Now sift through your information, selecting examples which best illustrate your message.

4. In pairs or groups, assign writing tasks. The aim is to draft a range of different kinds of writing to get your message across to different kinds of audiences.

5. Share your draft writing and review each other's work. Be helpful and make suggestions for alterations to improve the impact of the message.

6. Redraft, using others' suggestions, then edit for spelling, punctuation, and "good English".

7. Together with your illustrations, advertisements, and so on, publish your campaign kit in a form which can be used by students in other classes.

UNIT 6: English

SUBJECT : English
YEARS : 11 and 12
TOPIC : Poetry
SOURCE : *Mainly Modern, This World*, or an appropriate Text

PRELIMINARY WORK: Have students bring in their favourite poems for day one.

WEEK	DAY 1	DAY 2	DAY 3	DAY 4	DAY 5
1	1. Selections of poetry read aloud in class by students and teacher. 2. Introduction to poetry by looking at the Structured Overview, ALL POEMS HAVE. 3. Handout sheet to be completed as independent study.	1. Discuss independent activity work. 2. Review and discuss the previous lesson. 3. Read *The Death of The Bird*. 4. Students to complete cloze exercises. (Thinking Through)	1. Discuss and "correct" cloze exercises. 2. Oral discussions of poem.	1. Read *The Night of the Moths*. 2. Individually, students complete the Three-Level Guide (Thinking Through) 3. Discuss responses to the Three-Level Guide.	1. Complete and discuss responses to exercises A and B on *Men in Green* (Extracting and Organizing Information) 2. Discuss poem. 3. If possible role play the two groups.
2	1. Complete and discuss responses to exercises A,B, and C on *The Surfer*. (Extracting and Organizing Information.)	1. Students *Own Choice Poem* 2. Students choose poem and complete the outline sheet. (Consolidation of work done, especially Structured Overview ideas.) 3. Individual oral poetry reports.	*The unit may be continued if desired with further poems and activities.*		

Appendix

STRUCTURED OVERVIEW:
   All Poems Have

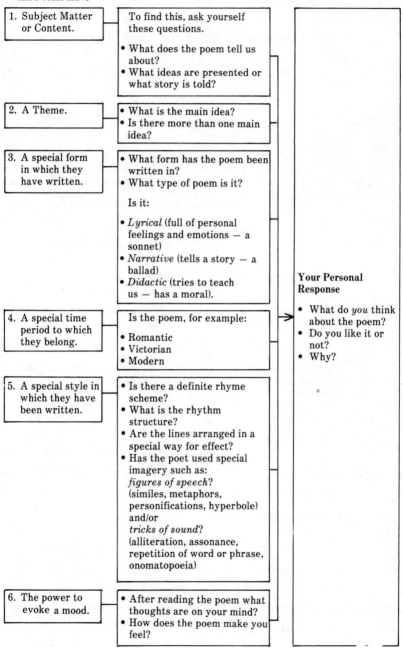

1. Subject Matter or Content.	To find this, ask yourself these questions. • What does the poem tell us about? • What ideas are presented or what story is told?	
2. A Theme.	• What is the main idea? • Is there more than one main idea?	
3. A special form in which they have written.	• What form has the poem been written in? • What type of poem is it? Is it: • *Lyrical* (full of personal feelings and emotions — a sonnet) • *Narrative* (tells a story — a ballad) • *Didactic* (tries to teach us — has a moral).	**Your Personal Response** • What do *you* think about the poem? • Do you like it or not? • Why?
4. A special time period to which they belong.	Is the poem, for example: • Romantic • Victorian • Modern	
5. A special style in which they have been written.	• Is there a definite rhyme scheme? • What is the rhythm structure? • Are the lines arranged in a special way for effect? • Has the poet used special imagery such as: *figures of speech*? (similes, metaphors, personifications, hyperbole) and/or *tricks of sound*? (alliteration, assonance, repetition of word or phrase, onomatopoeia)	
6. The power to evoke a mood.	• After reading the poem what thoughts are on your mind? • How does the poem make you feel?	

Learning to Learn from Text

POETRY: Independent Exercise

Fill in the blank spaces, selecting words from the list below.

Poetry roughly divides into two sections.

Poems of action or story: .... verse.	Words to Choose from word or phrase repetition simile lyrical ballad alliteration metaphor narrative assonance sonnet onomatopoeia personification hyperbole	Poems of thought and feeling: .... verse.
This is the earliest type of narrative poem, simple in language, often with a refrain, always with a definite rhythm and rhyme to help recitation. This narrative type of poem is known as the		This lyrical form has proved most popular in English verse. It contains fourteen lines with a distinctive rhyme scheme. This lyrical form is known as the ....

All poems can contain

Figures of speech such as:	Devices (tricks) of sound such as:
(a) .... — a comparison beginning with 'like' or 'as'.	(a) .... — for emphasis of ideas or feelings.
(b) .... — a comparison, without 'like' or 'as', in which one thing is said to be another.	(b) .... — the deliberate repetition of consonants. It may occur anywhere in the words and often helps to suggest mood or tone.
(c) .... — the giving of human qualities to non-human things.	(c) .... — the deliberate repetition of identical or similar vowel sounds.
(d) .... — deliberate exaggeration for dramatic effect.	(d) .... — the use of words whose sounds resemble the sounds they describe. For example, hiss.

DAY 2/DAY 3

FOCUS: Some Modern Poetry

The Death of the Bird

A.D. Hope (1907-   )

Page 294, *Mainly Modern*
Page 62, *This World*

After reading this poem, complete the following by providing words for the blank spaces. When you have finished, discuss your "answers" with someone, compare your work, and change or add anything you want. Your teacher will then go through the passages.

Appendix

1. Subject Matter or Content

The first .... stanzas tell us about one ...., frail bird being stirred by the mating .... Each year, mysteriously, this instinct asks her to .... far away to .... her nest and feed her .... Without question, this .... bird follows her .... path.

The last .... stanzas deal with her approaching .... when 'the guiding spark of instinct winks and dies'. The .... and .... become a vast .... and she feels lost. Finally, she can't .... the darkness and .... anymore. Inevitably, she .... and .... to the earth.

2. The Theme

The restlessness of the bird symbolizes the .... of the human spirit which is always seeking something until .... The poem deals with this vital life-force which is present in every .... thing.

3. Type of Poem

The poem tells a story. It is, therefore, a .... poem.

4. Time Period

The Death of the Bird can be thought of as an example of early modern Australian poetry. When was it probably written?

....

5. Style in which the Poem Has Been Written

The poem is ordered or regular in form. Each of the .... stanzas has .... lines of fairly .... length.

Every stanza has the same rhyme scheme — (a) (b) (a) (b) ....

(Stanza One)	last migration	(.................)
	her heart	(.................)
	summer station	(.................)
	across the chest	(.................)

The poet's use of figures of speech is limited but .... He makes no use of similes and very limited use of metaphors. One metaphor might be "*lost in the blue unfriendliness of space*". The word "sky" could be used instead of the underlined words; this means that it is a direct comparison. One .... he does effectively make use of, is personification; "*a speck on the map summons her to come*". A good example in the last stanza is ....

....

With regard to tricks of sound, A.D. Hope mainly uses alliteration and assonance. The second line of the poem gives us an example of his use of ...., while the third line shows his use of ....

6. Mood or Atmosphere

After reading the poem, I felt .... because ....

7. Your Personal Response

A.D. Hope's *Death of the Bird*, ... effective because ....

....

DAY 4

The Night of the Moths

Douglas Stewart (1913-   )

Page 295, *Mainly Modern*
Page 65, *This World*

- *On your own*, read through the poem and complete the following Three-Level Guide as directed.
- *In a small group*, compare your responses, exchange reasons, and discuss choices.
- *As a class*, share your ideas with your teacher.

Three-Level Guide: The Night of the Moths

LEVEL 1: LITERAL LEVEL

Tick the statements which *say* what the poet says in his poem. Be prepared to justify your choices.

_____ 1. The giant moths are like sparrows.
_____ 2. It is midnight.
_____ 3. Most of the moths die in the storm.
_____ 4. The black mass of moths blends in with the storm and trees and the mountain.
_____ 5. The moths are like a swarm of bees.

LEVEL 2: INTERPRETIVE LEVEL

Tick the statements which you think *mean* what the poet meant in his poem. Be prepared to justify your choices.

_____ 1. The moths are born into a loving world.
_____ 2. The world tries to crush the moths back into the earth at the same time as it flings them forth.
_____ 3. The moths that survive do so only to fly out of sight and die.
_____ 4. The atmosphere is oppressive, dark and troubled.
_____ 5. Every living things' struggle for life is noticed and seen by most people.

LEVEL 3: APPLIED LEVEL

Tick the statements which you think the *poet would agree with or support*. Be ready to give your reasons when you discuss your choices.

_____ 1. The theme of this poem does more than just tell us something about moths.
_____ 2. All living things are important.
_____ 3. Life does not have to involve struggle for survival.
_____ 4. No-one should lose contact with nature.
_____ 5. The Australian bush is the home of many fascinating things.

DAY 5

Men in Green

David Campbell (1915-   )

Page 56, *Mainly Modern*
Page 117, *The World*

Appendix

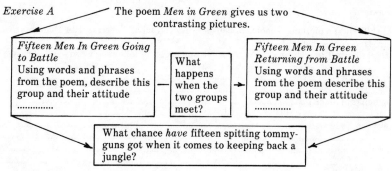

Exercise A — The poem *Men in Green* gives us two contrasting pictures.

Fifteen Men In Green Going to Battle
Using words and phrases from the poem, describe this group and their attitude
....

What happens when the two groups meet?

Fifteen Men In Green Returning from Battle
Using words and phrases from the poem describe this group and their attitude
....

What chance *have* fifteen spitting tommy-guns got when it comes to keeping back a jungle?

Exercise B

Words are a poet's only tools. Campbell uses his words very carefully to create vivid pictures for us. *Men in Green* abounds in figurative language. Campbell has used similes and metaphors, in particular, to achieve added effect.

List every simile and metaphor that you can find and draw pictures to show the two things being compared in each of them.

DAY 6

The Surfer

Judith Wright (1915-   )

Page 22, *Mainly Modern*
Page 101, *This World*

Exercise A

Read through the poem carefully and complete the following by using words and phrases from the poem where possible.

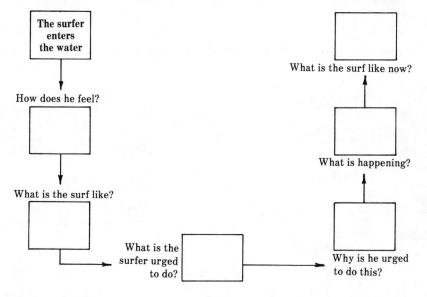

The surfer enters the water

How does he feel?

What is the surf like?

What is the surfer urged to do?

What is the surf like now?

What is happening?

Why is he urged to do this?

247

Learning to Learn from Text

Exercise B

Judith Wright's diction — choice of words — is original and precise. Her thoughts are expressed very effectively.

Explain what you think she means when she uses the following words and phrases:

thrust his joy: ....
....

long banks of foam: ....
....

hawthorn hedges: ....
....

brown strength: ....
....

hollow and coil: ....
....

weirs of water: ....
....

long muscle of water: ....
....

leaf of gold: ....
....

shoulder: ....
....

grey-wolf sea: ....
....

splits the waves' hair: ....
....

the bones: ....
....

sea crouches on sand: ....
....

its broken toys: ....
....

Exercise C

According to the poem, is the sea our friend or our enemy, or both? Explain.

Appendix

DAY 7

Now, how much have you learnt? Choose any other poem you like and complete the following overview.

POEM: ....

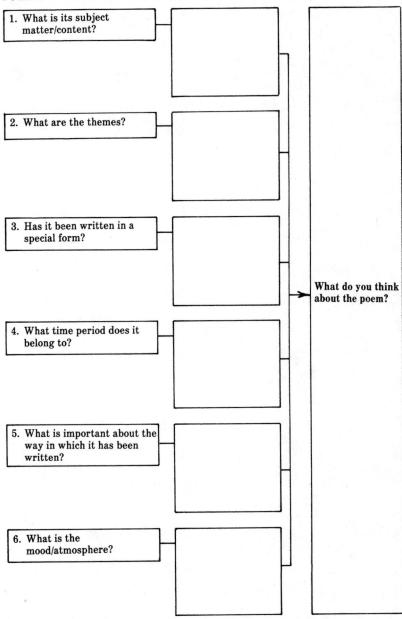

1. What is its subject matter/content?

2. What are the themes?

3. Has it been written in a special form?

4. What time period does it belong to?

5. What is important about the way in which it has been written?

6. What is the mood/atmosphere?

What do you think about the poem?

Bibliography

REFERENCES, ARTICLES AND PAPERS

ANDERSON, R.B. "Education as Experimentation: A Planned Variation Model." *Final Report (of Project Follow-Through)*. United States Office of Education, Department of Health, Education and Welfare, 1977.

ANDERSON, R.C. "The Notion of Schemata and the Educational Enterprise." in *Schooling and the Acquisition of Knowledge*. Anderson, R.C., Sprio, R.J., and Montague, W.E. (Eds.), Hillsdale, N.J., Erlbaum and Associates, 1977.

ANDERSON, R.C., and PICKERT, J.W. "Recall of Previously Unrecallable Information Following a Shift in Perspective." in *Journal of Verbal Learning and Verbal Behaviour*, vol. 17.1 1978(b), pp. 1-12.

ANDERSON, R.C., and FREEBODY, P. "Vocabulary Knowledge." in *Comprehension and Teaching: Research Reviews*. Guthrie, J.T. (Ed.), Newark, International Reading Association, 1981.

ANDERSON, R.C., SPIRO, R.J., and MONTAGUE, W.E. (Eds.). *Schooling and the Acquisition of Knowledge*. Hillsdale, N.J., Erlbaum and Associates, 1977.

ANDERSON, R.C., SPIRO, R.J., and ANDERSON, M.C. "Schemata as Scaffolding for the Representation of Information in Connected Discourse." *American Educational Research Journal*, vol. 15 (Summer 1978(a)), pp. 433-440.

APPLEBEE, A.N. "Writing and Reading." *Journal of Reading*, vol. 20 (April 1977).

AUKERMAN, R.C. *Reading in the Secondary School Classroom*. New York, N.Y., McGraw Hill Inc., 1972.

AUSUBEL, D.P. "The Use of Advance Organizers in the Learning and Retention of Meaningful Verbal Material." *Journal of Educational Psychology*, vol. 63 (1960), pp. 267-272.

AUSUBEL, D.P. *The Psychology of Meaningful Verbal Learning*. New York, N.Y., Grune and Stratten, 1963.

AUSUBEL, D.P., and ANDERSON, R. *Readings in the Psychology of Cognition*. New York, N.Y., Holt, Rinehart and Winston, 1965.

BAKER, L., and STEIN, N. "The Development of Prose Comprehension Skills." in *Children's Prose Comprehension: Research and Practice*. Santa C.M., and Hayes, B.L., Newark, International Reading Association, 1981.

BARNES, D., BRITTON, J., and ROSEN, H. *Language, the Learner and the School*. London, Penguin, 1969.

BARNES, D. *From Communication to Curriculum*. Harmondsworth, Penguin Education, 1976.

BARRON, R.F. "Research for Classroom Teachers: Recent Developments on the Use of the Structured Overview as an Advance Organizer." in *Research in Reading in Content Areas: Fourth Year Report*. Herber, H.L., and Riley, J.D. (Eds.), N.Y., Syracuse University, 1978.

BARTLETT, B.J. "Top-Level Structure as an Organizational Strategy for Recall of Classroom Text." (Unpublished Doctoral Dissertation), Arizona State University, 1978.

BARTLETT, B.H., TURNER, A., and MATHAMS, P. "Top-Level Structure: A Significant Relation for What Fifth Graders Remember from Classroom Text." Paper Presented at the American Educational Research Association Convention, Los Angeles, 1981.

BENNETT, B., and WALKER, A. "The Development of Writing Abilities 15-17: Research in Progress." *English in Australia*, No. 44 (June 1978), pp. 5-15.

BERGET, E. "Two Methods of Guiding the Learning of a Short Story." in *Research in Reading in Content Areas: Second Year Report*. Herber, H.L., and Barrow, R.F. (Eds.), N.Y., Syracuse University, 1973.

BERLINER, D.C. "Academic Learning Time and Reading Achievement." in *Comprehension and Teaching*: Research Reviews. Guthrie, J.T. (Ed.), Newark, International Reading Association, 1981.

BERMAN, P., and MCLAUGHLIN, M.W. "The Rand Corporation — Federal Programs Supporting Educational Change." vol. 3, *Implementing and Sustaining Innovations*. U.S.O.E., Santa Monica, California, Rand Corporation, 1978.

BOBROW, D.G., and COLLINS, A.M. (Eds.), *Representation and Understanding: Studies in Cognitive Science*. New York, N.Y., Academic Press, 1975.

BORMUTH, J.R. "Readability: A New Approach." *Reading Research Quarterly*, Spring 1966, pp. 79-131.

BRADDOCK, R., LLOYD-JONES, R., and SCHOER, L. *Research in Written Composition*. Urbana, Illinois, N.C.T.E., 1963.

BRANSFORD, J.D., and JOHNSON, M. "Contextual Prerequisites for Understanding: Some Investigations of Comprehension and Recall." *Journal of Verbal Learning and Verbal Behaviour*, vol. 11 (1972), pp. 717-726.

BRITTON, J. *Language and Learning*. London, Pelican, 1970.

BRITTON, J. "The Student's Writing." in *Explorations in Children's Writing*. Evertts, E. (Ed.), Urbana, Illinois, N.C.T.E., 1970.

BRITTON, J., BURGESS, T., MARTIN, N., McLEOD, A., and ROSEN, H. *The Development of Writing Abilities (11-18)*. London, Macmillan, 1975.

BRITTON, J. "Language and the Nature of Learning: An Individual Perspective." in *The Teaching of English, Seventy-sixth Yearbook, Part 1*. Squire, J.R. (Ed.), Chicago, N.S.S.E., University of Chicago Press, 1977.

BRUNER, J.S., GOODNOW, J.J., and AUSTEN, G.A. *A Study of Thinking*. New York, N.Y., John Wiley, 1956.

CALKINS, L. McL. "Children Learn the Writer's Craft." in *Language Arts*, February 1980.

CARRE, C. (Ed.). "Science", Number 4 in *Language, Teaching and Learning*. Torbe, M. (Gen. Ed.), London, Ward Lock Educational, 1981.

CARROLL, J.B. "Developmental Parameters of Reading Comprehension." in *Cognition, Curriculum and Comprehension*. Guthrie, J.T. (Ed.), Newark, International Reading Association, 1977, pp. 1-15.

CARROLL, J.B. "Development of Native Language Skills Beyond the Early Years." in *The Learning of Language*. Reed, E. (Ed.), New York, N.Y., Appleton-Century-Crofts, 1971.

CASHDAN, A. (Ed.). *Language, Reading and Learning*. Oxford, Blackwell, 1979.

CASSIDY, J. "Project C.A.R.E." *Teacher*, vol. 94, No. 8 (January 1977), pp. 70-72.

CASSIDY, J. "Teaching Reading and Writing — Fact and Fancy." Paper presented at Ninth World Congress on Reading, Dublin, August 1982.

CASSIRER, E. *Essay on Man*. New Haven, Conn., Yale University Press, 1944.

CRAIG, F.I.M., and Tulving, E. "Depth of Processing and the Retention of Words in Episodic Memory." *Journal of Experimental Psychology: General*. vol. 104 (1975), pp. 268-294.

DAVIS, F., and PARKER, R. *Teaching for Literacy: Reflections on the Bullock Report*. London, Ward Lock Education, 1978.

DAVIS, F.B. "Fundamental Factors of Comprehension in Reading." *Psychometrika*, vol. 9 (1944), pp. 185-197(a).

DAVIS, F.B. "Research in Comprehension in Reading." *Reading Research Quarterly*, vol. 3 (1968), pp. 499-545.

Department of Education and Science. *A Language for Life*. Report of the Committee of Inquiry, London, H.M.S.O., 1975.

DIXON, J. *Growth Through English*. Rev. ed. London, Oxford University Press, 1975.

DOAKE, D.B. "Comprehension: Reading Outcomes and Teaching Strategies." in *New Directions for Reading Teaching: Selected Proceedings of the Fifth New Zealand Conference on Reading*. Doake, D.B., and O'Rourke, B.T. (Eds.), 1976.

DOCTOROW, M., WITTROCK, M.C., and MARKS, C. "Generative Processes in Reading Comprehension." *Journal of Educational Psychology*, vol. 70 (1978), pp. 109-118.

DOOLING, D.J., and LACHMAN, R. "Effects of Comprehension on Retention of Prose." *Journal of Experimental Psychology*, vol. 88 (1971), pp. 216-222.

DURKIN, D. "What Classroom Observations Reveal about Reading Comprehension Instruction." *Reading Research Quarterly*, vol. 14 (1978-79), pp. 481-533.

EARLE, R.A. "Use of the Structured Overview in Mathematics Classrooms." in *Research in Reading in the Content Areas: First Year Report*. Herber, H.L., and Sanders, P.L. (Eds.), Syracuse University, 1969(a).

EARLE, R.A. "Cognitive Readiness: An Overview of Research." in *Research in Reading in the Content Areas: Second Year Report*. Herber, H.L., and Barron, R.F. (Eds.), Syracuse University, 1973.

EMIG, J. *The Composing Processes of Twelfth Graders*. Urbana, Illinois, N.C.T.E., 1971.

EMIG, J. "Writing as a Mode of Learning." *College Composition and Communication*, vol. 28, May 1977.

ESTES, T.H. "Use of Prepared Guide Material and Small Group Discussion in Reading Ninth Grade Social Studies Assignments: Pilot Study Report." in *Research in Reading in the Content Areas: First Year Report*. Herber, H.L., and Sanders, P.L. (Eds.), N.Y., Syracuse University, 1969.

ESTES, T.H., MILLS, D.C., and BARRON, R.F. "Three Methods of Introducing Students to a Reading-Learning Task in Two Content Subjects." in *Reading in the Content Areas: First Year Report*. Herber, H.L., and Sanders, P.L. (Eds.), Syracuse University, 1969.

EVANECHKO, P., OLLILA, L., and ARMSTRONG, R. "An Investigation of the Relationships between Children's Performance in Written Language and Their Reading Ability." *Research in the Teaching of English*, vol. 8, Winter 1974.

FAW, H.W., and WALLER, T.G. "Mathemagenic Behaviours and Efficiency in Learning from Prose Materials: Review, Critique and Recommendations." *Review of Educational Research*, vol. 46, No. 4, Fall 1976, pp. 691-720.

FILLMORE, C.J. "The Case for Case." in *Universals in Linguistic Theory*. Back, E., and Harms, R.G. (Eds.), New York, N.Y., Holt, Rinehart and Winston, 1968.

FLANDERS, N.A. (1962) in *Interaction Analysis: Theory, Research and Application*, Amidon, E.J., and Hough, J.B. (Eds.), Addison-Wesley, 1967.

FRASE, L.T., and SCHWARTZ, B.J. "Effect of Question Production and Answering on Prose Recall." *Journal of Educational Psychology*, vol. 67 (1975), pp. 628-635.

FRASE, L.T. "Learning from Prose Material: Length of Passage, Knowledge of Results, and Position of Questions." *Journal of Educational Psychology*, vol. 58, 1967, pp. 266-272.

FRY, E.B. *Graphical Comprehension: How to Read and Make Graphs*. Providence, N.J., Jamestown Publishers, 1981.

GAGNE, E.D. "Long-Term Retention of Information Following Learning from Prose." *Review of Educational Research*, vol. 48, 1978, pp. 629-665.

GARDNER, P. *Words in Science*. Melbourne, Australian Science Education Project, 1972.

GEVA, E. "Facilitating Reading Comprehension through Flowcharting." *Technical Report* No. 211, July 1981, University of Illinois at Urbana-Champaign.

GLASER, R. "Foreword." in *Cognition, Curriculum and Comprehension*. Guthrie, J.T. (Ed.), Newark, International Reading Association, 1977, pp. ix-xi.

GOODMAN, K.S. "Behind the Eye: What Happens in Reading." in *Theoretical Models and Processes of Reading*. Singer, H., and Ruddell, R.B. (Eds.), Newark, International Reading Association, 1970.

GOODMAN, K.S. "Reading: A Psycholinguistic Guessing Game." *Journal of the Reading Specialist*, vol. 1, 1967, pp. 126-135.

GRANT, P. "The Cloze Procedure for Improving Sixth Grade Students' Reading Comprehension and Understanding of Social Studies Materials." 1976, (ED 141 754).

GRAVES, D. (1975) cited in *Donald Graves in Australia.* Walshe, R.D. (Ed.), Sydney, P.E.T.A., 1981, pp. 9, 15, 125.

GRAVES, D. (1975) cited in *Every Child Can Write.* Walshe, R.D. (Ed.), Sydney, P.E.T.A., 1981.

GRAY, S., and KEECH, C. "Writing from Given Information." *Classroom Research Study No. 3, Bay Area Writing Project,* University of California, Berkeley, 1980.

GRIMES, J.E. *The Thread of Discourse.* The Hague, Mouton, 1975.

GUTHRIE, J.T. (Ed.), *Cognition, Curriculum and Comprehension.* Newark, International Reading Association, 1977.

GUTHRIE, J.T., and TYLER, S.J. "Cognition and Instruction of Poor Readers." *Journal of Reading Behaviour* vol. 10, No. 1, 1978, pp. 57-58.

GUTHRIE, J.T. (Ed.), *Comprehension and Teaching: Research Reviews.* Newark, International Reading Association, 1981.

GUNN, V.P., and ELKINS, J. "Diagnosing and Improving Silent Reading Using 'Cloze' Techniques or So What!" Paper presented at the World Congress on Reading, International Reading Association, Singapore, 1976.

HARPIN, W. *The Second R: Writing Development in the Junior School.* London, Unwin Education Books, 1976.

HARTLEY, J., and DAVIES, I.K. "Pre-Instructional Strategies: The Role of Pre-Tests, Behavioural Objectives, Overviews, and Advance Organizers." *Review of Educational Research,* vol. 46, No. 2, Spring 1976, pp. 239-265.

HERBER, H.L. *Teaching Reading in Content Areas.* Englewood Cliffs, New Jersey, Prentice-Hall, 1970; 1978.

HOFFMANN, M. *Reading, Writing and Relevance.* London, Hodder and Stoughton, 1976.

HUGHES, T.O. "Sentence Combining: A Means of Increasing Reading Comprehension." 1975, (ED 112 421).

HUNTER-GRUNDIN, E., and GRUNDIN, H.U. (Eds.). *Reading: Implementing the Bullock Report.* London, United Kingdom Reading Association/Ward Lock Educational, 1977.

JACKSON, E. "Surveying: Is It Easily Applied in Today's Textbooks?" Paper presented at the annual meeting of the Illinois Reading Council, Peoria, Illinois, 1980, (ED 184 099).

JENKINS, J.R., and PANY, D. "Instructional Variables in Reading Comprehension." in *Comprehension and Teaching: Research Reviews.* Guthrie, J.T. (Ed.), Newark, International Reading Association, 1981.

JOHNSON, D.D., and BARRETT, T.C. "Prose Comprehension: A Descriptive Analysis of Instructional Practices." in *Children's Prose Comprehension: Research and Practice.* Santa, C.M., and Hayes, B.L. (Eds.), Newark, International Reading Association, 1981.

JONGSMA, E.A. *Cloze Instruction Research: A Second Look.* Delaware, International Reading Association, and Illinois, ERIC, 1980.

JUDY, S.N., and JUDY, S.J. *The English Teachers' Handbook: Ideas and Resources for Teaching English.* Cambridge, Mass., Winthrop Pub., 1979.

JUDY, S.N. *Explorations in the Teaching of Secondary English: A Sourcebook for Experimental Teaching.* New York, N.Y., Harper and Row, 1974.

KAMLER, B. "One Child, One Teacher, One Classroom." *Language Arts,* September 1980.

KARLIN, R. *Teaching Reading in High School: Improving Reading in Content Areas.* 3rd ed. Indianapolis, Bobbs-Merrill, 1977.

KELLY, G.A. *A Theory of Personality.* New York, N.Y., The Norton Library, 1963.

KIERAS, D.E. "Good and Bad Structure in Simple Paragraphs: Effects on Apparent Theme, Reading Time and Recall." *Journal of Verbal Learning and Verbal Behaviour,* vol. 17, No. 1, 1978, pp. 13-28.

KINTSCH, W., and KEENAN, J.M. "Reading Rate and Retention as a Function of the Number of Propositions in the Base Structure of Sentences." *Cognitive Psychology,* vol. 5, 1973, pp. 257-274.

KINTSCH, W. *The Representation of Meaning in Memory.* Hillsdale, N.J., Erlbaum and Associates, 1974.

KINTSCH, W., and VAN DIJK, T.A. "Toward a Model of Text Comprehension and Production." *Psychological Review,* vol. 85, 1978, pp. 363-394.

KINTSCH, W., KOZMINSKY, E., STREBY, W.J., MCKOON, G., and KEENAN, J.M. "Comprehension and Recall of Text as a Function of Content Variables." *Journal of Verbal Learning and Verbal Behaviour,* vol. 14, 1975, pp. 196-214.

KIRBY, D., and LINER, T. *Inside Out: Developmental Strategies for Teaching Writing.* Rochelle Park, N.J., Hayden, 1980.

KLEIN, M. "The Development and Use of Sentence — Combining in the Reading Program." Paper presented to the International Reading Association Twenty-fifth Annual Convention, St. Louis, 1980, (ED 186 845).

KRULEE, G.K., FAIRWEATHER, P.G., and BERQUIST, S.R. "Organizing Factors in the Comprehension and Recall of Connected Discourse." *Journal of Psycholinguist Research,* vol. 8, No. 2, 1979.

KRESS, G. *Learning to Write.* London, Routledge and Kegan Paul, 1982.

KUNTZ, M.H. "The Relationship between Written Syntactic Attainment and Reading Ability in Seventh Grade." Doctoral Dissertation, University of Pittsburgh, 1975.

LA BERGE, D., and SAMUELS, S.J. (Eds.). *Basic Processes in Reading Perception and Comprehension.* Hillsdale, N.J., Erlbaum and Associates, 1977.

LA BERGE, D., and SAMUELS, S.J. "Towards a Theory of Automatic Information Processing in Reading." in *Theoretical Models and Processes of Reading.* Singer, H., and Ruddell, R. (Eds.), Newark, International Reading Association, 1976.

LANGER, S.K. *Philosophy in a New Key.* 3rd ed. Cambridge, Mass., Harvard University Press, 1960(a).

LANGER, S.K. "Speech and Its Communicative Function." *Quarterly Journal of Speech,* April 1960(b).

LAZDOWSKI, W.P. "Determining Reading Grade Levels from Analysis of

Written Compositions." Doctoral Dissertation, New Mexico State University, 1976.

LEHR, F. "Content-Area Reading Instruction in the Elementary School." *Reading Teacher*, April 1980.

LEHR, F. "Writing as Learning in the Content Areas." ERIC/RCS Report, *English Journal*, November 1980.

LESGOLD, A.M., MCCORMICK, C., GOLINKOFF, R.M. "Imagery Training and Children's Prose Learning." *Journal of Educational Psychology*, vol. 67, 1976, pp. 663-667.

LEVIN, J.R., and PRESSLEY, M. "Improving Children's Prose Comprehension: Selected Strategies that Seem to Succeed." in *Children's Prose Comprehension: Research and Practice*. Santa, C.M., and Hayes, B.L., Newark, International Reading Association, 1981.

LOBAN, W. *Language Development: Kindergarten Through Grade Twelve*. Urbana, Illinois, N.C.T.E., 1976.

LUNZER, E., and GARDNER, H. (Eds.). *The Effective Use of Reading*. London, Heinemann Educational Books for the Schools Council, 1979.

LURIA, A.R., and YUDOVICH, F.I. *Speech and the Development of Mental Processes in the Child*. 1959. Translated by J. Simon, Harmondsworth, Penguin Books, 1971.

MCLURE, J. *Spike Island*. London, Pan Books/Macmillan, 1980.

MCCONKIE, G.W. "Learning from Text." in *Review of Research in Education*, vol. 5, 1977, pp. 3-48.

MALING-KEEPES, J., and KEEPES, B. *Language in Education: The Language Development Project, Phase 1*. Canberra, Curriculum Development Centre, 1979.

MALLETT, M., and NEWSOME, B. *Talking, Writing and Learning, 8-13*. Schools Council Working Paper No. 59, London, Evans/Methuen Education, 1977.

MARINO, J.L. "Cloze Passages: Guidlines for Selection." *Journal of Reading*, vol. 24, No. 6, March 1981, pp. 479-483.

MARLAND, M. *Language Across the Curriculum*. London, Heinemann Education, 1977.

MARSHALL, N., and GLOCK, M. "Comprehension of Connected Discourse: A Study into the Relationships between the Structure of Text and Information Recalled." *Reading Research Quarterly*, vol. 16, 1978-79, pp. 10-56.

MARTIN, N., D'ARCY, P., NEWTON, B., and PARKER, R. *Writing and Learning Across the Curriculum 11-16*. London, Ward Lock Educational for the Schools Council, 1976.

MERRIT, J.E. "Reading: Seven to Eleven." *Education*, vol. 2, No. 1, 1975, pp. 3-13.

MERRITT, J.E. "Developing Higher Levels of Reading Comprehension." Paper presented at the First Annual Conference of the Reading Association of Ireland, Dublin, 1976.

MERRITT, J.E. "Contexts, Concepts and Reading Outcomes." Paper presented at Processing of Visible Language Conference, Eindloven, Netherlands, 1977.

MERRITT, J.E., WHITE, F., and MOORE, S. "Reading Purposes, Reading Outcomes and Comprehension." in *Growth in Reading*. Thackray, D. (Ed.), Proceedings of the Fifteenth Annual Course and Conference of the United Kingdom Reading Association, 1978, London, Ward Lock Educational, 1979.

MILLER, G. *The Magical No. 7. Plus or Minus 3: The Psychology of Communication*. London, Penguin, 1966.

MILLER, R.B., PERRY, F.L., and CUNNINGHAM, D.J. "Differential Forgetting of Superordinate and Subordinate Information Acquired from Prose Material." *Journal of Educational Psychology*, vol. 69, No. 6, 1977, pp. 730-735.

MILLIGAN, J.R. "Schema Learning Theory: An Approach to Perceptual Learning." *Review of Educational Research*, vol. 49, No. 2, Spring 1979, pp. 197-207.

MEYER, B.J.F. "Identification of the Structure of Prose and Its Implications for the Study of Reading and Memory." *Journal of Reading Behaviour*, vol. 7, No. 1, 1975, pp. 7-47.

MEYER, B.J.F., and FREEDLE, R. *The Effects of Different Discourse Topics on Recall*. Princeton, N.J., Educational Testing Service, 1979.

MEYER, B.J.F., BRANDT, D.M., and BLUTH, G.J. "Use of Author's Schema: Key to Ninth Grader's Comprehension." Paper presented at the meeting of the American Educational Research Association, Toronto, March 1978.

MOFFETT, J. *Teaching the Universe of Discourse*. Boston, Houghton Mifflin, 1968.

MOFFETT, J. "I, You, and It." *College Composition and Communication*, vol. 16, No. 5, December 1965, pp. 243-248.

MORRIS, A., and COPE, R.G. "Australian Secondary Reading Programmes: Whose Responsibility?" in *Perspectives on Reading: Proceedings of the Second Australian Reading* Conference, 1976. Levi, R., Forrest, G., Watson, A., and Bishop, B. (Eds.), Sydney, Ashton Scholastic, 1977.

MORRIS, A., and STEWART-DORE, N. *Assigning Reading as a Teaching Strategy*. Brisbane, Kelvin Grove C.A.E. Press, 1981.

National Assessment of Education Progress. cited in *Education U.S.A.*, 16 November 1981.

NOLAN, F. "How Do Children Write? Let's Ask Them." *English in Australia*, No. 50, November 1979.

O'HARE, F. "Sentence-Combining: Improving Student Writing without Formal Grammar Instruction." *N.C.T.E. Research Report No. 15*, Urbana, Illinois, N.C.T.E., 1973.

OMANSON, R.C., WARREN, W.N., and TRABASSO, T. "Goals, Inferential Comprehension and Recall of Stories by Children." *Discourse Processes*, vol. 1 No. 4, 1978, pp. 337-354.

OWENS, A.M. "Generative and Passive Questions in Learning from Text." *Perceptual and Motor Skills*, vol. 51, 1980, p. 714.

PARK, J. *Biology Reading Guide: Grade 11*. McGregor State High School, Brisbane, 1979.

Learning to Learn from Text

PEARSON, P.D., and CAMPERELL, K.B. "Comprehension of Text Structures." in *Comprehension and Teaching: Research Reviews*. Guthrie, J.B. (Ed.), Newark, International Reading Association, 1981.

PEARSON, P.D., HANSEN, J., and GORDON, C. "The Effect of Background Knowledge on Young Children's Comprehension of Explicit and Implicit Information." *Technical Report No. 116*. Champaign-Urbana, Centre for Studies of Reading, University of Illinois, 1979.

PEARSON, P.D. "A Retrospective Reaction to Prose Comprehension" in *Children's Prose Comprehension*, Santa C.M., and Hayes, B.L., Newark, International Reading Association, 1981.

PEARSON, P.D., and JOHNSON, D.P. *Teaching Reading Comprehension*. New York, N.Y., Holt, Rinehart and Winston, 1978.

PERFETTI, C.A. "Language Comprehension and Fast Decoding: Some Psycholinguistic Prerequisites for Skilled Reading Comprehension." in *Cognition, Curriculum and Comprehension*. Guthrie, J.T. (Ed.), Newark, International Reading Association, 1977.

PIAGET, J. *Language and Thought of the Child*. 1951, Rev. ed., translated by M. Sabain, London, Routledge and Kegan Paul, 1959.

READANCE, D.W., and MOORE, J.E. "Accommodating Individual Differences in Content Classrooms." *High School Journal*, vol. 64, No. 4, January 1981, pp. 160-165.

REDER, L.M. "The Role of Elaboration in the Comprehension and Retention of Prose: A Critical Review." *Review of Education Research*, vol. 50, 1980, pp. 5-53.

RESNICK, D.P., and RESNICK, L.B. "The Nature of Literacy." *Harvard Educational Review*, vol. 47, 1977, pp. 370-385.

RIBOVICH, J.K. "Developing Comprehension of Content Material through Strategies Other than Questioning." Paper presented at the International Reading Association Annual Convention, Florida, May 1977.

RICHARDS, J. *Classroom Language: What Sort?* London, Unwin Education Books, 1978.

RICKARDS, J.P., and DENNER, P.R. "Inserted Questions as Aids to Reading Text." *Instructional Science*, vol. 7, 1978, pp. 313-346.

RICKARDS, J.P., and HATCHER, C.W. "Interspersed Meaningful Learning Questions and Semantic Cues for Poor Comprehenders." *Reading Research Quarterly*, vol. 13, No. 4, 1978.

RICKARDS, J.P. "Adjunct Postquestions in Text: A Critical Review of Methods and Processes." *Review of Educational Research*, vol. 49, No. 2, Spring 1979, pp. 181-196.

RILEY, J.D. in *Research in Reading in Content Areas: Fourth Year Report*. Herber, H.L., and Riley, J.D. (Eds.), N.Y., Syracuse University, 1978.

ROBINSON, F.P. *Effective Study*. New York, N.Y., Harper and Row, 1967.

ROBINSON, H.A. *Teaching Reading and Study Strategies: Content Areas*. Boston, Allyn and Bacon, 1975.

RODE, S.S. "Development of Phrase and Clause Boundary Reading in Children." *Reading Research Quarterly*, vol. 10, 1974-1975, pp. 124-142.

ROSEN, H. in *Handbook for English Teachers 2: Talking and Writing*. Britton, J. (Ed.), London, Methuen, 1967.

ROSEN, H. "The Language of Textbooks." in *Language in Education*. Cashdan, A., and Grugeon, E. (Eds.), London, Routledge and Kegan Paul and the Open University Press, 1972.

ROTHKOPF, E.Z. "Writing to Teach and Reading to Learn: A Perspective in the Psychology of Written Instruction." *Psychology of Teaching Methods*, National Society for the Study of Education, Seventy-fifth Yearbook, 1976.

RUDDELL, R.B. *Reading-Language Instruction: Innovative Practices*. Englewood Cliffs, N.J., Prentice-Hall, 1974.

RUMELHART, D.E. *Toward an Interactive Model of Reading*. University of San Diego, California, 1976.

RUMELHART, D.E. "Understanding and Summarizing Brief Stories." in *Basic Processes in Reading: Perception and Comprehension*. La Berge, D., and Samuels, S.J. (Eds.), Hillside, N.J., Erlbaum and Associates, 1977.

RUMELHART, D.E. "Schemata: The Building of Cognition." in *Comprehension and Teaching: Research Reviews*. Guthrie, J.T. (Ed.), Newark, International Reading Association, 1981.

SAPIR, E. *Culture, Language and Personality*. Berkeley and Los Angeles, University of California Press, 1961.

SCHACHTER, S. "An Investigation of the Effects of Vocabulary Instruction and Schemata Orientation upon Reading Comprehension." Unpublished Doctoral Dissertation, University of Minnesota, 1978.

SCHANK, R.C. "Identification of Conceptualizations of Underlying Natural Language." in *Computer Models of Thought and Language*. Schank, R.C., and Colby, K.M. (Eds.), San Francisco, Freeman, 1973.

Schools Commission. *Schooling for 15 and 16 Year Olds*. Canberra, Schools Commission, November 1980.

Schools Council Projects. "Writing Across the Curriculum 11-16." *From Information to Understanding: What Children Do with New Ideas*. London, Ward Lock for the Schools Council, 1976.

SCOTT, E. *et al. The Report on School-Based Assessment*. Brisbane, Board of Secondary School Studies, 1978.

SHABLACK, S., and DIXON, C.A. "The Effects of Different Types of Guide Materials on Students' Written Response to Short Stories." in *Research in Reading in the Content Areas*. Third Year Report, Herber, H.L., and Vacca, R.T., Syracuse University, 1979.

SHAFER, R.E. "Children's Interactions in Sustaining Writing: Studies in an English Primary School." Paper presented at the Ninth World Congress on Reading, International Reading Association, Dublin, August 1982.

SHEPHERD, D.L. *Comprehensive High School Methods*. Columbus, Ohio, Merrill, 1973.

SINGER, H., and BALOW, I.H. "Overcoming Educational Disadvantagedness." in *Comprehension and Teaching: Research Reviews*. Guthrie, J.T. (Ed.), Newark, International Reading Association, 1981.

Learning to Learn from Text

SINGER, H., and DONLAN, D. *Reading and Learning from Text*. Boston, Little, Brown and Co., 1980.

SMELSTOR, M. (Ed.). *A Guide to the Relationship between Reading and Writing*. Madison, Wisconsin, University of Wisconsin, 1979.

SMITH, F. *Understanding Reading*. New York, N.Y., Holt, Rinehart and Winston, 1971.

SMITH, F. *Psycholinguistics and Reading*. New York, N.Y., Holt, Rinehart and Winston, 1973.

SMITH, F. *Writing and the Writer*. London, Heinemann Educational Books, 1982.

SNOUFFER, N.K., and THISTLETHWAITE, L.L. "The Effects of the Structured Overview and Vocabulary Pre-Teaching upon Comprehension Levels of College Freshman Reading Physical Science and History Materials." Paper presented at the Annual Meeting of the National Reading Conference, San Antonio, Texas, 1979. (ED 182 728).

SQUIRE, J.R., and APPLEBEE, R.K. *Teaching English in the United Kingdom: A Comparative Study*. Urbana, Illinois, N.C.T.E., 1968.

SQUIRE, J.R., and APPLEBEE, R.K. *High School English Instruction Today: The National Study of High School English Programs*. Urbana, Illinois, N.C.T.E., 1968.

STAUFFER, R.G. *Directing the Reading-Thinking Process*. New York, Harper and Row, 1969.

STAUFFER, R.G. *The Language-Experience Approach to the Teaching of Reading*. New York, Harper and Row, 1970.

STEBBINS, L.B., ST. PIERRE, R.G., PROPER, E.C., ANDERSON, R.B., and CERVA, T.R. in *Education as Experimentation: A Planned Variation Model*. Anderson, R.B., vol. IVA: *An Evaluation of Follow-Through*. Final Report, U.S.O.E., Department of Health, Education and Welfare, 1977.

STEVENS, K.C. "Chunking Material as an Aid to Reading Comprehension." *Journal of Reading*, vol. 25, No. 2, November 1981.

STICHT, T. "Learning by Listening." in *Language Comprehension and the Acquisition of Knowledge*. Carroll, J.B., and Freedle, R.O. (Eds.)., New York, N.Y., John Wiley, 1972.

STUBBS, M. *Language, Schools and Classrooms*. London, Methuen, 1976.

SWABY, B. "The Effects of Advance Organizers and Vocabulary Introduction on the Reading Comprehension of Sixth Grade Students." Unpublished dissertation, University of Minnesota, 1977.

SWANSON, C.C. "Readability and Top-Level Structure: Effects on Reading Comprehension." Unpublished Ph. D. dissertation, University of Arizona, 1979.

TAKAHASHI, B.L. "Comprehension of Written Syntactic Structures by Good Readers and Slow Readers." Master's Thesis, Rutgers University, 1975.

THORNDYKE, P.W. "Cognitive Structures in Comprehension and Memory of a Narrative Discourse." *Cognitive Psychology*, vol. 9, 1977, pp. 77-110.

TIERNEY, R.J., and BRIDGE, C. "Inference and Reading Comprehension:

Theory, Research and Practice." in *Communication Through Reading*, Page, G.M., Elkins, J., and O'Connor, B. (Eds.), Brisbane, Australian Reading Association, 1978.

TORBE, M. *Language Across the Curriculum: Guidelines for Schools*. London, Ward Lock Educational, 1976.

TOUGH, J. *Focus on Meaning*. London, Allen and Unwin, 1973.

TOUGH, J. *The Development of Meaning*. London, Unwin Education Books, 1977.

TRABASSO, T. "On the Making of Inferences during Reading and Their Assessment." in *Comprehension and Teaching: Research Reviews*. Guthrie, J.T. (Ed.)., Newark, International Reading Association, 1981.

VAN DIJK, T.A. *Some Aspects of Text Grammar*. The Hague, Mouton, 1972.

VYGOTSKY, L.S. *Thought and Language*. translated by Hanfmann, E., and Vakar, G., Cambridge, Mass., M.I.T. Press, 1962.

WALBERG, H.J. HARE, V.C., and PULLIAM, C.A. "Social-Psychological Perceptions and Reading Comprehension." in *Comprehension and Teaching: Research Reviews*. Guthrie, J.T. (Ed.), Newark, International Reading Association, 1981.

WALKER, C. *Reading Development and Extension*. London, Ward Lock Educational, 1974.

WALKER, C., and MEYER, B.J.F. "Integrating Information from Text: An Evaluation of Current Theories." *Review of Educational Research*, vol. 50, No. 3, Fall 1980, pp. 421-437.

WATERS, H.S. "Superordinate — Subordinate Structure in Semantic Memory: The Roles of Comprehension and Retrieval Processes." *Journal of Verbal Learning and Verbal Behaviour*, vol. 17, 1978, pp. 587-597.

WATTS, G., and ANDERSON, R.C. "Effects of Three Types of Inserted Questions on Learning from Prose." *Journal of Educational Psychology*, vol. 62, 1971, pp. 387-394.

WERTSCH, J.V. "Adult-Child Interaction and the Roots of Metacognition." *Quarterly Newsletter of the Institute for Comparative Human Development*, vol. 2, 1978, pp. 15-18.

WILDER, G. "Five Exemplary Reading Programs." in *Cognition, Curriculum and Comprehension*. Guthrie, J.T. (Ed.), Newark, International Reading Association, 1977.

WITTROCK, N.C., MARKS, C., and DOCTOROW, M. "Reading as a Generative Process." *Journal of Educational Psychology*, vol. 67, 1975, pp. 484-489.

WOLFE, R.F. "An Examination of the Effects of Teaching a Reading Vocabulary upon Writing Vocabulary in Student Compositions." Doctoral dissertation, University of Maryland, 1975.

RESOURCES

These texts have been used when selecting extracts for developing the various ERICA strategies.

ADDISON-WESLEY SCIENCE SERIES, LEVEL 6. Menlo Park, California, Addison-Wesley, 1980.

ANDREWS, R.L. *A Geography of Natural Landscapes.* 2nd ed., Melbourne, Geo. Philip and O'Neill, 1973.

ANDREWS, R.L. *Resources in the Social Sciences. 1. The Nuiginians.* Melbourne, Geo. Philip and O'Neill, 1978.

BALDWIN, D. *Human Biology and Health.* London, Longman, 1978.

BARR, B.B., and Leyden, M.B. *Life Science.* Menlo Park, California, Addison-Wesley, 1980.

CULL, R.G., and DRAKE, W.A. *Concepts in Science 1.* 3rd ed., Brisbane, Jacaranda/Wiley, 1979.

GIBSON, G. *et al. The Australian Economy: An Overview.* Melbourne, Pitman Australia, 1979.

HENDY, A. *et al. Foundations.* Melbourne, Nelson, 1976.

MARVIN, M., MARVIN, S., and CAPPELLUTI, F. *The Human Adventure.* Menlo Park, California, Addison-Wesley, 1976.

PRIDDLE, A.G., and DAVIES, T.H. *Mathematics: A Systematic Approach.* Brisbane, Wm. Brooks and Co.

STANNARD, P., and WILLIAMSON, K. *Exploring Science 1.* Melbourne, Macmillan, 1979.

STEWART-DORE, N. *The Reporter.* The Mount Gravatt Developmental Language/Reading Program, Level 5. Sydney, Addison-Wesley, 1981.

TEASDALE, T.C. *Social Psychology.* Melbourne Lloyd O'Neil, 1977.

WYLLIE, P.J. *Dynamic Earth: Textbook in Geosciences.* John Wiley, 1971.

Glossary

ANAPHORA: a term used to describe the use of COHESIVE TIES in a text to refer to something which has already been stated. ANAPHORIC REFERENCING means referring back. For example: Allan felt ill. *He* went home. Where 'he' refers to Allan. Anaphora may be applied to more than one word: to a phrase, or a complete sentence.

ANNOTATED BIBLIOGRAPHY: See BIBLIOGRAPHY.

APPLIED COMPREHENSION: the level of understanding of a text demanding application and TRANSFORMATION of ideas to more general situations and instances. To effectively operate at this level, a reader needs to have proceeded, albeit sub-consciously, through the stages of LITERAL and INFERENTIAL COMPREHENSION.

AUTOMATICITY: a term coined by David La Berge and Jay Samuels to describe a person's instantaneous recognition of a word in print. The more automatic the recognition the more chance the reader has of understanding the text.

BIBLIOGRAPHY: a list of books or references, usually listed at the end of a work in alphabetical order according to author. An ANNOTATED BIBLIOGRAPHY includes a short summary statement of the contents of the reference as a guide to the reader.

CATAPHORA: a term used to describe the use of COHESIVE TIES in a text to refer to something which will be mentioned subsequently in the text. The reader needs to *read ahead* to find out what is being referred to. Many context clues, particularly definitions, require CATAPHORIC REFERENCING. For example: Cataphoric referencing means reading ahead to find out what is meant.

CHECKING: a process of returning to a text to CONFIRM that PREDICTIONS are realized, or to disconfirm hypotheses formed about an author's intentions. Checking requires re-reading and is encouraged through small group discussion of texts as for example, when using a THREE-LEVEL GUIDE.

CLOZE EXERCISE: a way of using CLOZE PROCEDURE as a teaching strategy. Students first complete a *cloze passage* individually and then compare inserted words and justifications for their choice with other students to arrive at a 'best' solution.

CLOZE PROCEDURE: a technique whereby selected words are deleted from a printed passage. The prepared *cloze passage* is then given to a reader who is asked to fill in each blank with a word which he or she thinks makes most sense, using the remaining context clues.

CLOZE TEST: a method of measuring a reader's understanding of a prose passage. Also use as a measure of READABILITY by administering a CLOZE TEST to a group of students. The text indicates which students were able to use the material at an INDEPENDENT level, which at an INSTRUCTIONAL level, and which at a FRUSTRATION level.

COHESION: a text is said to display cohesion when it 'hangs together' by a series of COHESIVE TIES or referents across or within sentences. When teachers comment that the 'expression' of student's written work is faulty, they are often showing that they know intuitively from their experience of language structure (SYNTAX) that a piece of writing is not cohesive or lacks COHESION.

COHESIVE TIES: words which connect ideas within and across sentences and paragraphs. Cohesive ties give a passage of text COHESION so that it 'hangs together' and makes sense.

COMPREHENSION: defined by Lunzer and Gardner (1977) as a unitary skill involving the willingness or capacity to REFLECT on what is being read. Numerous TAXONOMIES of reading comprehension have been devised, but the most useful and straightforward for instructional purposes seems to be that used in constructing THREE-LEVEL GUIDES viz. LITERAL, INFERENTIAL and APPLIED levels of comprehension. See Herber, H., (1978).

CONCEPT LOAD: the density or difficulty level of (new) ideas in a passage. Usually determined by the number and frequency of CONTENT WORDS in a passage.

CONFIRM: a reading strategy whereby a reader sets out to PREDICT or make hypotheses about the text being read, and verifies what is expected against information presented in the text.

CONNECTIVES: FUNCTION words which connect ideas in a text — for example, conjunctions, such as 'and', 'but', 'so', and so on.

CONTENT-AREA READING: reading in subject areas where the reader 'reads-to-learn'. It is usually expository in nature, seeking to explain and teach the content of the subject to the reader.

CONTENT OBJECTIVE: a brief statement of what content you, as teacher, want students to learn by reading. The starting point for the development of THREE-LEVEL GUIDES and for establishing READING PURPOSES.

CONTENT WORDS: a term used to distinguish words which convey meaning from those which link ideas or show relationships (FUNCTION WORDS), e.g. 'heart' and 'kinesiology' are CONTENT WORDS: 'the', 'because', and 'thus' are FUNCTION WORDS.

CONTEXT: the surrounding textual or pictorial/graphic information in a passage.

CONTEXT CLUES: items of information in the text surrounding a word or group of words which can be used to help understand the meaning of unfamiliar words in a passage.

CONVERSING (WITH A TEXT): a phrase used to describe an INTERACTION between a reader and the text he or she is reading which demands:
- REFLECTING READING.
- Confirming PREDICTIONS.
- Discussing propositions.
- Drawing INFERENCES.
- CHECKING on intended meaning.

CRITERION REFERENCED TESTING: assessment using specific items to measure students' mastery of particular criteria. For example: knowledge of specific vocabulary, and ability to use a dictionary.

CUES: aids to reconstructing an author's message. Cues may operate linguistically within a text (SEMANTIC, SYNTACTIC CUES, GRAPHO-PHONIC); or within a reader (LANGUAGE EXPERIENCE or background knowledge); or between the reader and the print itself. For example: GRAPHIC AIDS.

DECODING (WORD-ATTACK SKILLS): the process of working out sound-symbol relationships or other elements in a word which is not already familiar (SIGHT WORD or VOCABULARY).

DEVELOPMENTAL READING: reading instruction aimed at helping all students improve their reading skills using increasingly sophisticated and varied material.

DIAGNOSIS: methods used to determine an individual's strengths and weaknesses in reading.

DICTIONARY SKILLS: those skills necessary to be able to use a dictionary efficiently. They include knowledge of alphabetical order, guide words, pronunciation keys, SYLLABICATION, word meanings and usage, and derivations.

DIRECTED READING ACTIVITY (DRA): a teaching strategy for helping students focus on aspects of text to promote comprehension. A DRA sets out READING PURPOSE, METHOD, and OUTCOME.

ETYMOLOGY: the study of the origin of words.

EXPOSITORY PROSE: a piece of explanatory or elaborative prose structured to clearly set out relationships between ideas, and which contrasts with NARRATIVE PROSE.

EXTRACTING INFORMATION: the process of reading in a discriminating way to sift out irrelevant or redundant information; the process of applying a READING PURPOSE and matching it to the stated READING OUTCOME, noting relationships between ideas, and constructing a means for RETRIEVING needed information.

FIXATIONS: brief pauses in eye movement during reading.

FRUSTRATION LEVEL: the level of reading at which little if any information is gained because of print material difficulty, inadequate background experience, or unfamiliar content.

FRY READABILITY GRAPH: a method used to gauge the difficulty of text material, developed by Edward Fry, based on the number of syllables and the number of sentences in a 100-word passage. Level of difficulty is calculated by reading from a graph to equate with school year levels.

FUNCTION WORDS: (c/f CONTENT WORDS): words which link ideas and express relationships between CONTENT WORDS. For example: 'however', 'therefore', 'if'.

GLOSSARY: an alphabetical listing, at the end of a book or a chapter, of selected words and their meanings as used in the text which it accompanies.

GOOD ERRORS: mistakes or MISCUES which indicate that the reader has made good use of existing CONTEXT CLUES although not arriving at the words used by the author in the original text. Good errors can be acceptable SEMANTICALLY (according to the total meaning) and/or syntactically

Learning to Learn from Text

(according to the word order or grammar).

GRAPHIC AIDS: pictorial supplements to print material which explain, illustrate, or elaborate on the content. They can take many forms and require some degree of VISUAL LITERACY to interpret and gain information from.

GRAPHIC OUTLINE: a visual representation of the structure and content of a chapter of a textbook or similar instructional material. It shows main headings, sub-headings, and so on, together with the relevance or otherwise of graphic illustrations. It is used to help students understand the way an author has organized information.

GRAPHO-PHONIC INFORMATION: information which aids word identification; comprises word and letter shape, letter sequence, and SOUND-SYMBOL RELATIONSHIPS.

GROUP READING INVENTORY (GRI): an informal, teacher-made test for use by classroom teachers to determine whether students can perform various reading tasks. For example: use an index, glossary, or table of contents; use context clues to derive meaning; or extract information from graphic aids. The teacher determines the areas to be tested and the test is administered to a group. Results show individual and group strengths and weaknesses in the areas tested.

GUIDING READING: the process or means whereby students are DIRECTED in their reading to maximize the use of efficient READING-TO-LEARN strategies. Comprises strategies which include THREE-LEVEL GUIDES and CLOZE PROCEDURE.

INDEPENDENT READING LEVEL: the level of reading understanding at which at least 90 per cent information gain is achieved. No teacher assistance is required. Most frequently achieved on material which is selected for recreational reading, but should also occur on wisely selected material used for independent study, i.e. at a level which is easier to understand than that used for classroom instruction.

INFERENCE: the process of reasoning to connect ideas, and judge or draw conclusion. Inferences need to be made when an author implies, but does not explicitly state, specific information.

INFERENTIAL COMPREHENSION: the level of understanding of a text which requires that the reader 'read between or beyond the lines' and fills in for himself or herself, ideas which are suggested, but not directly stated by the author. Demands that a reader makes connections between ideas which the author has assumed; requires making explicit, ideas that are merely hinted. Sometimes called INTERPRETIVE COMPREHENSION.

INFORMAL READING INVENTORY (IRI): a means of observing and informally monitoring students' reading behaviour, and strategies for reconstructing meaning. MISCUE ANALYSIS is one tool used.

INSTRUCTIONAL READING LEVEL: the level of reading at which a reader achieves between 50-75 per cent understanding/information gain. The reader needs teacher assistance and guidance to learn at this level.

INTERACTION: an engagement between reader and text whereby the reader responds to text information and actively seeks to make sense of it by reflecting, challenging, drawing inferences and conclusions, and recreating the author's intended meanings in various ways. (Refer also to CONVERSING WITH A TEXT.)

INTERPRETIVE COMPREHENSION: see INFERENTIAL COMPREHENSION.

LANGUAGE EXPERIENCE: a term used to refer to the body of knowledge about language and its structure which a native speaker of a language has. Language experience is promoted and developed by frequent opportunities to explore everyday experience orally and in writing, through small group discussion and by setting up various opportunities to read and to write for different purposes.

LANGUAGE EXPERIENCE APPROACHES: commonly, methods of reading teaching, whereby the learner's own language is recorded and used to create instructional materials and experiences. This may be done in various ways, but at the core is the learner's personal experience/language.

LANGUAGE DEVELOPMENT: the life-long process of learning language (usually one's mother tongue), learning through language and learning about language.

LITERAL COMPREHENSION: recognition, understanding, and recall by the reader of what the author has actually said. Often regarded as the most basic level of understanding, and a prerequisite for INFERRING and hypothesising (PREDICTING).

MAIN IDEA: the essential idea or thought, usually in a paragraph; may be stated in a TOPIC SENTENCE or INFERRED (see INFERENCE).

MISCUES: oral reading responses which differ from expected responses to a written text.

MISCUE ANALYSIS: a means of analyzing the kinds of reading 'errors' made in oral reading (see CUE SYSTEMS).

MODELLING: a graphic representation of a person's understanding of what he or she has read: it is one READING OUTCOME, which can take a variety of forms. For example: RETRIEVAL CHART, graph, or diagram. Designed to show how the reader has created connections between ideas; requires also that the reader verbalizes his or her 'model' to explain how it was constructed and the reasoning behind the inclusions and omissions. Refer also CONVERSING (WITH A TEXT).

MORPHEMES: the smallest meaningful element of a word, morphemes may consist of PREFIXES, SUFFIXES, and ROOTS. A morpheme may also serve as a word. For example, book.

NARRATIVE PROSE: connected writing form in which an author tells a story.

NORM: a statistical term used to indicate the 'average' level of performance. Individual performances can then be compared to the 'norm' as in talking of a 'Year 6 Reading Level'. Use of the norm leads to frequent misunderstandings since it hides the fact that a range of performances is the more natural occurrence.

ORGANIZATIONAL PATTERNS, EXTERNAL: identifiable features of a text such as title page, index, table of contents, chapter headings, GLOSSARY, introduction, and preface. Necessary reference points for efficient use of a textbook or resource/reference book.

Learning to Learn from Text

ORGANIZATIONAL PATTERNS, INTERNAL: features of a chapter of a text or reference book which include the structure or organization of ideas. These comprise such patterns as cause/effect relationships, comparative or contrasting situations, simple listing or enumeration of ideas, or time or event sequencing. (Refer also to TOP-LEVEL STRUCTURE.)

OUTLINE: a point form summation of the MAIN IDEAS and SUPPORTING DETAILS of a text.

PHONIC ANALYSIS: a method of teaching word identification by matching letters or combinations of letters with their sounds.

PHONICS: the study of sound-symbol (letter) relationships and using this information to recognize and pronounce words. Not to be confused with reading which is an interactive, language process.

PREDICTION: when native language users read, they predict on the basis of their knowledge of language: its structure or syntax and its meaning. They do not read one word at a time, but 'chunk' according to their knowledge of what to expect. Fluent readers are predictive readers who use a variety of CUE SYSTEMS to anticipate what will follow.

PREFIXES: MORPHEMES added to the beginning of ROOTS of words which alter their meaning. For example, 'pre' in *pre*cede (meaning 'go before').

PREPARATION FOR READING: may be equated with READING READINESS; implies that before reading a passage of text, a reader needs to be familiar with prerequisite concepts, have some understanding of content vocabulary, and can recognize the way in which content is organized. PREPARATION FOR READING involves preparation by the teacher *and* the student.

PSYCHOLINGUISTICS: the interdisciplinary field of language and cognitive psychology in which language behaviour is examined. Sometimes generally used to refer to the process of making meaning from print material, where the reader uses his or her tacit knowledge of language and the way it works, to think about and make sense of what he or she is reading.

RANGE OF READING ABILITY: any normal group of people, for example a school class, necessarily contains a spread of READING ABILITY. It is a mistake therefore to expect that all students will read 'up to' their year level. As a rough guide, a teacher could expect a range of reading abilities in any average mixed class to be about two-thirds the average chronological age of the class.

READABILITY: a term used to describe the ease with which a reader can read a text meaningfully. Often given in terms of year level of difficulty as indicated by applying a READABILITY FORMULA to prose material. Most readability formulae (for example, FRY GRAPH) use elements of language (sentence and word length) over samples of 100 words, to gauge degree of difficulty.

READING AGE: a term to describe the level of reading ability achieved by a reader stated in terms of age. A reader who reads as well as it is expected of a 7 year old would be considered to have an RA of 7.0 years despite his actual (chronological) age.

READING DEMANDS: text variables which contribute to the ease with which a reader understands, assimilates, and uses information: READABILITY level is a reading demand, as is CONCEPT LOAD, ORGANIZATIONAL PATTERNS, and LANGUAGE EXPERIENCE. Reading demands can be minimized by teachers paying attention to adequate PREPARATION FOR READING and developing GUIDING READING activities.

READING METHOD: a term applied to the way in which a reader might proceed to read a text according to his or her READING PURPOSE. Reading methods include SKIMMING and SCANNING, and may incorporate SQ3R. Reading method can also refer to any of several steps used to teach reading or aspects of it.

READING OUTCOME: what is done as a result of reading. A reading outcome might be a piece of writing in summary, point, or extended prose form. It might be a diagram, a chart, or a table. The reading outcome should match the READING PURPOSE.

READING PURPOSE: the term used to identify why a reader is assigned a reading task. Establishing a *reading purpose* prior to beginning to read a passage of text provides a reader with an idea of where he or she is going and focuses attention on relevant material.

READING READINESS: a term (often misused) to indicate the prerequisites for a reader to understand and gain from reading a text. Readiness includes background experience/knowledge, concept development, familiarity with vocabulary, knowledge of the structure of the text, and so on.

READING-TO-LEARN: a term used to distinguish between learning-to-read, and using reading capacities to EXTRACT INFORMATION to acquire knowledge and deepen and develop understandings. Sometimes used as an alternative to CONTENT-AREA READING.

READING VOCABULARY: sight vocabulary which a reader needs, to be able to effectively understand print materials. Some vocabulary items encountered in content area reading may be in a student's oral vocabulary, but he or she may not recognize them in print. See VOCABULARY.

REDUNDANCY (REDUNDANT): redundancy in language refers to that information in text which is repeated or expressed in different ways. An author, in order to be explicit, may need to repeat what has already been said to maintain COHESION. Redundancy helps readers to PREDICT what is to come.

REFERENTS: the words which refer backward or forward to the same idea in a text. The most common referents are pronouns: he; she; it; they; that. However, they can also be articles: a; the.

REFLECTIVE READING: a process whereby CONVERSING WITH A TEXT is promoted as a reader predicts, questions, confirms, and relates to his or her own experience of what he or she has read. Reflective reading requires a reader to challenge and think about the passage read; it is one means of learning through reading.

REMEDIAL READING: special programs designed for students with severe reading difficulties.

REMEDIAL TEACHER: a specially trained teacher who assists students with severe learning disabilities. In many places, remedial teachers have been replaced by RESOURCE TEACHERS, whose aim is to help the student indirectly through the class teacher in the normal classroom, rather than directly by withdrawing the student to a separate room or school.

RESOURCE TEACHER: a specially trained, experienced teacher who assists class teachers to provide for the range of student abilities found in a normal mixed-ability class. Resource teachers may on occasion, withdraw a small number of severely learning-disabled students for intensive help, but this is not the major aim of their role.

RETRIEVAL CHART: a means of organizing information into tables and charts under headings or categories. Allows a reader or writer easy and efficient access to information.

ROOTS: the basic component of a word from which meaning is derived. Root words in English derive from Latin and Greek in the main.

SCANNING: the search-reading of a text to locate specific information. See SKIMMING.

SCHOOL LANGUAGE/READING POLICY: a statement of aims and procedures which describes how the school intends to meet the language/reading needs of its students. May include sections on REMEDIAL READING, CONTENT-AREA READING and DEVELOPMENTAL READING. Sets out the steps which teachers are to follow to help meet the policy's objectives.

SEMANTICS: the MEANING SYSTEM of a language, usually tied to CONTENT WORDS.

SHORT-BURST READING: the practice of assigning a reading task for a specific purpose. For example: to locate a particular piece of information; Lunzer and Gardner (1976) found short-burst reading to be the norm in subject classrooms; the 'short-bursts' were often for only a period of seconds! A practice which does little to promote REFLECTIVE READING.

SIGHT VOCABULARY (SIGHT WORDS): vocabulary which is so familiar to the reader that it is instantaneously recognizable when encountered in print.

SKIMMING: the rapid surveying of material to gain an overall impression of its content, or to determine the MAIN IDEA or gist of a passage.

SOUND-SYMBOL RELATIONSHIPS: the correspondence between a sound in oral language and the way it is represented by letters (symbols) in print. For example: $/\bar{e}/$ as in meet, meat, mete.

STANDARDIZED READING TEST: a test which has been administered to various groups and for which NORMS have been calculated.

STRUCTURED OVERVIEW: a visual arrangement of words/concepts pertaining to a particular subject; shows relationships between key concepts and provides a ready reference for SUMMARIZATION and OUTLINING. Can be teacher-developed to introduce a topic or may become a learning device for students to develop as a READING OUTCOME. Developed by Barron. See Herber, H., 1978, *Reading in Content Areas*.

SQ3R (SURVEY, QUESTION, READ, RECITE (RECALL), REVIEW): a study strategy usefully applied especially to difficult or unfamiliar texts.

SUFFIXES: MORPHEMES added to the end of ROOTS of words to alter their function. For example: 'ly' added to slow = slowly, 'ness' added to hard = hardness.

SUMMARIZING: the ability to compose, from an OUTLINE, a piece of connected prose which encapsulates the MAIN IDEA of what has been read, together with relevant SUPPORTING DETAILS.

SUMMARY: a piece of connected prose which sums up the MAIN IDEAS and essential DETAILS of a longer piece of prose/EXPOSITION.

SUPPORTING DETAIL: those details of information — elaborative, exemplary, explanatory — which support or add weight to the MAIN IDEA of a paragraph.

SYLLABICATION: the method of dividing words into parts (syllables). Used as a pronunciation guide or word-attack skill.

SYLLABLE: the smallest divisible part of a word based on vowel sound.

SYNTAX: the way in which language is structured or organized; word order. Sometimes referred to as the 'grammar' of a language. The sentence: 'I'll home he because went was he' abuses the syntactic rule system of English and is not meaningful. Syntax or word order contributes to meaning.

TAXONOMY: the classification of items, especially relating to components of COMPREHENSION in reading. Usually arranged hierarchically according to degree of difficulty.

TEXT: any piece of connected prose or written discourse. OUTLINES (point form summations) are not TEXT because they do not COHERE (refer to COHESION).

THREE-LEVEL GUIDE: one strategy for GUIDING READING. It involves the designation of a CONTENT OBJECTIVE and the development of numerous statements in relation to the text being read at LITERAL, INFERENTIAL, and APPLIED levels of COMPREHENSION. THREE-LEVEL GUIDES require readers to INTERACT or hold CONVERSATIONS with the text, to challenge and justify statements about it. (See Herber, H., 1978, *Reading in Content Areas*.)

TOP-LEVEL STRUCTURE: a term used to describe the way ideas or propositions are ordered in text.

TOPIC SENTENCE: that sentence in a paragraph, which contains the MAIN IDEA. May occur anywhere in the paragraph, most typically, in predictable text, in the first sentence, although students should be alerted to other positions.

TRANSLATING INFORMATION: the term applied to various READING OUTCOMES emphasizing the use of information gained through reading; often involves writing and publication of material for various audiences and for different purposes, and should demonstrate a student's capacity to use extracted information in an original way to reveal his or her level of understanding of content. Stands in direct contrast to regurgitation or verbatim copying.

USSR (UNINTERRUPTED, SUSTAINED, SILENT READING): the practice of reading continuous prose/DISCOURSE without interruption and usually for pleasure. USSR programs are valuable for promoting positive attitudes towards reading because they give emphasis to the value of reading for reading's sake. It contrasts with SHORT-BURST READING often observed in subject classrooms.

VISUAL LITERACY: the ability to use GRAPHIC AIDS as a means of interpreting information to derive meaning. Relates to understanding the intent of photographs, drawings, graphs, diagrams, and tables.

VOCABULARY: the store of words which a person recognizes (when listening or reading) and/or uses (when speaking or writing). Thus we can distinguish between a person's listening, speaking, reading and writing vocabularies. See READING VOCABULARY.

WORD-ATTACK SKILLS: the methods of identifying and pronouncing words based on phonic or structural analysis, configuration clues, sight-work knowledge, or context clues.

Index

Active learning, 44
Adjunct questions, 179
Advance organizer, 53, 179, 180, 182
Affective objectives, 199
Analysis of text, 14, 149, 179, 187
Anderson, 181, 189
Anderson & Freebody, 185
Applebee, 192
Applied level, 207, 208, 211, 216, 217, 233, 238, 246
Approximations, 37
Assessment of student writing, 166
Assignment Writing, 13, 193
Assumptions, 185
Audiences,
  for student writing, 155, 156, 162, 163
Aukerman, 182
Ausubel, 179
Automaticity, 184

Baker and Stein, 22, 182, 186, 187, 189
Barnes, 32, 36, 38, 174, 191
Barr & Leyden, 41
Bartlett, 183, 187, 188
Beginning reading schemes, 184
Below average readers, 184
Below average students, 189
Bennett & Walker, 194
Berget, 176, 186
Berliner, 177, 189
Biology, 61
Bottom-up-approaches, 182
Braddock, 192
Bransford & Johnson, 189
British classrooms, 194
Britton, 151, 190, 193
Bruner, 190
Bullock Report, 37, 191

Calkins, 194
Careers Education, 153
Carre, 191
Carroll, 192, 193
Case grammar, 182
Case study approach, 194
Cashdan, 191
Cassidy, 193, 194
Cassirer, 190
Categorizing, 180, 189, 202
  exercise 205
Cause-effect, 183
Chunking, 186, 188
Classroom language interactions, 191
Cloze activities, 177
  exercises, 107-112
  research on the use of, 186

selective deletion, 107
using to develop comprehension, 107, 203, 205, 223, 224, 225, 226, 227
Cloze tests, 108
Cognitive objectives, 199
Cohesion, 188
Comparison - contrast, 183, 194
Composition:
  as process, 193
  as transaction, 193
Comprehension, 13, 14, 187
  applied, 98
  improving, 99
  interpretive, 98
  levels of, 100, 186
  literal, 98
  teaching, 102, 183, 184, 186
Concept maps, webs, hierarchies, 49
Conceptual overload, 188
Conference approach, 164, 165
Connectives, 187, 188
Consolidation, 176, 212, 228
Content area reading, 19
  what is content area reading, 21-23
  need to focus on, 25-30, 182
Content area writing, 167
Content focus, 180
Content objectives, 199
Context, 162
Context clues, 16, 109
  the importance of, 90, 91
  teaching the use of, 92
  using, 85
  vocabulary, 136, 185, 187, 200, 203
Copying, 13, 144, 146-147
Curriculum Development Centre, Canberra, 38

Davis & Parker, 191
Decision making, 186
Determining content objectives, 102
Diagrams, 121
  as aids to understanding, 134, 135, 136, 183, 184, 189, 200
Directed Reading Activity, 171, 174, 175
Directed Reading Thinking Activity, 171, 174, 175
Discussion, 31-37
  directed, 97
  mixed ability groups, 31, 176
  small group, 32, 34, 36, 52, 94, 108, 109, 135, 185
  structured, 31, 32
Dixon, 176, 177
Doake, 185
Doctorow, 189

Doctorow, Wittrock & Marks, 186
Draft, 159
Durkin, 95, 186

Earle, 49, 179, 180
Economics, 13
Editing, 159, 166
Education USA, 28
Educational practices, 114
Effect, 179
Emig, 193, 194
English, 242
ERICA,
  background to the model, 169-195
  development of, 174-176
  model, 31, 32, 33, 43, 45, 46, 171, 175, 183, 185, 199
Estes, 186
Estes, Mills, & Barron, 180
Evanechko, Ollila & Armstrong, 192
Expectations, 190
Exploratory writing, 152
Expository schemata, 183
Expository text, 21, 58, 182, 183, 184, 187, 188, 189
Extract & organize information, 33, 113-141, 116, 149, 180, 183, 187-189, 200, 211, 214, 218, 224, 225, 226, 227, 234, 235, 238

Faw & Waller, 179
Fillmore, 182
Final copy, 166
First draft, 149
Flanders, 33
Flexibility in communicating, 158
Flow charting, 135, 174, 189
Focusing questions, 179, 183
Form, 162
Frase, 179, 180
Frase & Schwartz, 180
Fry, 188, 189

Gagne, 179
Gardner, 38, 41
Gathering information, 185
General language ability, 192
Generating text, 193
Generative post-questions, 186
Generative post-reading activities, 189
Geography, 35, 66, 101
  MacDonnell Ranges, 102, 119, 161, 213
Geva, 189
Glaser, 178, 187
Glossary, 92, 94, 185
Goodman, 108, 179, 181
Grant, 176
Graphic formats, 135
Graphic organizers, 184
Graphic outline, 57-84, 183, 184, 199, 203, 213
  construction of a, 64-81
  examples of, 204, 210, 215, 221, 232

types of, 58
use of, 82, 213
value of, 83
  (i) to teacher, 83
  (ii) to student, 83, 84, 136, 137, 180
Graphical analysis, 188
Grapho-phonics, 15
Graves, 146, 151, 156, 164, 194
Gray & Keech, 194
Grimes, 182
Group cloze, 200
Gunn & Elkins, 176
Guthrie & Tyler, 184

Harpin, 191
Hartley & Davies, 179, 180, 182
Headings, 183
Herber, 98, 172, 174, 175, 176, 178, 181, 182, 185, 186
Herzberg's motivation hygiene theory, 131
Higher - level questions, 179
Higher - order conceptualizations, 182
History, 39, 40, 53, 62, 144, 163, 209
Home Economics, 230
Hughes, 192
Hunter-Grundin & Grundin, 191
Hypothesis - testing, 181
Hypothesising, 190

Illustrations, 183
Incidental learning, 179, 180
Independent learners, 27, 135, 139
Independent reading, 187
Index, 92
Inferences, 186, 188
Information processing, 182
Instructional Framework, 172, 174, 175, 185
Instrumentalist view of vocabulary, 185
Integrated approach, 182
Integrated reading & writing models, 193, 194
Interpretive level, 207, 211, 216, 217, 233, 237, 246

Jackson, 184
Jefferson Junior High School, 172
Jenkins & Pany, 177, 179
Johnson & Barrett, 187
Jongsma, 176, 186, 187
Journal writing, 193
Judy & Judy, 154, 156

Kamler, 194
Karlin, 182
Kelly, 190
Kieras, 188
Kintsch, 181, 188
Kirby & Liner, 193
Klein, 192
Knibe, 181
Kress, 194

Krulee, 182
Krulee, Fairweather & Berguist, 183, 187
Kuntz, 192

La Berge & Samuels, 184
Langer, 190
Language:
  and learning, 190
  and reasoning, 99, 175
  developments, 36-38
  environments, 31
  functions of, 42
  modes, 31
  oral, 176
  of secondary education, 38
  processes, 190
  registers, 22-24, 38, 41-43, 176, 194
  the central role of, 31
Language & learning theory, 190
Lazdowski, 192
Learning:
  active, 44
  by doing, 29
  climate, 31
  efficient, 48
  from text, 193
  processes, 35, 191
  techniques, 189
  to write, 149
Lehr, 193
Lesgold, McCormick & Golinkoff, 189
Less - able students, 184
Levin & Pressley, 178, 184
Literal level, 206, 207, 211, 216, 217, 233, 237, 246
Literacy, 18, 26
Loban, 192, 293
Logical connectives, 193
Low-level information, 182
Low-level questions, 179
Lunzer & Gardner, 30, 34, 95, 176, 186, 191
Luria, 190

Main ideas, 19
  identification of, 186, 189, 223
Mallett & Newsome, 191
Marino, 187
Marland, 191
Marshall & Glock, 183
Martin, 191
Mathematics, 104, 186, 219
McConkie, 177, 178, 179
McGregor's theory X and theory Y, 132
Meaningful context, 185
Meaningful - reception learning, 182
Memory, 183, 187
Merritt, 133, 134, 174, 189
Merritt, White & Moore, 189
Metacognition, 187
Meyer, 120, 177, 181, 182, 183, 188
Meyer & Freedle, 183
Meyer, Brandt, & Bluth, 183
Miller, 181, 186

Milligan, 181
Mixed ability group:
  discussion, 31, 36, 176
  small, 37, 96, 99
Modelling, 189
Moffett, 193
Morris & Cope, 171
Morris & Stewart-Dore, 176
Motivating, 96, 189
Mount Gravatt Developmental
  Language/Reading Program, 164

Narrative, 182, 189
Narrative text, 21, 58
National language development project, 38
Negotiating, 36, 149
Note-making, 187
Note-taking, 19, 174

Objectives:
  affective, 148
  cognitive, 148
  content, 148
  skill, 148
O'Hare, 193
Organizational patterns, 182
Organizing ideas, 149
Organizing information, 235
Oral language, 176
Outlining, 135, 200
Owens, 180, 186

Paragraph structures, 188
Paraphrasing, 186
Pearson, 181, 184
Pearson & Camperell, 22, 187, 188
Pearson & Johnson, 184, 186
Peer tutoring, 36, 96
Perfetti, 184, 186
Phonics, 181
Phrase boundaries, 186
Piaget, 190
Pictorial organizer, 189
Positive learning outcomes, 180
Post-questions, 179, 180
Pre-questions, 179, 180, 183
Pre-teaching vocabulary, 184
Pre-writing, 163
Predicting, 17, 181, 182, 183, 202
Preparation, 14, 175, 178-185, 183, 199
Primary schools, 186
Process of gaining information, 136
  objectives, 199, 200
  strategy, 145
Propositions, 183
Prose analysis, 188
Purpose setting questions, 179
Purposes for reading, 27, 162

Readability formulae, 174
Readence & Moore, 180
Reader generated questions, 180

Reading:
  and learning, 25
  as a thinking process, 27
  and writing, 152, 192
  content area, 85
  efficient, 48
  independent, 187
  preparing for, 47-94
  Primary school reading programs, 19
  process, 181, 201
  readiness, 178
  reading schemes, 18
  reflective, 189
  remedial reading, 192
  thinking through, 92-112
  time, 188, 192
  to generate questions, 179
  to learn, 21, 45, 48
  to review, 165
  what is reading? 14
  why teach reading? 18
  wide reading, 192
Recall, 179, 184, 188, 189
Recording, 152
Redrafting, 165
Rehearse, 36
Research skills, 13
Resnick & Resnick, 25
Retelling, 143
Retrieval chart, 132, 133, 134, 135
Review, 159
Ribovich, 193
Richards, 32, 42, 174, 191
Rickards, 179, 186, 189
Rickards & Danner, 179
Rickards & Hatcher, 179
Riley, 186
Robinson, 172, 182, 183
Rode, 186
Role, 35, 161, 163
Rosen, 38, 43, 176, 191
Rothkopf, 179
Rough drafts, 164
Ruddell, 186
Rumelhart, 22, 180, 181, 182

Sapir, 190
Schachter, 185
Schemata, 180, 181, 182, 183, 184, 185, 189
Schools:
  Commission, 27, 28
  Council, 43
  language use, 37, 191
  primary, 186
  secondary, 186
Science, 40, 41, 59, 63, 86, 87, 91, 120, 132, 150, 201
Scott, 147
Secondary schools, 186
Selective deletion cloze, 185, 186
Semantic clues, 16, 182, 192, 193
Sentence combining, 193
Shablack & Dixon, 176

Shafer, 194
Shepherd, 182
Signal words, 39, 40, 41
Singer & Donlan, 193
Skeleton outlines, 136, 137, 138, 139
Skill objectives, 199
Skimming, 183
Smelstor, 192
Smith, 108, 179, 181, 194
Snouffer & Thistlethwaite, 180
Social climate, 36
Social psychology, 122
Social science, 186
Specific learning, 179
SQ3R, 57, 172, 174, 183, 184
Squire & Applebee, 192
Staging of information, 193
Stauffer, 34, 171
Stevens, 186
Story grammar, 22, 182
Structured discussions, 31, 32, 175
Structured overview, 48-56
  as a preparatory activity, 118, 135, 136, 180, 181, 182, 183, 199, 201, 203, 209, 213, 222, 236, 243
  development of, 51, 52
  for ongoing reference, 54
  for revision or assessment, 55, 118
  student prepared, 54
  teacher developed, 53
  teacher & student developed, 53
  use of, 53-55
Stubbs, 191
Students; less able, 36
Study skills, 187
Subordinate, 181, 193
Summarizing, 14, 19, 187
Summary statements, 193
Superordinate, 181, 193
Surveying, 183, 199
Swaby, 185
Syntactic cueing, 192, 193
Syntactic maturity, 193
Syntax, 192
Synthesis, 179
Synthesize information, 185, 187

Takahaski, 192
Talking, 142
  to learn, 191
Teachers:
  assumptions, 178
  concerns, 175, 187
  English, 182, 184
  insecurity, 34
  primary school, 182
  strategies, 178
  subject area, 182
  talk, 33
  transmission, 36
Teaching framework, 186
Text analysis, 182, 188
  grammar, 182

structures, 182, 187
Thinking through, 33, 95-112, 175, 180, 185-187, 189, 223, 225, 229
Thorndike, 22, 182, 183, 184
Three level reading guide, 92-106, 186
  examples of, 202, 203, 206, 207, 211, 214, 216, 217, 223, 224, 225, 226, 227
Tierney & Bridge, 23, 26, 186, 187
Time on task, 177
Top-down approach, 182
Top-level structures, 118, 119, 121, 182, 183, 187
Topic-sentence, 188
Torbe, 191
Tough, 37
Trabasso, 182, 184, 186
Translate information, 33, 142-167, 190, 200, 203, 208, 212, 236, 239
Transactional mode, 151

Units of work:
  planning of, 45
  topics, 49, 199

Van Dijk, 182
Verbal aptitude, 185, 192
Verbal transformation 176
Verbatim recall, 179
Visual transformation, 176
Vocabulary:
  content vocabulary, 94, 185
  could words, 87
  identification chart, 88
  identifying content area, 86
  instrumentalist view of, 185
  knowledge hypothesis, 185
  learning new, 85-94

must words, 87
pre-teaching of, 185, 192, 200, 203
should words, 87
using context clues, 136, 205, 206, 207, 210, 213, 214, 216, 217, 218, 222, 229, 230, 231, 237
Vygotsky, 190

Walker, 34, 180, 184
Waters, 181
Watts & Anderson, 179, 186
Wertsch, 187
Wittrock, Marks & Doctorow, 184
Wolfe, 192
Writing:
  assignments, 13, 193
  essays, 136, 142
  extensive, 193
  fluency, 193
  form of, 145
  from given information, 200
  gains through reading, 194
  in subject areas, 147
  performance, 194
  processes, 194
  promoting the writing habit, 149-151
  publishing students' writing, 166
  real world writing demands, 160
  reasons for writing, 160, 161
  reflexive, 193
  response to writing, 166, 182, 190, 191
  sustained writing, 194
  we learn to write, 149
  workshops, 151
  writing environment, 159, 160
  writing teaching, 194